Leigh Anderson is an accomplished paramedic with 15 years of operational experience and first-hand, extensive knowledge of how to perform and thrive in high-stress, unpredictable situations.

Outside of an ambulance, Leigh has a keen desire to improve the human experience of stress to set people up to flourish. He has a Bachelor of Paramedic Science and a Graduate Certificate of Emergency Health. He has lectured and tutored at university level and been a peer reviewer of scientific journal articles.

Leigh lives in Brisbane with his family.

'*The Paramedic Mindset* is a must-read book. Through the use of personal experiences, both his own and a range of subject matter experts, Leigh delivers an engaging, evidence-based, and practical book on not only how to survive under pressure, but how to flourish. At a time of skyrocketing mental health issues in our first-responder communities, *The Paramedic Mindset* offers the tools to turn the tide.'

Dr Dan Pronk, co-author of *The Resilience Shield*,
Special Forces veteran and Emergency Doctor

'Leigh Anderson has written: The. Definitive. Book. On this vital subject. I know of no other book that will provide this degree of lifesaving information to this vital audience. This book is "required reading" for all paramedics, and should be used as a textbook for training all medical first responders.'

Lt Col Dave Grossman, USA (ret.), author of *On Combat, On Killing, On Spiritual Combat*, and *Assassination Generation*

'Leigh has set out to describe the often confronting and challenging role of being a front-line emergency health care responder. A combination of apprehension, performance anxiety, satisfaction, and exhilaration! He most ably transcends his unique experiences, providing a bird's eye view of the "job", its challenges and how to cope. I would highly recommend for anyone interested in how to deal with a high-pressure environment.'

Dr Stephen Rashford, Specialist Emergency Physician and
Queensland Ambulance Service Medical Director

'Leigh pulls the curtains back on one of life's biggest skills: how to keep your mind when you should be losing your moorings. The mindsets and capabilities needed to be a top performer in any field are critical and not widely known – Leigh has bottled some of that magic in this hard-scrabbled account. Brilliant.'

Mark Wales, Special Forces veteran, business CEO, author of
Survivor and *Outrider*, and winner of *Australian Survivor* TV show

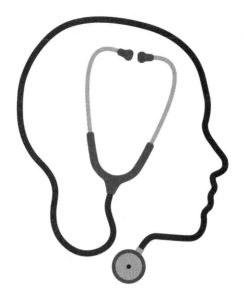

The
Paramedic
Mindset

LEIGH ANDERSON

MACMILLAN
Pan Macmillan Australia

Pan Macmillan acknowledges the Traditional Custodians of Country throughout Australia and their connections to lands, waters and communities. We pay our respect to Elders past and present and extend that respect to all Aboriginal and Torres Strait Islander peoples today. We honour more than sixty thousand years of storytelling, art and culture.

Some of the people in this book have had their names changed to protect their identities.

First published 2024 in Macmillan by Pan Macmillan Australia Pty Ltd
1 Market Street, Sydney, New South Wales, Australia, 2000

 A catalogue record for this
book is available from the
National Library of Australia

Typeset in 11/16 pt Sabon LT Pro by Post Pre-press Group, Brisbane
Printed by IVE

Internal illustrations by IRONGAV
Paramedic's Poem on page ix © Paul Oliveri. Reprinted by permission.

 The paper in this book is FSC® certified.
FSC® promotes environmentally responsible,
socially beneficial and economically viable
management of the world's forests.

To all emergency service workers who continuously give
to others without regard for their own wellbeing.
I hope this resource gives to you as you have given to many.

Contents

Have you seen a beautiful dawn break through bloodshot nightshift eyes;
a baby take its first breath;
a person brought back from death's edge from what you have done;
the look of the person who knows they are dying.
Have you seen the pain and devastated looks on the family of the dead.

Have you eaten a meal speeding through traffic
with lights flashing and sirens wailing;
gone to work when most are going home;
made light of injury and death;
relieved the pain of the adorable young child with a broken bone;
eaten meals reheated two, three, and four times over.
Have you ever been too tired to sleep.

Have you learnt to put a 4-1/2 tonne ambulance
sideways in a controlled skid;
to watch your partner's back and know that they are watching yours;
that you are different from others to be able to do the job;
not to think about your own mortality.
Have you learned this does not always work.

Have you stood in a line of white shirts, epaulettes and
shining medals, holding back your tears, honouring
your colleagues who did not finish the shift.

We have;

We are Paramedics.

By Paul Oliveri
Australian Paramedic

Author's Note

The opinions and observations in the book are my own. The personal experience stories were written from a personal perspective and not as a representative or employee of a particular business, emergency service or private company. During a rigorous editing process, all names and locations were changed to protect both patient confidentiality and my colleagues.

This book contains an individual narrative of my own experiences working as a paramedic. Some of these descriptions can be graphic – or simply gross. If graphic descriptions of injuries or other upsetting symptoms can be a trigger for you, reader discretion is advised.

Prologue

They say the day your child is born is the happiest day of your life. My experiences as a paramedic and as a father left me questioning this belief. Without the knowledge and skills I have developed as a paramedic, in particular my mindset, I wouldn't have been able to function during this nightmare.

It started with a phone call from my wife. She had severe lower abdominal pain. We knew she was about nine weeks pregnant. My paramedic brain in overdrive, I immediately thought it might be an ectopic pregnancy. I swear I could physically feel my pupils dilate and my heart race as she was telling me her symptoms.

I waited impatiently at work, 450 kilometres away, as she had her scan. The phone rang. I took a deep breath, expecting the worst as I answered. I heard laughter on the other end of the phone. I was confused. My body went through drastic physiological changes in that moment. I went from feeling fear and panic to jubilation and excitement – then suddenly fear again as I realised we were having twins.

Ten weeks later, we were together for our next ultrasound. I couldn't wait; this was going to be the first time I saw the twins.

The only problem was that the sonographer found a strange mass on one of the twins, whom we'll call Twin B. 'Here we go again,' I thought. A spiral of negative self-talk kicked in. 'This pregnancy thing will be the end of me,' I said to myself, 'and I'm not even the one pregnant.'

Three weeks after that, we found ourselves back at the doctor. Twin B had a tumour near her tailbone – a sacrococcygeal teratoma, a type of tumour that develops before birth and grows from a baby's coccyx. Because the tumour demands a lot of blood, the biggest risk was that it could overwhelm Twin B's small heart, causing heart failure. I vividly remember my wife and me both crying our eyes out in the hospital parking lot.

We tried to focus on the positives. Twin A wasn't affected by it. They were fraternal twins, meaning they each had their own sacs, placentas and umbilical cords. At least Twin A was safe. I later discovered what we were doing – trying to find any positives in the situation – is called reframing (which we will cover later in the book).

We packed up our house and moved everything to Brisbane for the impending birth. Weekly hospital visits had turned into multiple times a week. The wait became overwhelming as I kept thinking of the worst-case scenario. The doctors warned us of the potential negative outcomes. Do we sacrifice Twin B to save Twin A's life?

At thirty-six weeks, it was time. The obstetrician decided we couldn't wait any longer as the tumour was growing and pushing up against the abdominal organs, specifically the bowel and rectum, risking the loss of the sphincter muscle that controls bowel movements. We were warned that it was highly likely Twin B would have to live with a colostomy bag for her entire life.

I was in the birthing suite, ready for the balloon catheter, a device used to induce labour, to be removed. We opted for a natural birth as recommended by the obstetrician. I felt like a duck floating on a pond. Everything was still and calm on the surface – I was trying to remain calm (as paramedics do in emergencies) and stay composed for my wife – but under the water, my mind was going a million miles an hour.

The obstetrician removed the balloon device then immediately froze for what felt like an eternity. He told the midwife that it was a cord prolapse, a rare obstetric emergency, and to hit the emergency button now. This is where being a paramedic is not advantageous, because we know a little about a lot of medical conditions, but we're not experts in any field of medicine. I knew what a cord prolapse was, all the bad stuff about it, and I was not optimistic.

I saw the doctor insert his hand inside my wife's vagina which was yet to be fully dilated; her screams are still with me today. I'll never forget the fear in her eyes as six or more people ran into the room ready to rush her through to the operating room – they'd have to perform an emergency caesarean instead. I quickly kissed her and told her it was going to be okay. I'd seen a lot of people die in front of me before, but never had I seen such panicked eyes. Perhaps I was just more emotionally attached this time.

It was like an episode from *Grey's Anatomy*. My wife was being wheeled down the corridors of the hospital into surgery with a doctor sitting between her legs, a hand where it shouldn't be, and about six medical staff chasing them down. The obstetrician came up to me and I could see he wanted to reassure me, but all he said was, 'You'd be used to this, wouldn't you, Leigh?' He showed sympathy, not empathy.

A nurse told me I might be able to join them in the operating room despite all the chaos. I didn't want to, to be honest, but I thought I would lose my wife and the twins and regret it if I didn't. So I put on the surgical scrubs they gave me, shaking frantically as I tried to get dressed. I couldn't for the life of me put the boot covers over my shoes. I had to use my elbows to help stabilise my tremors.

After all that, the doctors wouldn't let me in. I was relieved. I imagined blood and guts everywhere, a scene out of a horror movie. As a paramedic, I tend to think of worst-case scenarios all the time.

A nurse escorted me to an empty waiting area and made me a cup of tea. As I sat down in the recliner, alone, I tried to drink the tea, but I just spilled hot water all over me. I was still shaking too much, and my palms were pouring sweat. I put the tea down with two hands before looking up and realising I was put in a pre-op area. An elderly gentleman rolled out in his hospital gown and paper shoes to ask me what surgery I was having this morning. He was having a colonoscopy. At that moment, I would have preferred to have had a colonoscopy.

It was the longest wait of my life. I was disassociated from reality and time slowed down. Everything felt like it took twice as long.

The nurse walked out to tell me that two beautiful girls had been born via caesarean and were very much alive. What a relief. I was allowed to walk in and see them. It was a surreal moment, meeting my daughters for the first time, not knowing which way to look, and not wanting to have a favourite already.

They were each placed in a neonatal trolley and wheeled out of the surgical room with their own team of three medical personnel. I had a quick glance at the tumour. The size of a golf ball, it looked huge on a baby who weighed less than 1.8 kilograms.

When we came to the elevator, the doors opened and a member of the medical team asked me where I wanted to go. Twin A was going to the Special Care Unit. Although she was doing well, it was still a premature birth. Twin B, on the other hand, was going to the Neonatal Intensive Care Unit. I froze. I didn't know what decision to make.

The medical staff looked rushed so I had to decide quickly. I went with Twin B. My justification was that she was the one with the tumour and the sicker baby (sorry, Twin A). It felt very wrong watching my newborn child get wheeled away from me down the other end of the corridor, in the hands of complete strangers, but I made my decision. I had to focus on Twin B.

I felt useless throughout this entire endeavour, watching the medical professionals help stabilise my daughter. Normally I'm the one in the trenches getting to intervene, but this was different, having to stand back and watch. I felt hopeless. The hardest part was that I had no control over the outcome.

A nurse walked in asking if I was Twin A's father, as I needed to sign a waiver to allow them to feed Twin A with formula milk, since my wife was unable to breastfeed.

Then the light bulb went on: 'How's my wife?' I asked.

I was informed that she had been moved to recovery but wasn't doing well. She was having a post-partum haemorrhage. When was this day going to end? At this point I had only seen Twin B for a precious few seconds, but I felt I had to go back upstairs to see my wife. I'd already left one twin, so this decision was easier to make.

My wife was in the care of our obstetrician, who told me that they had been unable to control her bleeding. She was now experiencing hypertension (high blood pressure) as well due to pre-eclampsia. The obstetrician thought this was because of retained products, bits left behind from the delivery, trapped in the uterus. But he didn't want to go back into surgery after just recently closing my wife's wounds from the caesarean.

He told me that he was going to insert his hand and scrape inside the uterus to remove any retained products from the birth. Again, I had to witness this awful procedure, but thankfully this time my wife was still affected by the general anaesthetic and couldn't feel it.

This procedure worked and the bad news ended for that day. Twin B had surgery on her tumour ten hours after birth. It was another adrenaline-pumped adventure, saying goodbye before I had barely said hello. Another lingering wait ended with my wife answering the hospital room phone. All I heard was her saying, 'Yes, okay,' before she hung up the phone and fell back to sleep. I had to shake her awake to tell me the news. I couldn't bear it. The surgery was successful, and the surgeon managed to save Twin B's sphincter as well. 'She can poo!' I screamed. She was going to be all right.

We named Twin B Evolet – meaning 'the promise of life'.

This experience catalysed my fascination with the human factors that influence our decision-making and how we function under high stress. I thought I was pretty good at it until I felt the full spectrum of emotions, hormones and impulses on this journey. During my daughters' birth I was exposed to personal stress, not work-related stress, but I realised that the skills and mindset I had as a paramedic really helped me get through it.

In this book, I hope to draw both on my lived experience as a paramedic, and on existing scientific research and interviews with people who have experienced and thrived in difficult situations, to give you tools, strategies and behaviours you can implement to improve your own ability to perform under stress. After all, you don't have to be a paramedic to need to learn how to flourish while faced with great stress and adversity. You only have to be human. We all go through the same responses to stress, no matter the situation.

What to Expect in This Book

This book has two components – personal experiences and science-based research. The stories I share with you are some of my most calamitous failures and wonderful successes. They are true stories that are entertaining, shocking, revealing and at times funny, but they all serve a purpose in helping you in your quest to flourish under stress.

As much as I wanted to hide certain details and close the door to vulnerability, I thought it only fair – if I'm asking you to be courageous and vulnerable – that I also enter the arena. I have dared greatly to publish this book. I hope you join me and dare too.

Each chapter leads with an anecdote about a personal experi-ence to illustrate a real-world application of the science-based research. The aim is to make sense of the science and outline its relevance to performing under stress. Each chapter ends with a call to action. The quotes provided within the calls to action are generated from interviews with high-performing people, also explored in the Afterword.

As a paramedic I like evidence. Before believing or acting on anyone's information, I want to know the *why* behind the decision. Here I've attempted to explain logically how the evidence underpins each chapter's key takeaways.

I've shared numerous practical tools which you can implement in your daily life, not only to manage your stress but also to improve your mental health. This toolbox (see page 289) full of useful skills and strategies is designed to combat any challenge. It may seem geared towards flourishing under stress in the professional environment, but I can't emphasise enough that it applies to everything. No matter where we go, we take our physiology with us.

You may be surprised to find that the first few chapters have more to do with personal wellbeing than psychological skills for debunking stress. It's crucial that I highlight this, because it's a common theme among people who flourish in high-stress, high-consequence environments. Having positive mental health is the first step towards achieving poise.

1

Understanding Poise

Personal Experience – The Fearful Student

I was a 21-year-old paramedic student when I found myself driving at 135 kilometres per hour down a country road to my first major car crash. We were told over the radio that we would be the first crew to arrive on the scene; backup was at least 30 minutes away. There would be six patients: three were children, two were unconscious and one deceased.

I was frightened of what I would encounter. I envisaged great suffering. I could feel the adrenaline pumping through my veins. My heart was racing; I felt like it was about to beat out of my chest. Images ran through my mind of what I would see – body parts scattered across the road, people crushed, blood and pain.

I looked to my left to find my mentor, an experienced paramedic, sitting calmly. She seemed to be in complete control and told me what to do when we arrived. She didn't seem nervous or worried.

On the other hand, I, as a novice, was apprehensive. The images that flooded through my mind worsened my fear. I began to doubt myself and my ability. Did I choose the right profession? Would I be able to cope with the pressure and the trauma mentally? Would I end up with post-traumatic stress disorder (PTSD)? What if I couldn't help someone and they died?

I had read the textbooks and done all the studying, but that was in a controlled environment. In my studies, we had air-conditioning and lighting; now we were out in the rain and wind. We had professors guiding us and the safety of knowing that if we made a mistake, the plastic mannikin would not call their lawyer. We weren't surrounded by distressed family members or bystanders.

This crash was going to be the real thing.

I distinctly remember wondering how my mentor was so relaxed as we travelled quickly towards the scene. How could she just sit there and talk about whether she put her lunch in the fridge or left it out on the table?

What does it take to be like that?

After this incident, I would no longer feel like a rookie. I had my first true encounter with suffering. Arriving on scene, we saw the carnage of the crashed vehicles ahead. I tried to take in as much as possible but it was hard not to become fixated on the two-year old having a seizure on the side of the road, with a clear injury to the head after being ejected from the vehicle.

There was rubbish everywhere – broken appliances, clothes, boxes. The people in one of the vehicles were moving house and the car was loaded to the brim. Frantic bystanders were on the scene, and as soon as we stopped, they rushed to us. I was thrown into the commotion of people yelling and pointing in all directions at once. The heat was in my face and the rush in my veins as we scrambled to the nearest patient.

A baby was crying, her voice small and wounded. We scrambled in the direction of the sound, my body cramping as we searched. The crying was coming from under a smashed television. Seconds crawled under my skin as I lifted up the TV, ghastly images flashing in my head. Miraculously the baby was fine after being ejected from the child restraint, apart from some superficial cuts and bruises. I couldn't believe it.

A married elderly couple was sitting in the front of another vehicle down an embankment 100 metres away. As I approached the vehicle, I could see that one of the patients wasn't moving. He was obviously deceased, crushed inside the vehicle. His partner was alive though.

She had minor fractures to her arm but she was trapped inside the vehicle. She was going to have to sit next to her husband until the fire service could cut her out.

My mentor wanted me with a woman who was hanging out from the door in her upside-down car, and I alone was to treat her. Doubt crept in even before the work began. The woman was conscious, mumbling but in severe pain.

After my assessment of her, I realised her back was most likely broken. The implications ran through my head in a long list. How severe was it? I looked at the angle by which she hung, and my mind came up with nothing. My heart froze. This wasn't the time to be empty. I could screw up and make things worse for her. 'My baby,' she mumbled. She was the mother of the crying girl. A quake started in my hands. Someone kept whispering in the back of my mind that I was going to mess up everything. *What do I even know? I'm just a student.*

Her baby was fine, but her back was broken and she couldn't move. I started with calm responses but even my voice wavered as I took her vital signs. I offered hope with my words as I remained with her. We were together for more than an hour before she was extricated from the vehicle.

Two helicopters had landed on site; I remember having a moment of realisation, understanding how severe my first major trauma was.

Why Paramedicine?

I became a paramedic by chance. Sport was my priority throughout high school. Rugby League was my passion and I had dreams of playing for Queensland in the State of Origin. It became an even stronger focus when my brother signed and debuted for the Melbourne Storm, eventually winning a premiership with them. School was a distraction from my sport until I blew my knee out. This was my first ride in the back of an ambulance, getting my kneecap popped back into place.

I was fifteen when I had my first knee operation, but it was the third operation that really ruined it for me. After being discharged from hospital I developed an infection that quickly spread throughout my body. I had high fevers, excruciating pain, and felt like a frail old man. I called an ambulance to take me back to hospital. After a fourth operation, a washout and clean of the knee joint, lying alone on the hospital bed, I knew my dream was over.

Two months later I still couldn't walk properly. My leg was as stiff as a fence post. I was only eighteen and I couldn't bend my leg past 30 degrees. Things started to really worry me. Reality hit me in the face – my sports dream was nothing compared to the inability to walk. A fifth and final operation ensued. This time it worked and I could bend my leg again.

I'm thankful for this experience. Without this suffering I never would have pursued an academic path and become a paramedic. Sport was all I'd thought about, but these injuries forced me to study. If it wasn't for these injuries I wouldn't be writing this book. The paramedics who took care of me were amazing; they showed great compassion and care. It impacted me greatly and I came to realise the importance of suffering, because without it we wouldn't grow.

A Witness to Suffering

Life constantly puts obstacles in our path. If we want to flourish under stress then we must face these obstacles. We constantly seek comfort but simultaneously want to achieve great things. Comfort isn't a good enough goal to wade through the pools of pain. If we don't choose to face the suffering we will suffer in any case – not physically but psychologically, as we feel aimless and lack purpose.

The ultimate role of a paramedic is to reduce pain and suffering. Every person who calls for an ambulance calls because they are in distress and are desperately searching for someone to take it away. It doesn't matter whether it's physical or emotional, it's all suffering. After responding to thousands of calls, I understood that I was becoming a witness to suffering and I had to learn to bear it.

Through this exposure, I realised that suffering is the most certain thing in life. Tragedy strikes us all. It happens to the righteous and evil, from innocent children to criminals. It's unavoidable. I have seen people die in all manner of ways, from cancer to murder, drugs and suicide (the comedy film *A Million Ways to Die in the West* has some merit). Life is clearly difficult. There would be no need for the existence of a paramedic if that wasn't true. For that matter, suicide wouldn't exist if suffering wasn't a reality.

One of the saddest cases I have ever attended was an 86-year-old woman who wanted to kill herself because she was suffering alone and unable to leave her room without assistance. Her family had stopped visiting her and her husband of over 60 years had died. She was a strong woman with no signs of dementia. The nursing home staff were aware that she was suicidal, so they took everything potentially harmful away from her.

She was so desperate to end her suffering that she started eating her makeup. I arrived to find her chewing on lipstick because there was nothing else in her drawer. She was crying uncontrollably, telling me that she just wanted to end her pain. She no longer had a purpose. I had never felt so empathetic before.

People are constantly subject to all sorts of terrible things that are unfair. When you witness a six-month-old with cancer who has only weeks to live, it's fair to say inequality exists. It's especially hard to accept when they are as innocent and undeserving as this baby. It's difficult to explain to a loving mother, but it's a fact of life and we must be frank about it.

From the moment a human comes into being, life is challenging. For a newborn to survive during birth it must go through significant changes over a period of seconds and minutes. While the foetus is in the womb its lungs are full of fluid and are being delivered oxygen through the placenta. The newborn baby must clear the fluid and take its first breath or it will not survive.

Once the newborn is released into the world they immediately face challenges. The womb is an entirely sterile environment, but now they are vulnerable to infection. They have a poor ability to maintain body temperature, losing heat twice as fast as an adult. They must constantly adapt to the outer world or they won't survive. Suffering starts at the beginning.

The best way to overcome life's obstacles is to have a worthy enough goal to justify the pain. Canadian clinical psychologist Dr Jordan Peterson, who has studied suffering to the deepest level of anyone I know, has concluded that having a strong goal is the best defence against suffering. It means we become less tormented by adversity and uncertainty.

If you want to feel positive emotion and flourish then you need something to aim for, something you can achieve. Finding your best possible goal will engage you with the suffering and force you to struggle through it. A worthy goal will make the pain, anguish and trauma worth it.

This is why a cancer victim voluntarily engages in chemo-therapy treatment. I remember attending to a teenage cancer victim who was too weak to stand, had no hair and was wearing an adult nappy because she had lost control of her bowels. She was attached to a permanent morphine drip that seemed to have no effect, yet she continued to receive the chemotherapy in her other arm.

The treatment uses powerful chemicals to kill the dangerous cells in the body, but it does this at a great cost. The potential side effects are so numerous I don't have time to list them here, but my point is this: despite the suffering caused by the treatment, the patient believes that the suffering is worth it. Their goal is to live, and that's a powerful enough goal to endure the hurt.

As difficult as it is, find the positive aspect of why you are suffering. For me, bearing witness to suffering as a paramedic is a burden I am happy to carry because the goal of saving someone's life is strong enough to get me through it. I don't enjoy looking at someone who has just fallen off a horse and is most likely paralysed from the waist down, but I can get through it because the purpose of a paramedic is to shine a light in the darkness. It gives me the resilience to witness the tragedies of life.

This rule also applies to my personal life. When I was in my early twenties I was diagnosed with a condition called ankylosing spondylitis, an inflammatory disease that can mimic arthritis and cause your bones in your back to fuse. I am in physical pain nearly every day. I wake some mornings and feel like a stiff old man, with swelling and constant pain in my joints.

At its peak, the disease has affected my mobility and ability to play with my children. I am unable to throw them in the air or run with them at the playground. There is no cure for my condition but there are treatments – strong medication that causes unwanted side effects, especially if taken long term. One day, getting ready for work, my foot was in so much pain I couldn't put my shoes on. I had to find another way.

I heard about the anti-inflammatory effects of ice baths. I read about Dutch motivational speaker Wim Hof, The Iceman, and decided to buy a freezer. I hate ice baths; they are far from enjoyable. I consider sitting in it for three minutes at three degrees every day to be a form of suffering. I'm a Queenslander, anything under 20 degrees is considered freezing. But the anti-inflammatory effects it gives me are worth the three minutes of pain. It's worth it if it lets me be a more active father.

You need to make yourself capable, prepared, educated and trained to face what might come. To flourish in life is to not be comfortable or sit in a paradise that doesn't exist. It's to thrive in spite of the suffering. It's to carry the weight of the suffering on your shoulders and progress with ease until it no longer becomes a weight but a blessing.

A paramedic voluntarily signs up for the profession – it's an opt-in career. If you choose to do it, then you are accepting all of what it brings. This applies to any choice. If you want to be a great painter or a great athlete, then you accept the pain that is required to become great. You acknowledge the risk and happily take on the consequences of the role. For me, it was accepting the night shifts, abuse, trauma, responsibility and stress. If you don't think the suffering is worth it, then perhaps you need to change your goals.

Achieving Poise

First responders are committed to serving the community and caring for those in need. This motivation both drives our performance and equips us with the requisite coping skills to support our wellbeing. As a paramedic with fifteen years of field experience, I have come to understand the job's inherent challenges. Prevention and early intervention are critical to performance and longevity in stressful pursuits, and I hope that my book helps you with this.

This book is designed to complement the training and skills you already possess. Everyone is equipped with professional training or job experience; we learn how to respond to a particular situation. We are not as equipped with an understanding of how to manage the human factors that come into play. We develop this knowledge through our experiences and by looking to the experts. This book will demonstrate how to deal with your fear, stress and self-doubt.

I talk about topics and situations we all go through and deal with but rarely, if ever, discuss. We must start discussing them.

Paramedics are an ideal example of how to develop a mindset of composure and self-assurance, because we are under pressure every day. The struggle to perform under pressure is common in most professions, but in the emergency medicine environment, nothing is more important than making a correct decision, because the wrong one could be deadly.

When you find yourself in the middle of an emergency, you are faced with a daunting responsibility that is do or die. In this context, you know that any mistake or incompetence can have catastrophic outcomes. You don't get a second chance. The paramedic mindset will give you the tools so you don't need that second chance.

We all face similar struggles within our own minds – no matter the stressor placed upon us. We all have the same physiological response to pressure. If the outcome matters to you and time is against you, then the pressure will be on – no matter the situation. It could be a medical emergency, a job interview or a public speaking event. You don't have to be a paramedic to need poise.

Ballet is a completely different profession from paramedicine, but dancers need poise just the same. A ballerina creates a state of equilibrium between effort and ease. We are immersed in the beauty of a ballerina performing when they achieve the finest point of balance that is possible to attain.

Tiekka Tellier, a professional ballerina in New York for 16 years, believes ballet teaches us where and how to use our personal energy through complex movements that develop more than just muscular dexterity. In fact, the ability to move gracefully relies as much on the mental approach as the physical one.

The aim of the paramedic mindset is to generate poise – never being thrown off course despite the tremendous internal and external pressures being thrust upon you. Giving you the ability to bend but not break.

The paramedic mindset *is* poise.

History of Poise

Poise is not a new concept; it goes back a long time, and humans have always revered people who possess poise. If you think about the people society has looked up to and that history has remembered, all had poise. They may not have called it poise, though. Here is a list of notable characters throughout history from whom we can draw inspiration in developing poise.

Stoic Roman

The Stoic Romans were great thinkers of their time and continue to influence the behaviours of modern philosophers. Stoicism is a school of thought and teachings that centre around the endurance of pain or hardship without complaint. The Stoic Roman taught us that the key to a good life is the cultivation of mental health, which the Stoics identified as being virtuous and rational. The ideal attitude is of calm indifference towards external events.

Stoicism advocated self-control and fortitude as a means of overcoming destructive emotions. American author Ryan Holiday, the foremost researcher of modern Stoicism, defines its philosophy as trying to 'see things for what they are, do what we can, endure and bear what we must'. We need to learn to see obstacles as the way forward.

The philosophy focuses on the mental ability to overcome adversity, and physical and emotional obstacles. Stoics believe that the key principle for flourishing under stress is to love your own fate, no matter what it might bring. It's a school of thought that teaches us humility and strength. Holiday's beginner guide says that 'Stoicism doesn't concern itself with complicated theories about the world, but with helping us overcome destructive emotions and act on what can be acted upon.'

The most famous Stoic Roman is Marcus Aurelius. His work has generated thousands of quotes, but one of my favourites is: 'Today I escaped from anxiety. Or no, I discarded it, because it was within me, in my own perceptions – not outside.'

Laconic Spartan

The Spartans are famous for a lot of reasons but most notably for their fortitude during the battle at the Pass of Thermopylae. Their fortitude gave them the ability to become immoveable in adverse circumstances, and to endure pain and suffering when all looked lost. Fortitude comes from the Latin *fortitudo*, meaning 'strength'. Poise requires the courage to act but also the fortitude to withstand suffering.

The Spartans were famous for speaking in laconic phrases with a concise wit. The best example of the laconic Spartan showing poise is from the 300 Spartans who fought to prevent the Persians from invading their homeland. When the Spartan King Leonidas led the Greeks against an almighty Persian army, all the doubters and all those in fear told the Spartans that the archers were so numerous that their arrows would blacken the sun. The Spartan Dienekes smiled and said, 'All the better, we'll fight in the shade.'

When the battle seemed lost and the Spartans had no chance of survival, they still stood and fought, and for that reason we still talk about them today.

Inscrutable Samurai

Samurais embody virtues of courage, integrity and loyalty. They practised with an unwavering discipline to achieve these high virtues. The inscrutable samurais taught us the power of awareness and of the empty mind. An empty mind is one that is free of extraneous thoughts, one of stillness. Most people would only find the stillness state through meditation. Samurais show us that if we lose self-control and fill our heads with thoughts, we will most likely make a wrong decision.

One of the most famous samurais, Shiba Yoshimasa, wrote more than 600 years ago that the greatest art of war is calming our own thoughts and knowing those of others.

The samurais trained relentlessly, believing they should always be ready for battle. They possessed mastery, so when fear struck, they were able to act without thought.

Stiff-upper-lip Brit

The Stiff-upper-lip Brit is someone who has fortitude in the face of adversity. Over the centuries, the Brits have repeatedly displayed resolute calm during a crisis. The entire nation showed true grit and poise when struggling through the Blitz of World War II. The Germans dropped bombs on London for 57 consecutive nights. Civilians had to flee underground with little food, no electricity, limited bedding and poor sanitation facilities.

Hitler believed that he could break the morale of the British people and have them force Churchill to the negotiation table. He couldn't have been more wrong. They grew a stiff upper lip, fortifying their courage to fight and stay the course.

The Digger

The term Digger was first used during the gold rush in Australia to describe the miners but during World War I it became a name for an Australian or New Zealand soldier. After landing at Gallipoli, the ANZACs were instructed to dig, dig, dig. They became the best trench diggers in the British Empire. They dug in and held fast against great odds.

The term became synonymous with Australian grit. The Rats of Tobruk are regarded as some of the greatest Aussie Diggers. The Australian War Memorial says: 'surrounded by German and Italian forces, the men of the Tobruk garrison . . . withstood tank attacks, artillery barrages, and daily bombings. They endured the desert's searing heat, the bitterly cold nights, and hellish dust storms. They lived in dug-outs, caves, and crevasses. The defenders of Tobruk did not surrender, they did not retreat.'

Steven Bradbury is another Aussie who kept his poise while all others were falling around him. He dug into the ice as his four rivals collided, tumbled and collapsed, passing them all and becoming the first Australian to win a Winter Olympic Gold. Afterwards he said, 'I'll accept this gold medal. But not for the 90 seconds of the race – I'm going to take it for the 14 years of hard work.' He may have been an accidental hero, but without persistence and determination he never would have been in it to win it.

*

What can we learn from those who have displayed poise throughout history? The most important thing is that they worked on their mindset. They were able to flourish under pressure because they got the mental piece right.

Paramedics have advanced medical training, carry state-of-the-art equipment, and administer complex medication, but this is not what separates them from the average bystander.

What makes paramedics unique is their mindset.

There are many reasons why people find it difficult to perform under stress. Panicking will make you feel a sense of impending doom and an urge to flee. You will fear a loss of control, and experience feelings of being detached from your body and disconnected from the world around you. These reactions will negatively impact your ability to make good decisions. But with a few simple steps, you will be given the power of poise.

Personal Experience – At Breaking Point

During my university training, I honed my skills in treating a diverse range of emergencies, but nothing prepared me for the prevalence of self-harm and suicide-related calls. It became distressingly routine to encounter individuals in crisis. One evening, prompted by a concerned neighbour's call, we responded to a potentially suicidal patient. Upon arrival, we were met with anxious neighbours out the front, signalling the gravity of the situation. It was evident that the individual inside was in distress, as we could hear him yelling about wanting to kill himself even over the blaring music he was playing.

Despite our efforts to establish communication through the closed door, he adamantly refused entry. Tension was rising outside. What should we do next? How could we help if we couldn't get in? The arrival of the police provided crucial support. While we were hoping for a peaceful resolution, a neighbour helped us find a crowbar so we could smash open the door if needed. In the end, we had no choice but to breach the door – only to be met with the frightening sight of the patient charging towards us in a rage. Quick action from the police ensured his safety and that of others.

After we sedated the patient, we managed to facilitate a calm transfer to the hospital, hoping for the best outcome in his journey towards recovery. We had done our job. As we wrapped up the paperwork at the hospital, the pager suddenly sprang to life with another urgent call. To our disbelief, it was for a near identical situation – an out-of-town family member had called in a suicide risk. This time, though, it was different. I recognised the address. It was a colleague, someone I considered a friend.

When we arrived at the scene, the apartment complex was securely locked, barring our access. There was no group of concerned neighbours, no loud music, but the silence was even more tense. Despite many attempts to contact the person inside, our calls went unanswered. Undeterred, we resorted to knocking on neighbouring apartment doors and ringing every button on the intercom, trying to find someone to help us gain entry through the gate. Thankfully, our persistence paid off, but it felt like a lifetime when someone I knew might be in distress.

Approaching the front of the ground-floor apartment, we found a familiar obstacle: another locked door. I banged loudly and yelled out her name. I was starting to feel desperate. I walked around the side of the apartment and out the back, looking through the windows as I went, trying to peep through the curtains. I was looking for her bedroom to see if I could bang on that window to wake her up. Suddenly, I heard a noise and let out a sigh of relief. I thought she was stumbling towards the door half asleep. When the noise started to sound like a bark, I realised it was her dog inside the house.

My experience told me something was seriously wrong here. Those natural instincts began to kick in and my heart was pounding. I was trying to stay composed, as I knew I had a job to do, I couldn't let my emotions take over and freeze.

We broke into the back door of the apartment after climbing over the balcony via a neighbours' apartment. I still had hope in that moment, despite my spider senses telling me something bad was unfolding.

I walked straight to her bedroom, where I found a bed that was unslept in. I then jumped as I heard a snore. 'Thank God,' I told myself, as it sounded like a drunk person's snore. My wife always complains that I snore when I've been drinking. I turned around to find the dog had followed me into the bedroom and was making a snoring noise. It was the second time the dog had caught me out and dimmed my hopes.

By this time, I knew what I was going to find next. My heightened senses were trying to find anything to escape from the sickening feeling in my belly. I was trying to grab onto any good news, which is why the dog kept fooling me.

What happened next I will remember forever. Our colleague had committed suicide. She was dead.

I wanted to scream out loud and flee from the scene. It was hard to comprehend at first. Questions, thoughts and self-talk started racing through my mind. I was trying to search for an explanation. I was grateful to have my colleagues with me; they gave me strength and support in that moment. Having the ability to switch into paramedic and manager mode helped me cope with the traumatic situation before me.

As the team leader, it was my job to manage the scene. By focusing on being task-oriented, controlling what I could and letting go of the rest, I was able to function in that very high-stress situation.

My calls to our supervisors and colleagues to tell them what had happened are phone calls I thought I would never have to make. But one of the toughest things I have ever had to do as a paramedic was filling out my colleague's life-extinct form and handing it over to the police. I distinctly remember locking myself in the office to get away from everyone while I filled in the ambulance report form – detailing her death and noting my observations of the scene. I wanted to do it privately so as not to put this burden on anyone else.

The truth of being a paramedic is that we are constantly exposed to stress, trauma and grief. A study on paramedic health found that 27.2 per cent of paramedics had reported suicidal thoughts in the past year. In 2010, an Australian psychosocial health study revealed that the prevalence of suicidal thoughts in paramedics was nine times higher than in the general population.

In 2019, an Australian Senate committee reported on the mental health of emergency service workers and discovered that ambulance personnel have the highest prevalence of PTSD among all occupational groups of rescuers. Reasons for this include ambulance personnel being exposed to greater pressure and stress at work than other rescue teams, responding to more emergency calls and having closer contact with the victims.

The Senate committee made 14 recommendations for change to the Australian Government. At the time of writing this book, none of those recommendations have been implemented.

Unfortunately, this wasn't the first time I had experienced a friend commit suicide. In 2013, my school friend Dwayne Lally took his own life after suffering in silence. It was a great shock to the entire community, especially his close friends Casey Lyons and Sam Webb. They went on to create the mental health advocacy organisation LIVIN in tribute. LIVIN's motto is 'It Ain't Weak to Speak,' encapsulating their key message of breaking the stigma around mental health and encouraging open and honest conversations.

If anything has triggered you or you are experiencing hardship please contact:

Lifeline Australia: 13 11 14
Beyond Blue: 1300 224 636

The Poise Cycle

Through my research and development of the paramedic mindset I was able to build a model for acquiring poise, which I call the poise cycle. The model identifies the key necessary components in joining either the cycle leading to poise or the cycle leading to panic.

The diagram on the next page provides a visual representation of what is required to develop the paramedic mindset.

POISE CYCLE

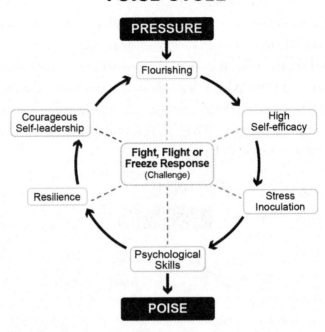

In the poise cycle, we are prepared and equipped with all the weapons necessary to remain composed and self-assured under pressure. It starts with a flourishing person who has positive mental health. They have a strong belief that they are more than capable of achieving the task at hand – in other words, they have high self-efficacy.

Through applying operational cognitive readiness to mentally prepare their mind for stress, using a technique such as stress inoculation (see page 130), they will be prepared for the unknown and embrace the challenge. Flourishing people have a complete toolbox of psychological skills that they can call upon to manage their fear and control their heart rate throughout any stressful encounter.

Being able to bounce back from a traumatic event with resilience allows people with poise to continue to move forward with growth. They are self-leaders, showing courage in the face of profound pressure, and they take positive action to resolve the difficult situation.

In the poise cycle, the fight, flight or freeze response is at the centre of everything. There is no hiding from our own physiology. We must work with it and try to manipulate it. To have poise we must see difficulties as a challenge rather than a threat.

I accept, though, that as with most things, there are aspects of dualism to this cycle. Where there is light, there is dark – and where there is poise, there is panic. The panic cycle occurs when we allow pressure to overwhelm us, and serves to highlight the responses we must avoid.

PANIC CYCLE

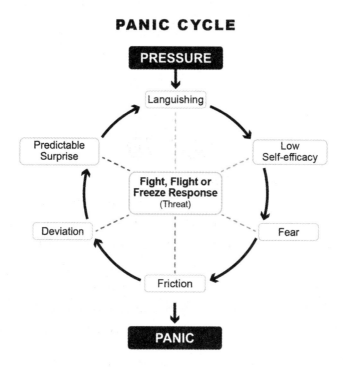

In the panic cycle, we join the loop of the fight, flight or freeze response but we see this process as a threat. It starts with someone who is languishing with poor mental health, which leads to a low self-efficacy – a belief that they are not good enough.

The immense pressure continues to build, manifesting as negative self-talk and a fear of failure, causing them to make decisions from a place of shame and unworthiness. Instead of resolving the problem, they feel an overwhelming agitation and friction that causes them to deviate from the standard, creating the perfect environment for a predictable surprise – a disaster.

In the chapters that follow, I will discuss, and break down in detail, each component of the cycle, revealing the essential role each one plays in having poise – or panicking – under stress.

These models are designed to be 'spun', by which I mean used over and over. If you encounter an issue under stress, refer to the cycle and identify at what stage of the cycle you break down. Then go back to the first step. Review the information and re-evaluate your initial response. This may help you develop a new direction and identify where you need more improvement. Spin the model, considering each step, until you have successfully mastered each issue.

INTERVIEW WITH THE AUTHOR
Have you ever killed anyone?

No, well not that I know of, but some of the mistakes I've made on jobs, in different circumstances, in the right conditions, could have. If you read my personal experiences throughout the book you will discover some of my worst failures. You could call it luck or fortune, but I like to think that if I was in different circumstances I wouldn't have made the mistake. I certainly won't now after learning from it.

A scenario I was taught a long time ago I think illustrates how the same mistake can have extremely different results in different circumstances. Imagine you have just poured a hot cup of tea and place it on the coffee table. You suddenly go to pick up the TV remote but knock over the mug. It falls to the ground and spills on the floor, no dramas. But what if your six-month-old daughter was lying in her bouncer on the floor next to the coffee table? You perform exactly the same error by knocking over the mug, it lands in the same spot and spills out the same way – but this time a baby is under it. Same mistake, different consequence. I think of that all the time.

Hopefully you can learn something from my near misses.

CALL TO ACTION

'I can't change what the world does to me. I can only change how I choose to respond, and we can turn those things into a positive, and that becomes our goal. That may be one of the greatest gifts we can give to anybody, is to embrace that mindset.' – **Lieutenant Colonel Dave Grossman**

Key Takeaways

- We all go through stress, no matter the situation.
- The Paramedic Mindset is having poise – possessing self-assurance and composure at a time when you are under a tremendous amount of stress, giving you the power to make good decisions.
- Mental wellbeing is just as important in having poise as specific psychological skills.

Key Tasks

- Name someone you know who possesses poise, and list three of their unique characteristics.
- For a perfect visual representation of poise, watch the movie *The Darkest Hour*. It's about Prime Minister Winston Churchill as Nazi Germany is preparing to invade and destroy Britain.

2

Mindsets and Mastery

Personal Experience – Decision Time

When you are isolated and alone, dealing with one critically ill patient is hard enough, but four was really going to test me. The fun all started just after 11 pm. That's when I was called to a 24-year-old female with abdominal pain: a fairly routine callout. After a thorough assessment of the patient, I could not confidently diagnose her with a specific cause of her severe pain. I had a few ideas, but no definitive diagnosis could be made without an ultrasound.

I was working on an island at the time. I requested a marine rescue boat to come to the island and transport the patient to the hospital. Because this generally takes about two hours, I had to work on my small talk. As I waited for the rescue boat, I received a call from my communications centre, informing me that I had a second patient: a 55-year-old male having a seizure.

It was normal to be dispatched to a second patient as I waited for the boat, so I knew what to do. I called a volunteer driver who would sit with the abdominal pain patient while I went to the man having a seizure – the higher-priority case.

I arrived on scene to find the patient in bed with what appeared to be seizure activity. He had tremors and was shaking uncontrollably, but he could look at me and follow my words. He would moan and groan when I asked questions. This didn't feel like seizures I'd seen before. My first thought was that he was faking it: what's called a pseudo-seizure. And that was something I had seen before. I spoke to the patient's wife, who informed me that he had a condition called functional neurological disorder. It is a condition that can't be explained by a discernible physical issue in the body, but causes significant distress and problems with functioning.

The patient became unable to communicate verbally; he went completely mute and couldn't tell me his concerns. You could see the anguish in his eyes. He couldn't write his thoughts down either, because of the tremors. He had lost complete motor control, and was unable to walk or even move.

As I was trying to manage this complex patient, I received a third phone call informing me that I had another patient. This time, it was an acute behavioural disturbance – behaviour that puts themselves or others in immediate harm. In this case, the patient was swimming naked in a pool, threatening suicide by drowning himself.

I already had two patients to deal with, so I rang the security guards for assistance – there were no police on the island. They managed to restrain the third patient and protect him from drowning while I moved the other patients to a central location. The security guard was able to drive the aggressive patient to me, which helped me manage all three patients at the same location. I was very grateful for this.

The aggressive patient was heavily intoxicated and verbally abusive towards me. He was very agitated, yelling and threatening harm. I placed the patient in a room with the security officer to help contain the situation. There were still two other sick patients in the back needing my attention. I rang a second ambulance volunteer to come and assist me.

I was reassessing the other patients when I received a fourth call: a patient with shortness of breath having an asthma attack. This patient was unable to drive and couldn't come to my location. I wasn't sure how I was going to get the patient to my current location, and I didn't want to leave the others. I couldn't ask the security or volunteers to leave, because their hands were full and they didn't have the medical knowledge or equipment to treat an asthma attack. I really didn't want to leave, but I couldn't just leave the fourth patient at home alone, could I?

I had no choice. I told one volunteer to watch the first two patients, then asked the security officer and another volunteer to stay with the aggressive patient while I drove, lights on and sirens blaring, towards the asthmatic patient.

It was probably the worst treatment I've ever given someone on the scene before. I pulled up outside their house and did a quick visual assessment. The patient was walking and talking, which meant they were well enough, given my other cases. 'That'll do,' I told myself. I put the patient in the ambulance and drove straight back to the house of chaos.

I rang my communications centre to ask for a situation report on the estimated time of arrival for the medivac. They informed me that the boat was delayed due to bad weather. It was going to be another hour at least, and the helicopter was still not available.

At this stage, I had the urge to curl up in a ball and forget what was going on, but I had a sudden moment of calm amid the chaos. I had a simple thought that made me smile: what an amazing challenge this stressful situation is, a great opportunity for growth and to allow me to apply my skills and test my abilities.

I began to laugh and giggle out loud at this thought. I'd read so much about mindsets, but I'd never actively applied the knowledge in real time. I was proud of myself for thinking of it at that moment. I felt as if I was stepping outside myself and could see the scene from a bird's-eye view. It was a very strange sensation. Even though the scene was busy and complex, I had a strong sense that everything was going to be okay. I felt grateful that I'd been able to rise to the occasion.

Another hour had passed as I walked back and forth between all four patients, but it was obvious that the aggressive and non-compliant patient was taking up most of my valuable time. They were not the sickest patient, but if I didn't manage to de-escalate their aggressive behaviour, I wouldn't be able to help anyone.

I tried various techniques: respecting their personal space, establishing a rapport, identifying wants and feelings, listening intently and trying to identify areas of agreement to offer choices and optimism. All of it was only enough to maintain the status quo.

Two paramedics eventually arrived on the boat to help me, which was fantastic, but we still hadn't solved all of the problems I faced. How were we going to transport four patients – including a potentially violent one – on a single boat?

We decided that we couldn't put the aggressive patient with the other three. Instead, the paramedics who arrived on the scene would transport three patients in their boat, leaving the aggressive one with me. I had to organise another boat to transport that patient.

Fortunately, my volunteer worked for a boating company and had a boat licence. We decided to take his boat. It's fair to say it was not designed for medical retrievals, but it was the best we were going to get.

After helping the other paramedics load and depart with their patients, it was now time to move the aggressive patient to the recreational boat. As soon as I mentioned that we were departing for the hospital, the patient suddenly snapped. Bellowing, he sent a big right hook for my face, and tried to follow it up by ramming the security officer into the wall.

The security guard and I had to quickly gain control of the scene. We managed to wrestle the patient to the ground and stop the assault. The security officer was able to hold the patient as I quickly drew up medication for sedation. The problem was that I really didn't want to sedate a patient in a confined space, spending the better part of an hour in the middle of the ocean, while operating alone. 'What's the alternative?' I asked myself.

I guess we could have sat there for a few more hours and hoped for a sudden change in attitude. By this time, though, we had already been there for several hours with no success. It had to be done.

The security officer was becoming fatigued and couldn't stay in this situation for the rest of the night; remember, he was operating outside of his normal day-to-day responsibilities just to help me out. I decided I had no other choice and administered the drug.

It was a long, hot and bumpy ride across the ocean in the middle of the night. Waves were forcing water over the bow, so we had to keep the front hatch closed, which meant there was no airflow. Not being able to look out, I became seasick. As someone who is a sailor, it wasn't my proudest moment, but we made it. I had to wait another 30 minutes for a crew to transport the patient to the hospital, but wasn't I glad to see them walking down the boat ramp at 5 o'clock in the morning!

As we drove back to the island watching the most beautiful sunrise over the ocean, we all felt a great sense of camaraderie and I no longer felt alone. The best way to fight loneliness is to dedicate your time and energy to working alongside other people to help other people. Despite feeling alone at the start, if it wasn't for the non-paramedics' help, I would have been completely lost at sea.

Habits of Mind

We all have varying mindsets, which we refer to throughout our daily lives and working environments. You will commonly hear of the financial mindset: ways to make more money and be rich. To achieve this goal you learn strategies and tools from financial experts. If you've ever been to Bali, you'd notice people very quickly develop the Bali mindset – they have the tattoos and the scars from crashing the scooters to prove it.

Mindsets help set us up for success. They shape the world around us, the actions we take, and the possibilities for our influence. In this chapter, we will explore a range of tools that you can use to rely on the paramedic mindset during an emergency, giving you the power to be mentally flexible and perform under immense pressure.

The word 'mindset' was first used in the 1930s to mean 'habits of mind formed by previous experience'. In simple terms, our mindset is our view of the world, the sum of all the assumptions we make, beliefs we hold onto and attitudes we show.

The way we act while under pressure depends on our previous experience and habits. If we've never had a positive experience during a pressure situation, we will find it exceedingly difficult to act in a positive way that will influence the outcome of the situation. We will need to shift our perception and develop strategies to act in an environment where we've had negative encounters or fears.

In this way, if you can create new pathways to deal proactively with a daunting crisis, you will develop a mindset that sets you up to flourish.

We see the world through the filter of our mind, which can distort reality and cause us to make misleading and mistaken decisions. Without strategies and tools to shift our mindset in that moment, we can fall into the trap of allowing our mind to deceive us.

I have witnessed paramedics overtreating their patients, administering drugs that were not warranted or necessary, because of the intense pressure of the situation. Their worldview became distorted, making them believe the injury was worse than what it really was.

An onlooker sees someone bleeding from a cut and believes the patient has lost copious amounts of blood, which requires immediate action, only for the paramedic to arrive and reframe that belief. For the paramedic, the blood loss is minimal, because they can compare it with past experiences. The outcomes of the paramedic's previous encounters tell them that the amount of blood this patient has lost is not going to cause life-threatening haemorrhagic shock – where the body loses enough fluid to cause organ damage and even failure. All that is required here is a simple dressing.

Experience shapes our mindsets, which shape our actions, which radiate out like ripples in the ocean. The ripple of our thoughts will build overtime and can result in a crash on the beach or a wave worth surfing. If you want to be able to perform effectively in pressure situations, then you must be willing to shift your thinking and develop a paramedic mindset.

My aim is to get you to make these subtle and deliberate shifts in thinking that will click on in your mind like a light bulb. This will allow you to see the world differently when exposed to a scene of carnage and trauma, changing how you perceive the incident.

Cultivating the paramedic mindset is extremely important in performing under pressure. Having all the knowledge and skills in the world becomes useless if we are unable to act in the moment with a clear and focused mind.

Have you ever wanted to buy a new car, and then suddenly it seems like you always see people driving your dream car on the road? You start seeing it everywhere, but in reality it was always there. Before you wanted to buy it, you never even noticed it, but now it seems everyone owns the same car. It's unlikely that the car unexpectedly had a massive increase in sales overnight. Your mind just did not perceive it earlier, as it didn't serve a purpose in your life at the time: you had a different mindset.

When you develop a paramedic mindset, your mind will actively shift its perception of the world to help you see things that will lead you towards achieving your goal. The mind actively searches for opportunities that will aid you in reaching your goal, ignoring other stimuli.

Growth Versus Fixed Mindsets

Professor Carol S. Dweck is the leading expert on fixed and growth mindsets. Her growth mindset theory is a critical component of the paramedic mindset and setting yourself up to flourish.

Dweck's research, which centres on human motivation and its relation to learning, shows the power of our most basic beliefs. Whether conscious or subconscious, those beliefs affect every aspect of our life, including our successes and failures. Our personality is to all intents and purposes our 'mindset'. It even determines whether we fulfil our potential.

How we see ourselves is of critical importance. If we have a fixed mindset and believe we cannot change, our lack of action will bear this out. This prevents us from succeeding or learning from our failures.

Her research identified that those with the growth mindset found success in doing their best, in learning and improving. And this is exactly what we find in champions.

A study completed by Dave Collins and his colleagues examined athletes from various sports who were classified as either super champions (they had won multiple championships or gold medals), champions (they had a single world championship or gold medal) or almost champions (athletes who compete at the elite level but don't win). They found that the main difference between the super champions and the almost champions was their mindset – the way they approached the challenge. The super champions, like Michael Phelps or Michael Jordan, loved the process; they enjoyed the hard work and going to training. The champions and almost champions, on the other hand, preferred game time, the competition, and didn't put as much emphasis on the day-to-day grind.

In other words, when we believe we can improve and become better, we understand that challenge makes us stronger. Doing something that we're passionate about and love goes a long way towards achieving success.

As Dweck explains, in a growth mindset, we see that our innate brain and talent are a jumping off point for growth and development through application and hard work. By fostering life-long learning, the growth mindset makes us increasingly resilient and takes us where we want to go.

In a fixed mindset, however, 'people believe their basic qualities, like their intelligence or talent, are simply fixed traits'. Rather than develop our innate strengths, we simply curate them. We fall into the trap of believing that people who succeed are more talented than we are, rather than more dedicated and hardworking.

The way we perceive a situation is what determines our physiological and cognitive response to it. Your mindset will significantly impact the way you read this book and whether you implement the strategies within it successfully. If you have a fixed mindset, you would believe that no matter what information you find in this book, it won't change your ability to perform under pressure. You will give up after the first chapter or not try to implement what you learn. But with a growth mindset, you will continually want to improve, and you will find this book enthralling.

What I also found interesting from Dweck's work is that people with a fixed mindset actively avoid continuous learning or challenges because they are afraid of failure or afraid of risking their current reputation.

For example, a paramedic with a fixed mindset who has graduated from university and has been working in the job for more than 10 years might avoid further challenges or opportunities for improvement because they would not want to risk failing at training scenarios and assessments when they are already considered successful. They would want to avoid looking like a fool at all costs, particularly in front of their peers. For this person, risking their reputation is too big a risk, so they will avoid taking action.

A brilliant paramedic who could, with further training, become a doctor, would avoid the challenge if they had a fixed mindset. Giving up their reputation as the best paramedic to become an only average doctor, one among many, would be too high a price to pay, despite the fact that becoming a doctor would be an amazing achievement.

As Dweck says, 'In the fixed mindset, everything is about the outcome. If you fail – or if you're not the best – it's all been wasted.' People with a growth mindset see value in what they do, whether they succeed or fail. They're always striving, meeting challenges head on and making important strides. They may not reach an imagined goal, but they treat failure as an opportunity for growth.

We each have neither a solely fixed nor completely growth mindset. We all possess a mixture of fixed and growth mindsets, depending on different contexts such as work and home and on attributes such as our personality and intelligence.

In this book I encourage you to cultivate a growth mindset, in order to chart a new course and tackle the challenges of stress, self-doubt and failure. As you will soon see, a commitment to continual learning and challenges is central to performing under pressure.

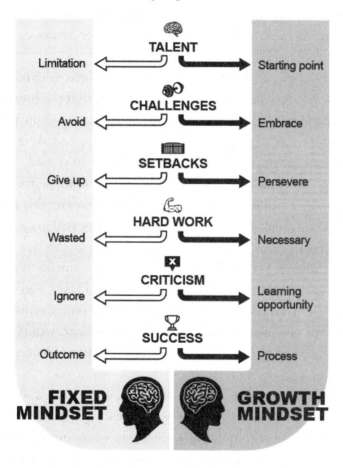

Your mindset shapes your beliefs about...

FIXED MINDSET		GROWTH MINDSET
Limitation	TALENT	Starting point
Avoid	CHALLENGES	Embrace
Give up	SETBACKS	Persevere
Wasted	HARD WORK	Necessary
Ignore	CRITICISM	Learning opportunity
Outcome	SUCCESS	Process

Figure 1. The two mindsets. Adapted from Carol S. Dweck, *Mindset: The New Psychology of Success* (New York: Random House, 2006, p. 245), original graphic by Nigel Holmes

Our Perception of Challenge and Threat

The challenge and threat model closely relates to the fixed and growth mindset. Mindset theory has proposed that mindsets can be induced through situational factors, such as whether an individual perceives their circumstances as a challenge or threat. When influenced by a stressor, a fixed mindset sees it as a threat, while a growth mindset perceives it as a challenge. In this model, our perception of stress determines whether we thrive under pressure or panic. It involves our individual evaluation of the situation and the demands of the task relative to our available resources to cope with it.

If we have a challenge perception, we believe we can handle the situation. We perceive that we can respond to the pressure in a positive way, and we realise that the pressure will benefit us. The situation is within our cognitive capacity, and we have the resources to manage the situation.

With the challenge perception we understand that we have a tremendous opportunity to improve and actively seek positive change. We understand and appreciate that the unknown is difficult, but instead of thinking it will lead us to a path of ruin, we feel we can respond to it.

By contrast, in threat perception mode, we believe we cannot handle the pressure. Our focus is on all the things that can go wrong. We're fixated on the negative because we fear failure. We feel like we're in danger. We feel trapped under the weight of so much uncertainty and paralysed by the unknown. The threat builds, cascading into fear, stress and anxiety. We develop a strong desire to fly away from the situation.

Research tells us that through seeing pressure situations as a challenge, we can improve our performance. In other words, the way we perceive stress impacts our response to it, in terms of improving or debilitating our performance.

When, for example, I get a call to respond to a patient who has just fallen 20 metres off a building, I can handle it because I perceive it as a challenge. If I were called to a patient who is stuck in a burning building, I would perceive this as a threat because I don't have a handle on the situation – I would need the fire service.

It's important to note that this approach only works if we're trying to achieve a particular outcome; it must be goal-relevant. If we're trying to achieve a particular goal, we will need a foundational skill set in that area. That's why the challenge and threat model is an excellent tool for athletes, paramedics, defence personnel and those in other goal-related professions and pursuits.

Simply perceiving all situations as a challenge without a goal and without any foundational knowledge and experience in that area won't help us achieve success. If I decided to be a ballerina tomorrow, perceiving it as a challenge probably wouldn't help me achieve success in the Paris Opera Ballet, because I can't dance and have no training in dancing. The thing perceiving it as a challenge would do, though, is prevent me from getting sad, angry or distressed over failing, because I wouldn't expect to do well.

In many situations, especially in the medical environment, the challenge or threat response is not all-or-nothing. We will transition through both stages, depending on our previous experience, knowledge, self-efficacy (belief that you can complete the task at hand), the required effort, the safety/danger level and many other factors. We will experience both stages of response; it's not a fixed and dichotomous state.

This theory tells us, though, that it's not enough to just be skilful and intelligent; we need the right mental mindset as well. A combination of all three helps us deal with pressure.

A 2019 study by John vonRosenberg found that 'Preparing for stressful situations is not only accomplished through the practice of skills and rehearsal of knowledge, but also cognitive readiness, mindfulness and encouragement of team members. Deciding to actively engage in problem-solving through the lens of overcoming obstacles and meeting challenges with confidence provides the mental framework that recruits the inevitable sympathetic surge [i.e. fight or flight] for benefit rather than impairment.'

When it comes to the paramedic mindset, it's about whether you perceive the pressure as a potential to gain or a potential to lose.

A Paramedic's Perception

My wife is constantly disappointed by me when she tells me she feels sick, has a headache or is going to vomit. I usually respond by telling her that she will be okay and continue doing whatever I was doing at the time. So she now tries to use more descriptive words when describing her suffering. Instead of saying, 'I'm in pain', she now says, 'I am in absolute agony.'

Because I have seen great pain and suffering, when my wife complains about a mild headache, I see it as a non-event. While I'm trying to be more empathetic, my individual perception of her pain is obviously very different from hers. My perception is clearly based on evidence, but it's obvious to anyone who's married that her assessment is 'right' and mine is 'wrong'.

Everybody perceives the world and approaches problems differently. Whatever we see and feel does not necessarily reflect the way things really are. A paramedic might not faint at the sight of blood – they're used to it. A bystander, though, might pass out. To paramedics, blood is simply plasma and red blood cells – nothing extraordinary.

Our perceptions are influenced by our needs. A paramedic's need is to fix the problem and be part of the solution. If you need to perform under pressure, then you have to change your perception of pressure situations in order to support your mission.

To have a paramedic mindset, you will need to change how you process information received from the outside world. You must choose to select, organise and interpret the meaning of that information differently. Changing your perception of information will result in decisions and actions that move you closer to your goal.

The first step is to select where you will focus your attention. Attend to the task rather than the pain and suffering. This will attract your attention to your mission of having composure and self-assurance in pressure moments.

The poised paramedic may look at a scene that involves a train crash with 18 victims scattered across the tracks, and perceive it as an opportunity to apply their training. A panicked paramedic, by contrast, will envisage what they might expect to see at a train crash – absolute chaos and misery.

What we interpret can be based on what we expect to see.

Personal Experience – Don't Drop the Baby

Most paramedics get frustrated over the media attention we get for delivering a baby. This is mainly because we do and see things far worse and more stressful that never get any attention or recognition. You can see the attraction of delivering a baby, bringing life into this world: it's always a beautiful thing, especially since we're often dealing with death. It is, however, a rare event, not something that we see every day. I know a paramedic who has been working for 25 years and is yet to catch a slippery, slimy baby.

Despite saying we paramedics don't like these stories, I would like to relate my own story of delivering a baby. I think the following case is a particularly good example of the power of perception, and of challenge versus threat mindsets.

Before this case, I had only delivered three other babies. Each of these jobs were different, and only one of them was 'normal' or by the book. On this particular day, I was called to a woman whose water had just broken (what we call prelabour rupture of membranes) with contractions five minutes apart. I was on call and had woken up to respond to this case, which isn't always great in the early hours of the morning as you're wiping the sleep out of your eyes.

When I arrived on scene, the mother was stable and the delivery didn't appear to be imminent, so I had time . . . some time, anyway.

What made this scene more difficult was that I was working by myself in a remote community. There was no access to a doctor, let alone a hospital, so I had to manage this case by myself. I requested backup, but the helicopter was unavailable – it was a classic case of Murphy's law in action. They still sent the helicopter, but it was going to be about a two-hour wait.

I asked how far along the pregnancy was, and was told that she was unfortunately only 31 weeks pregnant. This instantly changed the severity of the situation, as this baby would be a lot more premature than I'd have hoped.

For some reason though, I felt in control. In that moment, I was doing all the things to prepare for a delivery – and I was prepared for the worst, of course. I positioned the mother on the bed. I got all of my maternity equipment ready, placed the resuscitation equipment at the ready, just in case, and reassured the mother.

Then suddenly, the mother had the urge to pass her bowels – to poo. This is a classic sign that the baby's head is pushing on the mother's bowels, giving her this urge. (In fact, a lot of kids have been born in the toilet bowl because of this urge.)

I could see the head bulging; it was almost time. I quickly got dressed in my scrubs (the only time a paramedic would wear scrubs) and warned the father that the child's birth was close.

I looked up at the father quickly to find that he was as white as a ghost. He suddenly covered his mouth and ran outside to power vomit, which was followed by a sudden fainting episode. I took a quick look to see if he was breathing and 'okay', then left him to recover on the floor. Remember when expecting fathers used to wait at the nearest pub instead of being in the delivery room – why did we ever change that?

I could see the head and urged the mother to push as it came out first. Thank God it wasn't a leg. But the cord was wrapped around the baby's neck. SHIT (Send Help It's Terrible)! I managed to loosen the umbilical cord enough to pull it over the baby's head and free it from strangulation. Meanwhile, I was also trying to reassure the mother as well as the father, who, having recovered from his fainting spell, had made his way back indoors.

The baby's head was out, but I didn't want to stimulate the baby just yet: we still had the body to contend with. It felt like an eternity waiting for the next contraction to deliver the body as the baby sat there with its head out, neither breathing nor moving.

Then, suddenly, the next contraction came and the baby shot out like a rocket, so hard that the slippery little sucker fell right through my fingers. Did I really just drop a newborn? Whoops. Fortunately, the bed was there and saved the baby from a fall. I managed to gently 'place' the baby on the bed as I lost my grip.

The baby still wasn't breathing, so I went through the steps of stimulating it and checking its heart rate. Its pulse was a bit slow, so I used a bag valve mask (a mask with an attached hand pump) to ever so gently start breathing for the baby, willing the baby to take a breath. Then there it was, the most beautiful cry I've ever heard in my life, much better than the cries my own kids pester me with.

Once I'd wrapped the baby up, kept it warm, introduced it to its mother and ensured skin-to-skin contact, it was time for me to focus my attention back on the mother. Murphy's law decided to rear its head again as the mother started to bleed. Fortunately, though, through a few basic procedures, I managed to stop the bleeding.

Then, ten minutes later, the doctor and flight paramedic walked in.

The relevance of this story is that I had never experienced a birth like this with such complications before. I had never performed those procedures before, despite 10 years of experience. Despite all of this, for some reason I felt like I had things under control. Upon reflection, I believe that this was mainly due to the fact that I perceived this case as a challenge rather than as a threat.

Despite not being a midwife or an expert in obstetrics, I enjoyed the challenge of the case. It's one of those jobs that as a paramedic you read about all the time but think you'll never experience, so when it does happen, it creates an opportunity for growth. I had self-efficacy, which allowed me to realise that, despite my lack of experience in obstetrics, I possessed the skills to manage the challenge. I wasn't threatened by the case, and that was a great feeling, because I've certainly felt threatened in a bunch of other cases – which you will read about later.

The Contagious Nature of Mindsets

For a paramedic, determining whether your day is going to be good or a struggle can often depend on who you're going to be working with or partnered with. Generally, paramedics work in pairs, and you will be stuck together in the confined space of the ambulance for more than 12 hours.

The moment a negative person who is languishing jumps in the ambulance and starts with their pessimistic attitude, they instantly bring down the mood in the vehicle. You immediately feel the change in atmosphere, like you've been dragged into a pit of suffering. As a result, the negative self-talk begins and you run to your boss to ask for a roster change, telling them how horrible your day is going to be.

Mindsets are contagious; actions or emotions can be unconsciously transmitted from one person to another. Dr Michael D. Yapko, who has written several pieces on depression, highlights how our lives are filled with examples of catching behaviours and emotions from other people, such as depression, sadness, anger and frustration.

We feel what we reflect on; meaning our emotions come from our thoughts. If you're trying to provide medical interventions on someone who has just been hit by a bus, but you're panicking, sweating, and looking lost, out of control, nervous and in some cases frightened, then your emotions will permeate to the people around you and influence their actions. It's hard to maintain control and calm at the scene and provide lifesaving medical procedures if everyone is panicked, and worst of all, if that panic is being multiplied by your own panic.

Quite often, I've treated or 'cured' a patient's condition simply by walking into the room. This was not a miracle; instead, it happened because I walked into a panicked situation with poise, composure and self-confidence. Not only does the patient feel better, but their loved ones also experience a tremendous sense of relief. The patient has gone from a feeling of impending doom to safety, knowing they are going to be okay.

The people around you will consciously and subconsciously feel your emotional state and mimic your behaviour. The hour before the kids need to go to school creates mimicked behaviour. It usually starts off with my wife yelling at me to get the kids dressed because she is busy making lunches, packing their bags and basically doing everything. As I stumble down the stairs, I'm in a good mood and simply tell the kids to get dressed, but then we get distracted and start playing instead. After 45 minutes of burnt toast, lost homework and mismatched socks, though, I start yelling at the kids for not getting dressed, which puts them in a bad mood as well. Now we all walk out the door frustrated and annoyed.

The same is true in the opposite direction: 'You are the average of the five people you spend the most time with,' says American entrepreneur and motivational speaker Jim Rohn. This illustrates the power of those around us, and how our actions are shaped by the people who influence us. Eventually, we start to think as they think and behave as they behave.

If you want to have poise, then surround yourself with the knowledge of people who have achieved success before. By developing the paramedic mindset, you will be infecting yourself with the mentality and approach that helped them accomplish their success, making it more likely that you will achieve similar outcomes.

Master the Fundamental Skills

The one thing most books on mindset don't talk about is the absolute need to master the fundamental skills of your profession before learning mindset skills. If you wish to implement the mindset skills to perform under pressure then first you must work hard at mastering the competencies necessary to execute your tasks – the fine motor skills or the minimum standard of knowledge and understanding of your role. That role could be as a paramedic, a sculptor, a father or a mentor to a friend.

A skill is knowledge of the fundamentals and the ability to execute them properly and quickly, to be prepared and cover every little detail. That's what you must master if you want the mindset skills you're about to learn to optimise your performance.

Imagine you are in the middle of a war zone and you have to fight back or face death but you don't know the fundamentals of operating a gun. Picture yourself being able to remain calm because you have a brilliant mindset. In fact, you are very positive about the fighting and the bombs going off around you. Practising your breathing techniques and visualisation, you are centred and ready to fight. But to survive as a soldier, you need to operate your gun without hesitation. If you don't know how to load bullets into a gun, your calm mindset won't help you in battle. You'll be dead.

Athletes also understand that to succeed they must execute certain basic core skills. No rugby league player will succeed without the minimum standard fitness levels, muscular strength or catching, passing and tackling skills. No degree of mindfulness or visualisation can overcome the prerequisite for the fundamental skills needed to perform in your chosen profession.

As a paramedic the micro-skill of decompressing a patient's chest – by inserting a large needle between their ribs to puncture a hole in their lungs without puncturing the heart – requires hours of training to master the fundamental technique in order to implement it successfully in the moment.

But a critically ill patient has multiple complexities occurring at the same time, requiring multiple interventions, not just a single chest decompression. If a paramedic hasn't first mastered the fundamentals, the complexity will soon overwhelm them, manifesting as panic.

This book is focused on the mental and mindset skills of performance, but without a solid foundation, the roof will collapse and you won't be able to effectively execute any of the mindset skills required to master the paramedic mindset.

Four Levels of Competence

The best way to develop mastery of your fundamental skills is through the four stages of competence model. Drawing on the work of Martin M. Broadwell and Noel Burch, this model identifies the stages of learning and how our ultimate goal is to achieve unconscious competence – the mastery of skills.

The model is based on the premise that before a learning experience begins, learners are unaware of what or how much they do or don't know. As they learn, however, they move through four psychological states until they reach the stage of mastery.

Stage 1: Ignorance – Unconscious Incompetence

This is the lowest level of mastery. At this stage the person doesn't know or understand how to do the task. In some cases, they don't even recognise their deficits. The individual needs to acknowledge their own incompetence in order to learn the new skill.

Most paramedic students are at a level of unconscious incompetence when it comes to performing under stress. They get tunnel vision. They don't know it and usually they refuse to admit it. The first step in making them better is to get them to accept that they need experience and practise before they can be entrusted with human lives.

Stage 2: Awareness – Conscious Incompetence

At this level the individual acknowledges their deficit and takes accountability in developing the skills required. Paramedic students who arrive knowing that they need to learn will develop their skills much faster than those who are ignorant of that fact.

Stage 3: Learning – Conscious Competence

You can perform the skill, but it takes a lot of thought and is often broken down in steps – there's no flow to it. That is fine for many tasks, but when life-and-death skills need to be performed under stress, or you need to perform multiple tasks simultaneously, it's not good enough.

Stage 4: Mastery – Unconscious Competence

This is the highest level of mastery. As martial artist Bruce Lee put it, 'Learn it until you forget it.' This is what people mean when they say you need to develop muscle memory. The skill has become second nature.

This is the level you need to attain in order to flourish under stress.

INTERVIEW WITH THE AUTHOR
What's the worst thing you've ever seen?

This gets a bit graphic, so skip this Q&A if you're squeamish!

I find it hard to narrow this down to one scene; I've seen a bunch of bad things that all create their own unique circumstances. In general, I think cases involving children are more difficult than most because so much emotion is attached to the death of a child.

I vividly remember standing on the ramp at the hospital's emergency department when another ambulance reversed up to unload their patient. It was normal to open the door and help the other crew remove their patient from the ambulance. I opened the side door and

---

asked the crew if I could help. The paramedic inside was quick to say yes and handed me a dead child wrapped in a blanket. It was a shock to say the least, but the mother was watching me and I felt I had to put my emotions aside for her. Once they stepped down out of the ambulance, I handed the child back to the mother.

Or I could say the worst body I've seen is a months-old decaying, maggot-ridden, mummified corpse that excreted the most putrid smell. I remember walking into this house and noticing thousands of thousands of dead flies on the floor, just little black dots everywhere. Then suddenly turning the corner, there it was. The body had been there so long that the maggots had been transformed into flies and then even they died. Only cockroaches could survive that place.

Or other scenes where you experience these terrible sensations that are hard to forget, the ones that give you the shivers. Like walking to a car that has rolled into the bush, in long grass, you stand on someone's organ. Or doing CPR on a technically dead patient and having them suddenly open their eyes and stare right through you – only for them to go back to dead on the ground every time you stop compressions.

The one job though that will stick with me for the rest of my life is when I attended my work colleague, a fellow paramedic, who had committed suicide (see page 20).

People generally want to hear the stories like when I went to attend a father and son both shot, one in the head and one in the stomach, or cases that make the news like shark attacks or people jumping off balconies, but these are the types of cases I've trained for, that's my job.

I've always been able to move forward without concerns for my mental health a few days after these incidents, but it's the jobs where I've made a mistake that linger like a ghost.

CALL TO ACTION

'Challenge goes with discomfort and that fits with growth. If we're not willing to be uncomfortable, then we are not going to grow. And in the moment of performance, it's not physical discomfort. It's the discomfort that comes from knowing you might fail.' **– Dr Tom Evens, NSW Ambulance**

Key Takeaways

- The way you perceive a situation – as either a challenge or a threat – will greatly influence the outcome.
- Our beliefs affect what we want and whether we succeed in getting it.
- A growth mindset is a critical element if you want to perform under stress. It will allow you to solve problems, adapt and overcome.

Key Tasks

- Do you have a fixed or growth mindset? Take the mindset assessment to learn more about your mindset: <blog.mindsetworks.com/what-s-my-mindset>
- When you're placed under stress do you perceive it as a challenge or as a threat?
- Read the book *Mindset: The New Psychology of Success* by Carol S. Dweck.

3

From Languishing to Flourishing

Personal Experience – Feeling Blah

Standing alone in the backyard of the ambulance station during the early hours of the morning with nothing but my Batman boxer shorts on, I wondered how it had come to this. The only thing I was grateful for, as I ran out to fetch the garden hose, was that I didn't wake up with morning glory.

A fire had been intentionally lit, targeting my neighbours, the police station. As I looked around, my workplace looked more like a detention centre than an ambulance station. I felt my enthusiasm, passion and desire to go above and beyond drain out of me like the water coming out of the hose. I asked myself, why should I bother?

I had recently separated from my long-time girlfriend and was stuck out in a remote community isolated for eight days at a time – sleeping inside the station, working as a single officer and being a single man.

It was in this context that I was then sent to a patient who was having an acute mental disturbance (I wasn't far behind having my own). He was known to be aggressive and I was told that police were on scene needing assistance. I arrived to find no police car in sight, but I didn't miss the sight of a steel tyre rim being hurled towards the driver's windscreen seconds before it smashed into the front of the ambulance. Trying to gather my wits after jumping back in my chair, covering my face from the flying shards of glass, I glimpsed the patient sprinting towards me.

I hit the accelerator to get the hell out of there, but he seemed to be inspired by me fleeing the scene. He launched himself onto the side mirror, wrapped his arms around it and hung on for dear life. It looked like he was suspended from the side of a helicopter a thousand feet above the air, gripping tightly and determined not to let go. I kept driving, building up speed thinking he would have to let go at some stage, but as I started to go faster he was still hanging on. I was waiting for the thumping moment of driving over a couple of speed bumps as I ran over him.

That thought scared me more than him hitting me in the face, so I gradually slowed to a stop. Taking some advice from a friend who said all you have to do in these situations is to be louder than the opposition. I wound down my window and yelled at the patient as loud as I could, telling him to let the fuck go or I'd run him over.

It worked. As soon as he let go I sped away to wait for the police around the corner. Once the police came, I had to go back in, but this time I was armed. It was one of the more satisfying sedations I've done.

The next day, after getting little sleep while responding on call throughout the night, I arrived at a house to find a child who had been abused by their parents. With the lack of sleep and consecutive negative cases, it wasn't surprising that I found myself feeling blah.

I wasn't depressed or suffering from anxiety or another mental illness. I just lacked complete motivation and was disengaged from my work. I continued to see out the eight days, but I did it with little empathy. I did enough to get by, looking forward to my days off. I thought all I needed was a quiet couple of nights and a few days' rest. The only problem with my days off was that I went back to an empty house. My now ex-girlfriend had moved out and I was living 800 kilometres away from my hometown.

I would turn to alcohol as my coping mechanism. Back then, I wouldn't dare talk about how I felt and share my thoughts about the week. I thought I just had to deal with it myself, and the best way to do that was to go out and drink with my mates. Another problem was that my only mates in this town were paramedics, who also tried to mask their thoughts with alcohol.

As a student, the Martin Scorsese film *Bringing Out the Dead* was compulsory viewing. The story explores the depths of human misery as witnessed by a New York paramedic. To cope with the trauma, the main character, Frank, turns to alcohol to survive. The film shows a bleak but necessary insight into the life of a paramedic.

At this time, I felt like Frank. 'I was good at my job: there were periods when my hands moved with a speed and skill beyond me, and my mind worked with a cool authority I had never known. But in the last year, I had started to lose that control. Things had turned bad. I hadn't saved anyone for months.'

When I first started working as a paramedic, I framed my mindset around saving lives, and when that rare occurrence happened it was like the best drug in the world. But I soon realised that the job is less about saving lives than it is about bearing witness to tragedy. I struggled to cope with this reality. Constantly exposed to trauma and death, I no longer saw the value in my treatment. Sometimes I felt more broken than the patients I wheeled into the back of the ambulance.

I was in limbo and felt stuck. Living in a foreign town, single, I was a supposedly tough male who would just carry on. I had no sense of direction. I could still function, I wasn't in complete despair. I still cleaned my room and washed my clothes. I could go to work and perform my tasks, but I did the minimum – I reached the KPIs and then stopped. I was set in a downward spiral that made everything a struggle. If I didn't do something quickly, I would tumble into depression.

It wasn't until a couple of years later that I discovered the term for this – languishing. I was languishing in life, the opposite of flourishing. I wasn't diagnosed with a mental illness; I just had no energy or drive to perform well. I had an unhealthy social network and was just getting through the day. I discovered that more than 50 per cent of people who are languishing will fall into depression or other mental illnesses.

Mental Illness versus Mental Health

'Health is . . . not merely the absence of disease or infirmity,' the World Health Organization wrote in 1947, but instead incorporates 'physical, mental, and social wellbeing'.

Psychologist Dr Barbara Fredrickson's research on positivity has shown that people who flourish live within an 'optimal range of human functioning'. They are productive self-starters who are good to others, strive to grow and develop great resilience.

Goodness seems like a simple thing, but most of us rarely take the time to actually think about what goodness means. In 2002 the *British Medical Journal* asked its readers the question 'What makes a good doctor?' and received 102 letters in response.

An article in *Psychology Today* described a 'good' doctor as someone who is observant, listens and is eager to learn about their patients. They can tolerate uncertainty, maintain their composure and positivity while explaining medical concepts, and work to solve problems in order to achieve more favourable outcomes. Among other answers, an important component was respecting the values of people. In other words, the 'good' doctor is a glass-half-full kind of person. There was no mention of the good doctor being highly intelligent.

Before we take a look at a concept known as the mental health continuum, we need to understand the difference between mental illness and mental health. These two states are of course interconnected, but there's a big difference between the two.

Mental illness is more concerned with disease; it's a general term that refers to a group of illnesses that significantly affect how a person behaves, thinks and interacts with the world. Mental illness is diagnosed by professionals according to standardised criteria. Types of mental illness include clinical depression (major depressive disorder), anxiety, schizophrenia, bipolar disorder and others.

Mental illness has, at least recently, been the focus of mainstream medicine and society, but as a consequence, our mental health has been forgotten.

Mental health is a broader term that incorporates functioning beyond the threshold of clinical syndromes such as anxiety and depression. Factors that support good mental health include positive self-esteem, warm and trusting relationships, motivation and openness to learn from challenges and improve as a person. Mental health could thus be considered as a state in which our psychological functions allow us 'productive activities, fulfilling relationships with people, and the ability to adapt to change and cope with stress'.

Identifying the distinction between mental illness and mental health is important, because the absence of mental illness does not mean that a person is mentally well – i.e. flourishing. Mental health involves positive feelings and functioning well in life. It could be considered a precursor or enabling state that can support flourishing.

If someone suffers from poor mental health, they're likely to feel as though they're languishing and stuck. An absence of good mental health doesn't mean they're depressed. It just means they're in a mental state of stagnation. They can still go to work and complete day-to-day tasks, but they derive no satisfaction from it – it's a drag. If they were taking an exam, they would aim for 51 per cent and nothing more.

Sociologist and psychologist Dr Corey Keyes describes mental health as the presence of emotional wellbeing in conjunction with high levels of social and psychological functioning. A person with mental health has poise, which helps them flourish and thrive. Most of us are quick to judge and might diagnose ourselves with a mental illness when we are feeling low, but really we probably have poor mental health. By focusing on flourishing, we start to prevent mental illness rather than trying to find a cure after a diagnosis. Prevention is always better than a cure.

The Mental Health Continuum: From Flourishing to Languishing

We have two problems as a society: too much mental illness and not enough good mental health. Our biggest problem is this absence of good mental health. In general, society prioritises diagnosing mental illness over diagnosing positive mental health.

The mental health continuum model can measure an individual's status of mental health and categorises individuals as flourishing, or having good mental health; languishing, or having poor mental health; or moderately mentally healthy. Individuals who don't meet the criteria for flourishing or languishing are considered moderately mentally healthy.

A 2005 study using these definitions estimated that of the United States' general population, 16.9 per cent were languishing, 65.1 per cent were moderately mentally healthy, and 18 per cent were flourishing. Those who were flourishing scored higher in happiness scales, and showed no symptoms of depression or burnout.

Flourishing

Keyes describes flourishing as the ultimate state of mentally healthy adults. Such people have high levels of emotional wellbeing, and find satisfaction in their life, but still seek to grow. They have self-belief, feel like they know what they're doing, and are happy with who they are; 'they choose their fate in life, rather than see themselves as victims of fate'.

Not surprisingly, people who are flourishing are also less likely to suffer from premature death. This is thought to be because flourishing individuals are more likely to live a healthy lifestyle – they exercise, eat well and don't smoke or abuse substances. In turn, they have a lower rate of cardiovascular disease, fewer visits to the doctor and fewer missed days at work.

Around 80 per cent of the population is not flourishing, only 17.2 per cent of the population is flourishing. This is significant because if those who are flourishing have the lowest risk of developing a mental disorder, then flourishing is a protection against mental illness. Someone who is languishing has a three-to-fourfold higher risk of suicide and depression.

Barbara Fredrickson's research reinforced the value of this idea. She found that individuals who flourished had more significant peaks in positive emotion and thought. Having positive emotion is invaluable, as we see later in this book with the power that positive self-talk has over performance.

Flourishing is not a new term or concept. In the Ancient Greek and Roman philosophy of Stoicism, the aim was to achieve *eudaimonia*, which can be translated as human flourishing. Stoics believed that a life is eudaimonic when it is complete, when there is no further possibility of growth and we have fulfilled the human potential for excellence and poise. *Eudaimonia* relates directly to the paramedic mindset and poise – in order to perform well under stress we must first be flourishing.

Languishing

Unfortunately, a lot of people lack poise. Instead, their mindset leaves them in a state of languishing. Languishing may be conceived of as emptiness and stagnation. Those who are languishing are not mentally ill, but they show few signs of mental health or positivity.

Languishing people are those who are there in body but not in mind. They can function and complete their tasks, but not with a high level of effectiveness or satisfaction. They feel aimless. Languishing is not as demanding as depression, where we would feel sorrow or hopelessness. When we are languishing, we feel 'meh' or 'blah' – neither great nor terrible.

The risk of major depression is significantly higher among individuals who are at the languishing end of the mental health continuum. To avoid falling into the languishing state, we must deliberately plan and intentionally implement mindfulness strategies.

Several paramedics have been in a constant languishing state the entire time I've worked with them. They no longer derive joy or fulfilment from their work. I have seen these paramedics miss critical information or disregard a patient's cry for help because they are disengaged and seem to have lost empathy for their patients. These types of paramedics are the ones who get the most complaints from patients.

This is the mindset we must avoid. Some of the factors that enable us to move out of negative mental health states include resilience, positive social support, self-efficacy and positive experiences.

When I was languishing, when I tried to implement change and operational procedures within my community and ambulance station, I kept running into roadblocks and pushback. This made me very frustrated, as I was doing what I thought was best for patient outcomes but had no support from the people around me.

I became cynical towards my leaders, and laid blame and responsibility on other people. I let bureaucracy and red tape affect my mental wellbeing, which, in turn, started to affect my patient care. I wasn't as thorough with my assessments with patients; I had lost that care factor, that drive to go the extra mile. I was questioning why I should bother doing my best when no one around me was supportive. The languishing state has a snowball effect and creates a bad attitude.

The worst-case scenario of languishing is when you are in a group of languishing people – when your workplace is full of languishers. What results is collective negative rumination – repetitive and excessive discussion of adverse situations among members of an organisation. These discussions centre on the negative and uncontrollable aspects of their role.

I don't want to point the finger at any person, group or job, but if you've recently stood in line to renew your driver's licence or car registration, you'll know what a group of languishers look like.

In such a workplace we might turn to your colleagues for guidance or to vent our emotions, only to have them multiply those emotions. This is a vicious cycle of shared negative thoughts, which prevents us from resisting adversity by seeing it as a challenge.

A flourishing person is one who is self-accepting. They can form and maintain supportive, warm and trusting relationships. They see themselves as becoming a better person. They derive a sense of direction or meaning from the work they are doing. They can shape and influence the world around them. They believe that they are in control of what happens, rather than relying on luck or fate.

A languishing person lacks the motivation to do their job. They become short-tempered and lack patience. They have low enthusiasm. They are not highly engaged or passionate about their work. They tend to work towards goals that avoid something negative rather than achieve something positive. A languishing person is cynical about their leaders, colleagues and career, and will procrastinate.

All of these symptoms lead to mediocrity. You might be able to get by day-to-day but that's it. On the positive side, the majority of people who are languishing don't need therapy. They need support to develop their resourcefulness and get themselves unstuck. The goal of this book is to help you get unstuck and flourish.

It's normal to fluctuate between flourishing and languishing, and when we do lose flourishing, that should only occur as a result of a change in our life. It's a sign that we've gone through something difficult that has shaken our world. The key is identifying if this change is expected or unexpected.

Let's run on full and have loads of energy and confidence to perform at a high level. Let's focus on flourishing.

POISE CYCLE

PANIC CYCLE

Figure 2. The paths of poise and panic.
Which one are you going to take?

Focus on Flourishing

All humans live with a bias towards negativity – our status quo is to focus on the bad. We have negative bias to add more days to our lives, to survive. If you were stuck in the middle of Antarctica alone, with no jacket and no food, being positive about the situation won't change the fact that you'll die within minutes from hypothermia. But a negative bias will save your life, telling you you're in a terrible situation and you need to get out of it or die.

Barbara Fredrickson's research has shown that in order to offset one negative experience we need at least three positive experiences. Using this 3-to-1 ratio can help us develop a mental state where our survival mind and our flourishing mind collaborate for the best outcome.

When Fredrickson talks about positivity, she isn't just asking us to be stoic in the face of suffering. Positivity is beyond simple feelings of happiness: 'It consists of the whole range of positive emotions – from appreciation to love, from amusement to joy, from hope to gratitude, and then some.'

We need constant reminders in our daily life to focus on the positive, to add quality to the quantity. Otherwise, what's the point of life if we're not trying to add positivity to it? We need to rewrite the story that our innate negativity constantly tells us. This takes work and focus. Epicurus, a Greek philosopher, believed that we need constant reminders to be focused and stay focused on pursuing a better life.

Another interesting study by Barbara Fredrickson, in collaboration with Dr Lahnna Catalino, titled 'A Tuesday in the life of a flourisher', researched the role of positive emotional reactivity in achieving optimal mental health. Their theory was that flourishers thrive because they take advantage of experiencing greater positive emotions. They found that wellbeing may be fuelled by small yet consequential differences in the way people experience pleasant everyday events.

They focused their study on six positive activities that are known to elicit positive emotions. These included helping, interacting with others, playing, learning, engaging in spiritual activity and exercising. Their 208 participants comprised 108 flourishers, 67 non-flourishers and 33 depressed people.

Every group improved, and the non-flourishers and depressed groups had better days. But in comparison to non-flourishers and depressed people, flourishers experienced a 160 per cent higher positive emotional response when helping somebody. Across the board, flourishers far exceeded non-flourishers and depressed people in all areas tested. They had greater positive emotions during five of the six activities: helping, playing, interacting, learning and engaging in spiritual activities. The only activity that flourishing didn't change was exercise.

Fredrickson and Catalino concluded that if we do more of these five things throughout our day, we will improve our chances to overcome negative bias and flourish more and more. Ultimately, recurrent experiences of positive emotions make us more observant and less emotionally reactive.

Discover Your Wellbeing

Coming up is a quick questionnaire called the mental health continuum short form (MHC-SF) that many researchers have used to measure mental health. I strongly encourage you to take the time to complete this questionnaire. It's very valuable to measure our current mental status and have a better understanding of where we sit in the continuum. It can help us identify areas for improvement and what we need to focus on.

The Mental Health Continuum Short Form (MHC-SF)

The questionnaire comprises three categories – emotional, social and psychological – that test various aspects of mental health (the presence of emotional wellbeing) in conjunction with high levels of social and psychological functioning. There are 14 items, of which three were chosen to represent emotional wellbeing, six psychological wellbeing, and five items social wellbeing.

Mark your responses in the columns using the following guide.

- Never = 0
- Once or twice = 1
- About once a week = 2
- About 2 or 3 times a week = 3
- Almost every day = 4
- Every day = 5

Adult MHC-SF (ages 18 or older)

Please answer the following questions about how you have been feeling during the past month. Answer each question with a tick in the box that best represents your experience.

During the past month, how often did you feel . . .	Never	Once or twice	About once a week	About 2 or 3 times a week	Almost every day	Every day
Emotional wellbeing						
happy						
interested in life						
satisfied with life						
Social wellbeing						
that you had something important to contribute to society						
that you belonged to a community (like a social group or your neighbourhood)						
that our society is a good place or is becoming a better place, for all people						
that people are basically good						
that the way our society works makes sense to you						
Psychological wellbeing						
that you liked most parts of your personality						

During the past month, how often did you feel ...	Never	Once or twice	About once a week	About 2 or 3 times a week	Almost every day	Every day
good at managing the responsibilities of your daily life						
that you had warm and trusting relationships with others						
that you had experiences that challenged you to grow and become a better person						
confident to think and express your own ideas and opinions						
that your life has a sense of direction and meaning to it						

Source: C.L.M. Keyes, *Brief description of the mental health continuum short form (MHC-SF)'*, 2009. Available: <www.sociology.emory.edu/ckeyes>

Evaluating your results

Are you flourishing, moderately mentally healthy or languishing?

First, add up your scores. Your total score can range from 0 to 70 points, with higher points meaning higher levels of wellbeing.

To be diagnosed with **flourishing** mental health during the past month, you must have responded *every day* or *almost every day* to at least one of the three signs of emotional wellbeing (questions 1–3) and at least six of the remaining 11 signs of positive functioning (questions 4–14).

If you have been **languishing** during the past month, you will have responded to one of the three emotional wellbeing symptoms (questions 1–3) with *never* or *once or twice* and to six of the remaining 11 signs of positive functioning (questions 4–14) with *never* or *once or twice*.

If your responses show you're neither 'languishing' nor 'flourishing', then you are **moderately mentally healthy**.

The questionnaire isn't definitive, but completing it regularly can give you a good indication of whether you're improving or declining on the scale. It is possible to be flourishing but with a low score. If you take the test again in 12 months' time, you still might be flourishing, but with a higher score.

If you have scored low, don't be disheartened, as we will be working on improving mental health throughout the chapters to come.

If you would like to see my results and see an example of a completed questionnaire, refer to Appendix A.

INTERVIEW WITH THE AUTHOR
Have you ever been assaulted
or got into a fight with a patient?

Plenty of times, and I shit myself every time. I'm a lover, not a fighter. Once you're in the moment, though, the adrenaline sees you through. A lot of the time the patients are heavily intoxicated by either drugs or alcohol, so it's not a huge danger as they can barely stand. As much as I would love to hit them back I never have, but I do have the privilege of putting them to sleep with a sedative.

Having said that, you'd be surprised how strong a small and petite patient under the influence of drugs can be. I've been overpowered by people half my size.

I always imagine that one day I'll accidentally get hit just at the moment I'm trying to insert the needle in the patient's arm and accidentally inject myself and knock myself out. Wouldn't that be something?

CALL TO ACTION

'We are all capable of languishing, of finding ourselves in situations which are not really working for us, but we avoid making any kind of change because the stress of making that change is more uncomfortable than going along with the situation as it is'. – **Dr Wade Jacklin, psychologist**

Key Takeaways

- Mental illness and mental health are different paradigms.
- If you are languishing, you are at a greater risk of progressing into mental illness such as depression.
- Make flourishing your goal.

Key Tasks

- Complete the mental health continuum short form.
- Ask yourself what things you're doing to support flourishing. What would your pathway to flourishing look like?
- Watch Corey Keyes' TED talk, 'A positive approach to healthcare: Dr. Corey Keyes at TEDxAtlanta', TEDx Talks, YouTube, <www.youtube.com/watch?v=TYHOI3T32VA>.

4

Believe in Your Ability

Personal Experience – Crank Up the Adrenaline

Working in a remote community, I was dispatched to a 19-year-old male who was found lying unconscious three-quarters of the way up a staircase. Vehicle access to the property was limited, so I had to walk in. The apartment block was located on the side of a cliff. The view was scenic, but the walk up the hill was unbelievably steep. I felt like a pack horse carrying my five overweight medical bags up the staircase.

I arrived to find the patient lying face down. I checked his pulse; he had no radial pulse (the one in the wrist), but he did have a carotid pulse (the one in the neck). He was unable to respond to my questions; it sounded like he was talking in another language. I quickly dragged him up the top of the staircase so I had some room to work. At this stage, I had no idea why this healthy-looking 19-year-old had suddenly collapsed.

I flagged down his flatmate, who told me the patient had Addison's disease, which affects the body's ability to produce cortisol. He was suffering what is called an acute adrenal crisis as a result of his cortisol levels dropping too low. I was working alone, with no idea how to extricate him from his position up several flights of stairs on a steep hill, with no elevator nearby. I called for the volunteer fire service to help.

The patient's blood pressure was so low that I struggled to even record it; he was time-critical and needed advanced medical care. I had some medication in the toolkit, such as the steroid hydrocortisone, which could help with his condition, but he needed more than that. It was a terrible situation to be in, knowing the patient's condition could be treated, but being unable to give him the medication he needed.

I found myself on two separate phone calls at the same time, so I put them both on speaker. One was to request a medical helicopter, the other was to a doctor, who asked me to administer an adrenaline infusion and additional steroid medication. Both were outside my scope of practice.

I felt my stress levels rise as I tried to juggle the two phone calls. I was multitasking heavily: treating a critically ill patient and giving clear directions to the volunteers assisting me all at the same time. My own adrenaline levels were peaking: if only I could extract my excess cortisol and adrenaline to give to the patient!

Meanwhile, unbeknown to me, one of the volunteer firefighters present at the scene was friends with the patient. He decided to call the patient's father and handed the phone over to me just as I was sticking a needle into his son's arm.

I've never had to make so many phone calls on a job before. All I wanted to do was treat the patient: that's what I was trained for, and that's what I knew best. All of these outside distractions and scene-control requirements were becoming overwhelming. I had to be empathetic to the patient's father, but I didn't have time to talk to him either. I'd prefer him to be angry at me for being assertive on the phone and telling him I had to go and treat his son than to have a conversation explaining why his son died because I neglected his treatment. I hung up.

The phone call with the doctor was my priority. I'd requested the helicopter and given them a quick situation report; that was all they needed. Now I had to prioritise the treatment, because nothing I'd done up to this point had made a difference. In fact, he was getting worse.

I gave him an intravenous (IV) infusion of glucose, which he needed to boost his low blood sugar levels. I had hoped that it would improve his consciousness level, but it didn't seem to help.

Addison's disease created more and more challenges for me while treating the patient. A condition that develops from too much potassium in the blood, called hyperkalaemia, was just around the corner as well. Hyperkalaemia can result in cardiac arrhythmia and death.

By now I had given 1.5 litres of IV fluid to help improve his blood pressure and severe dehydration, but it wasn't working. I couldn't treat the cause of his condition; I was simply trying to manage the symptoms. His body wasn't producing enough of the stress hormone cortisol, which was causing all sorts of problems.

It was ironic that I found myself treating a patient who didn't have enough stress hormones. His condition is a perfect example of why we need stress hormones to survive: they are vital to maintaining our life-sustaining organs, such as the heart. Think of this patient if your goal in life is to be stress-free: you might find yourself unconscious on the stairs with no pulse.

The doctor on the phone instructed me to administer an infusion of adrenaline by injecting a vial of adrenaline into a bag of saline and running it through the IV until the patient's blood pressure improved – then turning it off for a while, then back on again when the blood pressure dropped. I was to repeat this process until the patient's blood pressure stabilised. Paramedics call this a dirty bag.

I was confident I could administer this, even though it was something I had never done before or even attempted in the classroom. I had given adrenaline a lot of times before and had also administered IV fluids often. I could rely on my previous experiences, I thought. I had never even witnessed other doctors do this procedure before, but I had at least heard of it. I was going to have to rely on that vicarious experience.

The doctor also asked me to administer an additional dose of steroids, more than what I'm normally permitted to administer. The only problem was that I didn't have any more vials of the medication in my kit. I had given them all, and we weren't permitted to carry any more due to the drug protocols.

I couldn't ask one of the volunteers to help me get more from the ambulance station – even though it was just a quick five-minute drive away. I had the codes to access the drug safe but I wasn't permitted to share them with anyone. Then I realised that the off-duty paramedic was in town and he might be able to help. I called him and he was happy to come in and assist. The ability to problem-solve in high-stress environments was a critical skill for me on this day.

The next challenge was to get the patient down to the ambulance as soon as possible. I could hear the helicopter hovering above, and they don't like to hang around and waste precious flying time waiting on the paramedic to get their act together.

Thinking back on this case, I believe that my self-efficacy – self-assurance in my ability to act – helped me save the patient's life that day. I was confident that I could pursue the recommended course of action, despite having no experience in doing so. That's why, despite having never treated an acute adrenal crisis before, and having to administer drugs outside my protocols, I was able to complete the necessary tasks.

A high level of self-efficacy is critical if you wish to complete a task under stress and flourish. Some people reading this may think that self-efficacy is just arrogance – it's not. There is a difference between self-assurance in your ability to act and blind arrogance that comes with a side of complacency.

Treating this case, I received one of the greatest compliments of my career. The flight doctor on the helicopter said that this patient received a better level of care on a stairwell than in some remote hospitals. Receiving this positive feedback increased my self-efficacy to combat any future challenges under stress.

Self-efficacy

Flourishing and positive mental health are clearly a vital contributor to positive functioning, productivity and resilience – but how do we attain them?

Recent research has identified a significant relationship between flourishing and high levels of self-efficacy. The opposite is also true; if we possess low levels of self-efficacy, then we are more likely to languish and have higher levels of emotional and mental distress.

The term 'self-efficacy' was coined by Canadian American psychologist Albert Bandura, who described it as 'the belief in one's capabilities to organise and execute the courses of action required to manage prospective situations'. In other words, it's our belief in our ability to succeed in a particular situation.

A paramedic with high self-efficacy believes that they can successfully save someone's life. A trader on Wall Street with high self-efficacy believes they can make an incredible purchase of shares to make an enormous profit.

Self-efficacy helps us exert control over our behaviours and actions. It helps us determine which goals to set for ourselves and what motivates us to pursue those goals. It's not just a belief in ourselves but a belief in our ability to meet the challenges we face. It's a belief in our own individual capacity to produce a performance good enough to obtain the outcome we seek.

Self-efficacy reflects the confidence we have in our own ability. Here's an example. I was working with a paramedic who had been in the job for more than 15 years and had seen a lot of trauma and sick patients before.

We were treating a patient who had sepsis, a potentially fatal condition where the body's inflammation response to an infection turns on the body itself. The patient was unwell but they weren't time-critical. If they were left untreated, however, their condition would have become life-threatening. The paramedic was sitting in the back of the ambulance getting ready to establish IV access to administer saline solution to combat the patient's low blood pressure and dehydration.

He went through the normal process of setting up the needle and equipment for the procedure, but he was searching frantically for a vein. I could see several obvious veins but he kept touching and rotating the arm, slapping the skin to try and raise the veins to make them even more visible.

He continued in this way for five minutes, which quickly became ten. Sweat began to run down his brow. Then, for no reason at all, he let go of the patient's arm and decided to ring the hospital to notify them that we were on our way. Despite having inserted hundreds of cannulas in the past and in more critically ill patients who were time-sensitive, in this instance he panicked and chose to divert.

I sat in disbelief. How did this simple task we do every day become so difficult for him? When I spoke to him afterwards, he told me he'd missed several cannulas recently and had lost his confidence, letting self-doubt dictate his actions. It's now apparent to me that this occurred because he had a low self-efficacy. He didn't believe in his ability to achieve his goal of cannulation.

Self-efficacy determines what goals we choose to pursue, how we go about accomplishing those goals, and how we reflect upon our own performance. In the example above, the experienced paramedic chose to pursue a different goal by calling the hospital. In other words, he chose to go about accomplishing his goal through avoidance.

Self-efficacy is essentially a personal judgement of ourselves. It's the personal beliefs we have regarding our own capabilities.

Boxers are often considered too arrogant, but without this self-efficacy regarding their ability to win the fight, they will be knocked out in the first round. It's common for a boxer who's experienced the first knockout in their career to never be the same fighter again. They've lost something. That something is their self-efficacy.

Having high self-efficacy doesn't mean that we will always succeed – we will still encounter life's setbacks. What it does help improve is our resilience to failure. People with high self-efficacy are more likely to bounce back from adversity, learn and try again. Great athletes have failures all the time; Serena Williams, Michael Jordan, Muhammad Ali and Michael Phelps all lost throughout their careers, but without high self-efficacy they would never have bounced back and kept going. Muhammad Ali is famous for his own self-belief; he knew within himself that he could achieve greatness, and this belief directed everything he did – his actions and choices.

High self-efficacy helps us interpret difficult goals as manageable. It makes significant challenges more attainable and helps us feel less stressed in challenging situations. According to Bandura, our self-efficacy can determine how we interpret situations, including stressful ones, and how we respond to the stress.

Our belief in our own ability to succeed under stress plays a substantial role in how we think, act and feel. It's also highly relevant to 'positive risk-taking'. When we're facing a challenge, positive self-efficacy enables us to back ourselves and visualise the possibility of a successful outcome.

The exciting thing is that research indicates a significant correlation between self-efficacy and mental health. It shows our self-efficacy is a good predictor of whether we're flourishing or languishing in life. As a result, if we improve our self-efficacy, we will improve our chances to flourish. This was confirmed in a study conducted by Australian researchers Amber Giblett and Gene Hodgins on the relationship between the mental health continuum and generalised self-efficacy. They concluded that 'a prospective belief in one's capacity to implement actions to succeed in future tasks may be associated with greater mental health'.

If our goal is to flourish, to remain self-composed under immense pressure, then we must determine whether we're high or low in self-efficacy. And if we're low in self-efficacy, we can implement some strategies to improve it.

German researchers Ralf Schwarzer and Matthias Jerusalem developed a generalised self-efficacy scale to correlate emotion, optimism and work satisfaction and give an indication of our general belief in our ability to solve problems and reach goals. They have generously allowed me to reproduce this self-report measurement in this book, so that we can use it to establish your baseline belief in yourself.

Generalised Self-efficacy Scale

Tick the box that best represents you.

	Not at all true	Barely true	Moderately true	Exactly true
I can always manage to solve complex problems if I try hard enough.				
If someone opposes me, I can find means and ways to get what I want.				
It is easy for me to stick to my aims and accomplish my goals.				
I am confident that I can deal efficiently with unexpected events.				
Thanks to my resourcefulness, I know how to handle unforeseen situations.				
I can solve most problems if I invest the necessary effort.				
I can remain calm when facing difficulties because I can rely on my coping abilities.				
When I am confronted with a problem, I can usually find several solutions.				
If I am in a bind, I can usually think of something to do.				
No matter what comes my way, I'm usually able to handle it.				

Source: R. Schwarzer & M. Jerusalem, 'Generalized self-efficacy scale', in J. Weinman, S. Wright & M. Johnston, *Measures in Health Psychology: A User's Portfolio*, Windsor, UK: NFER-NELSON, 1995, pp. 35–37.

Evaluating your results

Score your responses as follows:

NOT AT ALL TRUE = 1
BARELY TRUE = 2
MODERATELY TRUE = 3
EXACTLY TRUE = 4

Add these up to obtain a total score between 10 and 40. The higher your score, the greater your self-efficacy.

If you would like to see my results and an example of how to fill out the scale, refer to **Appendix B**.

Compare the Two Scales

Now compare your results from the mental health continuum scale (page 63) and the generalised self-efficacy scale. You should find the following:

- If you are flourishing, you will most likely be high in self-efficacy.
- If you are languishing, you will most likely be low in self-efficacy.
- If you are moderately mentally healthy, you will most likely be middle in self-efficacy.

Our goal is to flourish, so if your score on the self-efficacy scale is low, it's vital that you practise the strategies and tools covered throughout this book.

Personal Experience – Stuck in a Hard Place

We were dispatched, lights and sirens, to two men who had crashed their quadbike on the side of the road. It was dark and pouring rain. It was difficult to see as the water ran into my eyes, so I put my baseball cap on even though it was around midnight. I located the first patient, who appeared as if he was embedded into the side of the cliff, stuck up about 2 metres and curled in the foetal position. The patient looked like death: pale and grey – ashen.

The second patient was lying in a ditch and was easy to access, but had an obvious fractured femur (thigh bone) and a possible head injury. By the time we'd done a quick sweep of the scene and an initial triage, a crowd had started to gather. Bystanders came to observe the scene and were in shock at what they were witnessing. Things started to get disorderly.

At the time, I was a relatively new paramedic, with maybe about five years' experience, but I was working with two more senior paramedics at this scene. I initially thought one of them would take control of the scene and become the commander for the incident, but this didn't happen. The two experienced paramedics both started treating the patient lying in the ditch, so I told them I would take control.

I immediately began giving situation reports to our communications centre and requesting more resources. I spoke to the police to assist with crowd control, and coordinated with the fire captain to help with extrication. More importantly, though, we had a second patient who needed urgent treatment.

I walked up to the other paramedics and asked one of them to go and treat the other patient, but I was ignored. They were fixed on the other patient, who was admittedly critical. I didn't have a strong belief in my position as the forward commander, the controller. I lacked self-efficacy in managing the scene with more senior paramedics; I didn't have the louder voice that was required, so I didn't argue with them. Instead, I actually helped them by getting some equipment out of the ambulance.

I was getting anxious as I tried to hurriedly pull out the equipment they had requested from the ambulance. As expected, when someone starts to stress, the equipment began to get caught on belts and latches that normally wouldn't be a problem. I could only think of the patient half-embedded in the hillside, alone. What I was doing wasn't working. The other paramedics were fixated on their patient, most likely through fear, and weren't responding to my authority as a scene commander.

I gave up the role as scene commander, not that anyone noticed. I climbed up the embankment and started treating the patient on the hill as a bystander gave me a look to say 'Where have you been?' I found myself treating a patient, stuck on the side of a hill in the torrential rain, by myself. I had limited equipment and had to keep leaving him to go to the car to get more because the other paramedics were busy doing their own thing. The scene became disorganised, with no communication and a lack of appropriate resources.

This made me doubt my ability to manage the patient still further. It had a flow-on effect. I started questioning whether I could treat the patient at all, and how in the world I was going to get him off the hill. This lack of self-efficacy was clearly impacting my ability to perform by impacting my belief to implement effective actions.

I distinctly remember a firefighter came over to assist and called my name. Simply making eye contact with him and breaking my focus for a few seconds allowed me to snap out of my building anxiety and re-engage.

The firefighter helped me pull the patient off the hill and carry him to the back of the ambulance. It was the best thing we could have done. Once the patient was in the back of the ambulance, I felt safe and in control. This is what I was used to – working out of the rain in good lighting and air-conditioning with all the medical equipment within arm's reach. Outside, in the chaos, I had lost my moorings.

I'd needed to snap out of my lack of belief. The small, yet effective, involuntary cognitive pause that the firefighter unknowingly allowed me saved me from panicking. The roles were soon reversed. The firefighter was yelling at the patient to lift his arm so it didn't get stood on, but I had to inform him that the patient's arm was broken. It was almost at a right angle, so I was initially shocked that he could have missed it, but then I reflected on the minute before and what I'd missed.

Developing Belief in Your Ability

Bandura outlined four sources of information that we can employ to develop our self-efficacy.

Performance Outcomes

Performance outcomes or past experiences are our most important source of self-efficacy. Bandura wrote, 'Positive and negative experiences can influence the ability of an individual to perform a given task. If one has performed well at a task previously, he or she is more likely to feel competent and perform well at a similarly associated task.'

Bandura explains that this is the most important step because it provides the best evidence of whether or not we can achieve the goal in question. The best way to influence our performance outcomes is through positive past experiences. Athletes who have won a gold medal before know that they are good enough and have an inherent self-belief. This knowledge will significantly help them the next time they face off in a final for the gold medal. It took Formula 1 driver Mark Webber 130 race starts to win his first race. He said afterwards that he never really knew he was good enough to win until he did. After that moment, he arguably became a better driver and went on to win another eight races.

If you don't have any previous experiences of success you can draw on, the next best thing is to practise. Being successful within that training environment will help build your self-belief. By practising and training, repeating tasks and gradually improving, you are unknowingly teaching yourself that you can achieve your goal. You develop the skills and ability to influence the outcome. Through training and hard work, you will be able to create an atmosphere where you believe in yourself and that you are more than capable of learning something new.

Vicarious Experiences

Bandura wrote, 'People can develop high or low self-efficacy vicariously through other people's performances. A person can watch someone in a similar position perform, and then compare his own competence with the other individual's competence.'

This step is about having an example to follow, a positive role model. As mentioned earlier, we have contagious minds and are capable of absorbing the beliefs of those around us. The key here, then, is to find yourself a positive mentor or role model. Being able to measure yourself against a person you admire or who has already achieved what you are trying to achieve is essential. If they can do it, why can't you?

Most of our heroes are the ones who were the first to achieve something because we know they had no one to follow – no opportunity for vicarious experiences. We are constantly amazed by and rightfully praise the pioneers who were the first person to achieve a particular great thing. Such people include: Neil Armstrong, the first person on the moon; Roald Amundsen, the first person to reach the South and North Pole; Edmund Hillary and Tenzing Norgay, the first people to reach the summit of Mount Everest; and the Wright Brothers, the first people to create powered flight. We are inspired by these people because we can use them as a way to believe in ourselves. If a human can achieve that, why can't I as a human reach my goal?

Verbal Persuasion

Bandura wrote, 'Self-efficacy is also influenced by encouragement and discouragement pertaining to an individual's performance or ability to perform.'

Receiving positive feedback when you're attempting to complete a task gives you the belief that you can complete it, that you can do it. This is important to remember when we talk about the importance of positive self-talk. What we tell ourselves also influences our ability to complete a task.

The majority of sports teams win at their home ground, which has a lot to do with positive encouragement from their supporters. Receiving verbal persuasion from the fans gives them the belief that they can win, allowing them to go the extra mile.

The famous children's story *The Little Engine That Could* uses verbal persuasion to encourage the Little Blue Engine to pull the train carriages to the top of the mountain:

'I think I can climb up the mountain. I think I can. I think I can.'
Then the Little Blue Engine began to pull. She tugged and she pulled.

She pulled and she tugged. Puff puff, chug chug went the little engine. 'I think I can. I think I can,' she said. Puff Puff, chug chug. Up the mountain went the Little Blue Engine. And all the time she kept saying, 'I think I can, I think I can, I think I can . . .' Up, up, up. The little engine climbed and climbed. At last she reached the top of the mountain.

Don't underestimate the power of words. A simple statement of encouragement can make all the difference.

Physiological Arousal

We experience sensations from our body, and how we perceive this physiological arousal influences our beliefs of efficacy.

The way your physiological body responds to stress heavily influences our feelings and beliefs about a particular situation. The fight, flight or freeze response dramatically influences how we react to a task, which in turn influences whether or not we will achieve our goal. If we respond to our body's physiological arousal in a positive way, then we will be able to take positive action towards our goal (see Chapter 7 for more).

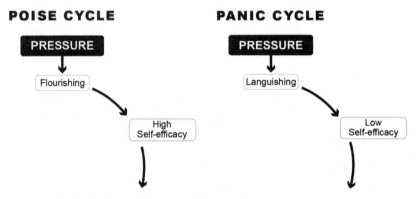

Figure 3. Self-efficacy influences which path we are going to take under pressure and correlates directly with a flourishing or languishing state. Having high self-efficacy cultivates the poise cycle, whereas low self-efficacy encourages the panic cycle.

INTERVIEW WITH THE AUTHOR
What's the scariest thing you've ever faced?

I love the marine environment and responding on water, but this particular night was quite scary. I was dispatched to a two-year-old child with life-threatening asthma. The patient was out in the middle of the ocean, about a one-hour boat ride away. Typically, a helicopter would be sent to this case as it's much quicker, but the weather had other ideas. It was pouring rain, the wind was roaring and the waves were the size of buildings, so they thought they would send us in a small boat not designed for medical retrieval.

Thirty minutes into the trip the boat broke down and was a floating duck. We lost steering and sprung a hydraulic leak. Having no control of the vessel and drifting in the middle of the ocean wasn't ideal. The hardest thing was the thought that a child was very sick and needed my help but I was hopeless to do anything. I wasn't scared for my own wellbeing though. I never thought we might be in danger. I was more scared about arriving on the scene to find a dead child.

We managed to slow the leak to a point, but it was still coming out. Luckily, we found 20 litres of spare hydraulic fluid in a jerry can. We had to stand in the engine room, topping up the fluid throughout the entire trip to make it to the patient. By the time we arrived, the mother had exhausted all of her prescribed medication. We got to them just in time. Fortunately, I think the child was too sick to be seasick.

CALL TO ACTION

'Stay focused on any thoughts where you see yourself being a better professional, doing your job, and any other thoughts that come in and take away from that, let them go.' – **Carol Fox**

Key Takeaways

- Self-efficacy reflects our confidence in our own ability, and is a critical piece of the puzzle when performing a task under stress.

- High self-efficacy not only improves our performance but is associated with positive mental health. It helps us flourish.
- We can develop self-efficacy through four key processes: performance outcomes, vicarious experiences, verbal persuasion and physiological arousal.

Key Tasks

- Complete the generalised self-efficacy scale (page 74) and compare your results with those from the mental health continuum scale (page 63).
- Write down the task you're trying to complete and answer the following questions:
  - Have you previously performed this task or a similar one successfully? If yes, how?
  - Has any other human ever achieved this task before? If yes, who and how did they do it?
  - Write down three positive self-talk sentences about achieving the task.
  - Share your task with at least one other person and ask for support.
  - List four psychological skills you will use when stressed.

5

Our Response to Stress

Personal Experience – Role Reversal

I never thought I would be the patient, but here I was. Lying on a stretcher, I felt the helicopter's vibrations as it took off. I had placed so many others in this situation, but this time was different. It was a role reversal.

I'm definitely the worst patient. I'm convinced the man flu is real. This belief made it certain that, when I was suffering from a gastrointestinal bug associated with severe vomiting and diarrhoea, I was dying. I wanted all the drugs. Stuck in bed, except for my trips to and from the bathroom, I called in sick for three days in a row. I asked the paramedic replacing me to help me out, but he just gave me medication to stop the vomiting and told me to remain hydrated.

I soon realised that I'd probably given exactly the same advice my colleague gave me a hundred times before. Being on the other side was different, though, and I didn't like it.

The moment I started to feel better, I decided to go back to work. I was halfway through an eight-day rotation and I told the paramedic covering me to go home. It wasn't long, though, before I started to feel very itchy. My back was killing me; it was like ants were crawling inside me. I took off my shirt and noticed that I'd started to develop a serious rash. The rash was spreading before my very eyes. My arms were now covered in welts and became itchy. I just wanted to scream (I think I was screaming).

I quickly called the now off-duty paramedic to come back and help me. I waited nervously to see if he'd left as I had told him to. Thankfully, he was still around, and he drove me back home. By this time, my face began to swell and my eyelids began to close.

I couldn't believe it. Surely, I wasn't suffering from anaphylaxis – a life-threatening allergic reaction! I'm not allergic to anything, so anaphylaxis didn't make sense in this case. I had seen a lot of allergic reactions before, though, and the symptoms were undeniable.

I could still breathe, which reassured me and helped calm my wife's anxiety as well. I took some antihistamines, thinking they would kick in and treat the rash and itching.

My colleague took me to the local doctor – I was usually working alongside her. It felt strange to be the patient this time. I wanted to act tough, like there was nothing wrong. Although they were treating me with great care, I was worried about being judged since I was so used to being on the other end.

I hung out for about an hour receiving some steroids and IV fluid. I was feeling exhausted by this time; I was still dehydrated and tired from the previous vomiting and diarrhea episodes. I decided to just tell them I'd sit there for another hour and then go home if it didn't get worse. Meanwhile, I informed my paramedic colleague – the one who had taken over my duties previously and who I called to bring me to the hospital – that he'd have to cover for me again.

Though I don't like it when my patients refuse to follow my advice, I became one of those patients that day. I refused to ride in the back of the ambulance and stubbornly walked out of the medical centre and sat in the front seat as we drove back home. I thought I just needed some rest, maybe just a good night's sleep, but as we pulled up in front of my driveway, my breathing issues started. I felt the full effects of the body's fight or flight response kick in.

I could feel a rush of panic coming over me. I wanted to grab at everything, scream and turn back time to a previous moment when I didn't feel like this.

I felt my throat start to narrow. I couldn't swallow, and I had the classic feeling of a lump in my throat. It blocked the life-sustaining air I needed to stay alive. I'd seen it happen to my patients, and now it was happening to me.

I'd seen the stare of panic in patients I've treated for anaphylaxis before; they would often reach to grasp their necks to tell me they couldn't breathe. Never did I think that I would someday be rushed to the stretcher in the back of an ambulance for the same thing – especially since I was 32 years old at the time and had never had an allergy in my life.

I held the needle for the paramedic to help him draw up the adrenaline. It was a surreal feeling to be on the receiving end this time. Those of you who have received adrenaline before: I have a much better appreciation for you now. It didn't take long for the heart palpitations to start, followed by uncontrolled tremors and untamed anxiety.

Wearing an ambulance uniform while being treated in an ambulance is not something I'd ever imagined. When I arrived back at the doctor's clinic – there was no hospital in this small town – she ordered a helicopter to take me to a hospital. She rightfully did not listen to my self-medication advice this time.

I felt embarrassed being placed in a helicopter and treated by paramedics I'd worked alongside for several years. When I was discharged from the hospital a few hours later, I was in an unfamiliar town with no way to get home. I booked a hotel for the night. My wife planned to drive down and pick me up the next day.

But the saga wasn't over yet. Around midnight, I woke up in the dodgy hotel room; I was itchy again. The rash was back, and I was struggling to breathe, but instead of doing the logical thing and calling an ambulance, I called a taxi.

I was too embarrassed to go through what I had during the original episode – or maybe my ego wouldn't allow it. I walked into the emergency department and was rushed to a room for another round of adrenaline injections. This time, I stayed in the hospital until the morning, finally getting some sleep.

I was discharged the next day and given scripts to fill at the pharmacy. The third time's a charm, I thought, as I started to have another reaction in the prescription queue. I had no idea what was going on: a third reaction within 24 hours? I still obviously hadn't learned my lesson, because I thought the logical thing to do would be to wait for my scripts to be filled and self-administer the medication in the shop.

Another five-minute wait for the drugs to be dispensed felt like an hour. Finally, the basket with my drugs arrived, and I bought a drink to gulp down the tablets. I walked back to the hotel and booked another night's accommodation just in case it started a fourth time. Thankfully, my wife had arrived by now and she could talk some sense into me, but fortunately, I didn't need to go back again. If any patient of mine had done this, I would have thought they were plain stupid. There's always a fine line between bravery and stupidity, and my actions had put me into the latter camp.

By the way, it turns out I'm still not allergic to anything. It was all a viral response to my gastroenteritis infection. At least I can still eat whatever I want.

The Survival Response

Discussing bad jobs has never been a problem for me. I've treated victims of rape, child abuse, shootings, stabbings, and a range of other things humans seem to experience. For the average person, these situations may seem impressively stressful to think about. But although others may be put off by blood, guts and gore, that's not what I lose sleep over.

I lose sleep over making mistakes – and most mistakes are made while performing under pressure when our rational decision-making ability is diminished.

Performing under pressure is getting the job done in stressful moments when the results and consequences matter. Pressure is a compelling force that can control our thoughts and actions. If we can't navigate our way through pressure (in both emergencies and the rest of our life), we will break down and lose control.

When a life is on the line, the results matter, and we will feel the pressure. *Everyone* feels this pressure. I still feel the pressure as an experienced paramedic. It doesn't go away; I can just implement strategies to deal with it.

In this chapter we'll take a look at human behaviour and the impacts of stress on performance. This knowledge applies to us all. Even if you're a paramedic, there's no changing your human physiological responses. But we can all develop tools and strategies for peak performance. We must hone our mental skills to perform under pressure.

So let's learn how to rise to the occasion.

Fight, Flight or Freeze

Stress, pressure, fear and agitation are meant to be triggers for action, not forms of suffering. The 'fight, flight, or freeze' mechanism is a system that developed over millions of years to inspire us to act, to survive in dangerous and challenging situations.

Fight, flight or freeze is the root cause of our reactions to pressure and fear. It's the fundamental model for how humans react to threats. The response is triggered by a release of hormones that prepare the body to either fight, flee or freeze. It's a mechanism that integrates the brain with the body.

First, the body judges a situation and decides whether it's stressful or not. When it perceives the situation as threatening, **no matter the threat**, this triggers a standard series of physiological reactions. Different stimuli can exert the same response: attending a car crash with a patient bleeding to death, telling someone you love them for the first time, attempting to score a winning goal in overtime.

Our autonomic (involuntary) nervous system has two components: the sympathetic nervous system and the parasympathetic nervous system. Stressful situations activate the sympathetic nervous system and trigger the fight, flight or freeze response. This releases adrenaline and other stimulant chemicals into the bloodstream to provide the body with a burst of energy so that it can respond to the danger. The parasympathetic nervous system acts in the opposite way, promoting the 'rest and digest' response that calms the body after the threat has passed.

When we're faced with stressful stimuli, our eyes and ears send images and sounds to a part of your brain known as the amygdala. The amygdala interprets this information and immediately sends a distress signal to another part of the brain, the hypothalamus.

There are two main stages of the stress response. The first, which involves rapid mobilisation of brain power to deal with stressful situations, occurs almost instantly after we're exposed to a strong stimulus. The second involves the release of hormones and takes time to come online.

The Instantaneous Stress Response

The first stage of the stress response is activated through a system called the sympathetic–adrenomedullary axis (SAM), which connects the hypothalamus in the brain with the adrenal glands, which sit on top of the kidneys. This occurs almost instantly after we're exposed to a strong stimulus. It's usually activated before we're even consciously aware of the threat.

The hypothalamus will send signals through the autonomic nervous system, which controls our involuntary body functions such as breathing, heart rate, and the dilation and constriction of blood vessels and air sacs in our lungs.

The hypothalamus activates the adrenal medulla within the adrenal glands. The adrenal medulla secretes hormones called catecholamines, namely adrenaline and noradrenaline, which are released in response to physical and emotional stress.

The release of adrenaline causes an increased heart rate; the opening of the airways in the lungs; mobilisation of glucose for energy; and shunting of blood away from the stomach, intestines and cerebrum (the rational thinking part of the brain). The rush of adrenaline also increases blood flow to skeletal muscles (the muscles we can control, that allow us to fight or run).

This physiological response happens so fast we don't even know it's occurred. In fact, the brain's wiring is so efficient that the amygdala and hypothalamus start this cascade even before the brain's visual centres have entirely had a chance to process what is happening. It's like jumping out of the way of a flying ball aimed straight at your head before even realising the ball was headed your way.

The Sustained Stress Response

To keep this fast-acting system going, the hypothalamus activates the second phase of the response, using a separate system called the hypothalamic–pituitary–adrenal (HPA) axis. Both phases are triggered at the same time, but the SAM system is much faster than the HPA.

The HPA first sends signals from the hypothalamus to the pituitary gland, which secretes a hormone called adrenocorticotropic hormone or ACTH. This travels in the bloodstream (which is a lot slower than travelling along the nervous system) to stimulate the adrenal glands, to produce the hormone cortisol.

Cortisol helps the body maintain heightened awareness and sustain the stress response. It enables the body to maintain a steady supply of glucose by releasing stores from the liver and suppressing the immune system.

These two responses – SAM and HPA – are coordinated, working together to prepare the body to respond to a stressful stimulus. The sympathetic response occurs within seconds and prepares us for a heightened level of response. It readies our body for a crisis that may require sudden action.

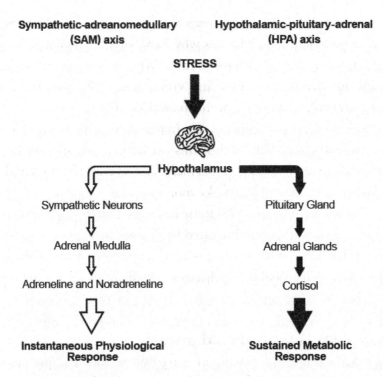

Figure 4. The sympathetic adrenal medulla (SAM) and hypothalamic pituitary adrenal (HPA) axes depicted above are at play in the human fight, flight or freeze response.

The lion analogy is probably the one most commonly used to describe the fight, flight or freeze response. That is, our system is designed to run away from a lion or fight it. But this analogy has been skewed and misinterpreted over the years. The fight, flight or freeze response did not just evolve to get us to run away from impending death, attempt to battle a lion in one-on-one combat, or freeze and act like a ragdoll.

It more likely evolved to make us get up and get moving. If we're hiding in a cave and are hours away from dying of starvation, fight, flight or freeze will encourage us to hunt. If we're about to go into a battle, it will give us courage. Our body is designed to act to enable us to survive.

When this system is activated, it occurs at the expense of our higher mental abilities. Our speech becomes inept (which isn't good if we're on a first date, which is why I always took my dates to the cinema, where we didn't have to talk). When our pupils dilate, we forfeit our depth perception and visual acuity. We lose our fine motor control, so we can't perform motions that require dexterity (such as medical procedures). We hyperventilate to increase our oxygen levels in the blood, but this causes hypocapnia (too little carbon dioxide), resulting in dizziness, lack of concentration and a feeling of detachment. We make more mistakes.

This finely tuned stress response has allowed us to survive under pressure, but if it's overstimulated for a prolonged period – when our cortisol levels don't subside – it has damaging effects. This can occur if we perceive non-life-threatening situations as threatening.

Surviving Goal-directed Stress

We take actions and behave in a particular way because we're directed towards a goal. It doesn't matter what the goal is, our behaviours will reflect what we're trying to achieve. You may not even be consciously aware of what your goal is but your behaviour will reflect it. Your goal might be to avoid pain, in which case you don't wake up early and go to the gym or spend an extra 30 minutes in the kitchen to cook a healthy meal. Avoiding things becomes your goal.

We seek out and engage in the things we're aiming towards. This is known as goal-directed behaviour. The problem comes when obstacles in our way cause us stress. We often make the mistake of changing our goal to avoid this stress, which in turn changes our behaviour.

Research completed by US psychologist Richard Dienstbier found that quickly mobilising the survival response during goal-directed stress via the SAM system rather than the HPA system was a marker for 'physiological toughness'. This was associated with favourable outcomes such as increased performance, more emotional stability and lower anxiety, which meant the physiologically tough individuals were more likely to see challenging situations in a positive way.

This brings us back to our earlier discussion of the challenge versus threat theory, because while the SAM system is activated in both challenge and threat perceptions, the HPA system is only activated in the threat system.

The SAM system is associated with increased cardiovascular stimulation – increased heart rate, better and more controlled heart contractions, improved cardiac output (volume of blood pumped around the body during a minute) and decreased peripheral vascular resistance (pressure in the arteries and blood vessels throughout the body: imagine the blood vessels widening). In simpler terms, the heart can pump better and move more blood around the body, carrying more oxygen to fuel our cells.

This means that if we can perceive goal-oriented stress as a challenge, our body's physiological response has far more positive effects: it allows us to rise to the situation with poise.

In a challenge state, the HPA system increases the peripheral vascular system, narrowing the blood vessels (this would be akin to comparing the size of the pipes bringing water to the kitchen tap with those releasing water from the dam). In a threat state, however, the purpose of this system is to stem the flow of blood if we've been injured, so we don't bleed to death. In the HPA response, blood flow to the brain decreases.

The HPA system gives a longer-term response. It can last for months or even years if we're constantly in a threat state. If this system becomes continuously activated in the absence of genuine threats, it can lead to cardiovascular diseases, and other conditions such as PTSD. Our blood pressure remains high, our heart rate remains increased, and our blood vessels remain constricted.

When there's no action or outlet for the stress to dissipate, it will become chronic and cause these normal control mechanisms to overwork.

As a result, the adrenal glands will continue to produce cortisol, which exhausts the stress mechanism and leads to fatigue and depression. Cortisol also interferes with mood-stabilising serotonin activity, furthering the effect of stress on the body.

Consistently high cortisol levels lead to suppression of the immune system through increased production of an immune system messenger and inflammatory molecule called interleukin-6. Not surprisingly, then, stress has a negative effect on the immune system, making us more vulnerable to disease.

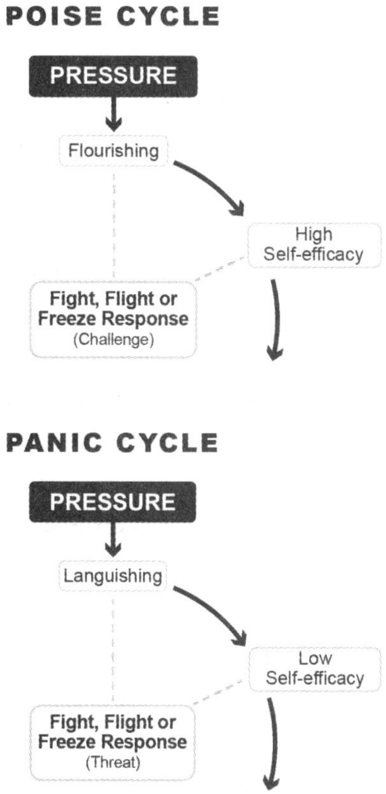

POISE CYCLE

PANIC CYCLE

Figure 5. The fight, flight or freeze response is at the heart of being placed under pressure; it controls our physiological and mental response to pressure. The poise cycle sees any pressure as a challenge whereas the panic cycle sees it as a threat.

Personal Experience – Patient A Deceased, Patient B Critical, Patient C Arrested by Police.

By this time I had been a paramedic long enough to have my heart rate suddenly rise at the sound of every pager tone. It went even higher once I read the message – vehicle roll-over with three patients. Sometimes you know it's going to be a bad case, just from the tone of the message or the voice of the operator on the radio.

My fight, flight or freeze response was in overdrive. I was working in a remote Indigenous community as a single officer, and there was no backup coming within the next two hours.

I always found it ironic that we respond to a major car crash in a car with lights and sirens on, driving above the speed limit, running through stop signs and breaking other road rules to keep us safe. One would think all the road trauma would stop you from driving, but I still enjoy it today.

I arrived on the scene and stepped out of the ambulance – or should I say leapt out – to find a patient had been ejected in front of the vehicle, as they hadn't been wearing a seatbelt. The car had, in fact, kept rolling and landed on top of them. The patient was trapped under the roof of the vehicle with the wheels facing the sky. Walking down the embankment to the car wreck, my heart was pumping. I knew as I got closer I wouldn't be able to forget the images I was about to be exposed to. It's a feeling of strong apprehension and angst, but courage as well. Knowing you're about to witness something terrible but still moving towards it is both exciting and terrifying.

I dropped down on my knees to look under the vehicle. All I could see was a young female's head crushed. There were no signs of life – her eyes didn't return a gaze full of light and life; they were fixed and darkened. I checked for a pulse in any case – there was nothing. I'm not sure how long I knelt there, as time begins to slow in those moments, but I managed to push myself up as the police car arrived and there were others to attend to. I left her alone.

A second patient was trapped inside the car, her eyes wide open, with a stare pleading for help. She was able to talk to me, which came as a great relief after what I'd just witnessed. A third was standing next to the car screaming, but not a scream of pain, the other kind. It was a scream of anger – deep and furious.

By this stage, my eyesight was laser-focused, almost tunnelled. I was breathing heavily and could feel my muscles twitching, ready to respond. Adrenaline was definitely being released throughout my body in copious amounts; the floodgates had opened.

I was doing a lot of sigh breathing (a breathing-based relaxation technique), trying not to let negative self-talk get inside my head when thoughts of whether I'd made the right decision to leave the deceased patient popped into my head. *Keep moving*, I had to say to myself, *stay focused*.

I moved on to the second patient, who was trapped and needed my care the most. The third patient was walking around screaming, which is a good sign they have a pulse and are breathing. I wasn't there long before I was called away by police. I had to leave the second patient hoping she would still be alive by the time I came back. I tried not to visualise walking back and finding her dead with the same face as her friend.

The third patient was completely disassociated with what was occurring. He was aggressive, becoming violent and threatening towards other bystanders and me. By this time, word had spread of the crash through the community and at least 50 people had arrived on scene. Things started to escalate.

A family member of the deceased patient ran over and started threatening the angry and lost driver. This didn't help, as the third patient was looking like he wanted to punch me in the head. Since he was talking and walking, it's a good guess he wouldn't drop dead in the next five or so minutes and was well enough to survive my next decision. I asked the police to arrest the patient and place him in the back of the police van. It wasn't a great look or a great feeling, to be honest: it went against the reason I wanted to be a paramedic. I wanted to help this man, but I couldn't help anyone if he continued to behave this way, and I didn't have time. It was a confronting sight as my patient was wrestled to the ground and cuffed. I asked the police to inform me if his condition deteriorated, and I walked away.

Time was speeding up in my mind; I had to slow it down. Darn adrenaline in my bloodstream. I finally walked back to the second patient still trapped in the car. The same anxious feeling crept in as I approached. I found her trapped in the same position but alive. I could finally start treating her and reducing her pain and suffering. I could still hear the driver kicking and screaming as I glanced over at the police car rocking back and forth. I saw this as a good sign.

And it's probably also worth mentioning that all of this was occurring at the same time as having to request assistance, provide situation reports to our communications centre, speak to doctors for clinical treatment advice, notify the local hospital and coordinate bystanders, fire personnel and police. And, of course, tell the tow-truck driver to get out of my way.

This experience helped me use my physiological skills to control my fight, flight and freeze response. It's an example of being hyperaroused. If I couldn't control the stress arousal within my own mind, it would have been easy to focus on one patient only and forget about the rest, and that most likely would have been the patient who was dead, ignoring the other two. I couldn't save the one who was already lost but the other patients lived to tell the tale.

Working Memory

Working memory refers to the capacity to selectively maintain and manipulate goal-relevant information without getting distracted by irrelevant information over short intervals.

If our working memory is disrupted by a traumatic event, then that will affect our capacity to perform under pressure. When exposed to a pressure moment, such as attending to a critically ill patient, we will experience the fight or flight response. Our heart will start to pound, and our thinking will become warped. If our mind is filled with thoughts of doubt, worry, negativity and failure, then there will be no room left for our knowledge to knock on the door; it'll stay hidden in the long-term memory bank.

This will be exacerbated if the situation and outcome matter. It will create fear and anxiety. The fear will compound, and as a result, we will lose control of our ability to think clearly, make sound decisions and execute our mission.

While many factors can lead to our mental capacity becoming distorted and affecting our performance, the most relevant to the paramedic mindset is our working memory: our ability to remember information that we need in the moment and perform a task.

I remember being interviewed as part of my final examinations; it was a simple voice assessment where I sat in front of an instructor who asked a couple of questions in relation to airway management. I was very familiar with the subject, as I'd studied and performed numerous scenarios to embed the skill in my brain, but when it came to answering a simple question under pressure, I went blank. It was as if there was nothing inside my brain, and an awkward silence fell over the room.

This built up more anxiety in my mind as I started to think I was going to fail, and if I failed, then I would not become a paramedic. I'd have to repeat the course, I'd be embarrassed among my peers, I'd be the laughingstock of the entire university – and on and on went this spiralling negativity.

What I should have done was apply some psychological skills training, and in particular, breathing techniques, to maintain composure, to retain poise. This would have allowed me to free up my working memory and bring forth the knowledge I had to perform the task and pass the exam.

If the knowledge and information are not automatic, as in the example of me sitting the exam, then in pressure moments, the working memory that stores the information we need will go blank. The working memory will be too overloaded with fearful thinking to recall any knowledge that's required.

The best way to free up the working memory is to make our skills and knowledge automatic. Automaticity allows the brain to reduce the cognitive load (our need to think), thus freeing up space for other information and allowing us to access the information we've already stored. That's why it's vital to study and train, to make our skills automatic.

Cognitive Bandwidth

Our cognitive bandwidth is our brain's ability to process the information within the working memory. Cognitive bandwidth, like a computer's RAM, determines how fast we can calculate, assess and process the information available to us.

Our conscious mind, the prefrontal cortex of the brain, oversees the work of the unconscious mind, always on the lookout for circumstances that don't precisely match a pattern. Our cognitive bandwidth is located within the prefrontal cortex, and studies have shown that it has a minimal capacity. Some studies suggest that we can only hold four to nine variables at a time, which means this system is easily overwhelmed.

The prefrontal cortex tries to rationalise the available information into a plausible explanation that fits into our previously formed patterns, but these patterns may not be real. Your prefrontal cortex is into plausibility, not reality.

We want to operate and make decisions in reality and leave enough room in our prefrontal cortex for the knowledge we need to make the right decision, not the data that will lead to cognitive overload and an overwhelmed decision-making system.

Ever walk out of a job interview and instantly think, why didn't I say this or that? That's because as soon as you walk out of the pressure cooker of a job interview, our cognitive bandwidth relaxes, leaving more room for processing the data stored in our brain. Suddenly, we can think of everything we should have said.

I remember arriving on scene to a patient in cardiac arrest.

We pulled up to the house and could see the grief-stricken family members standing on the balcony waving frantically for us to run up the stairs. I jumped out of the ambulance to grab my bags just as I received a call over the radio from our communications centre requesting our location. I promptly replied, 'At scene.'

They then told us that we were being diverted to another case because they believed this patient was an obvious death, meaning they had passed away a long time ago and CPR was no longer an option. The patient was gone. The dispatcher said they had another critical patient a few streets over and we were the closest unit. They were directing us to leave.

I looked up to the house and stared back at the family members; they must have been wondering why I was taking so long. Surely, I couldn't just get back in the ambulance and drive away.

I quickly ran upstairs to check the patient. I needed to make sure he was dead before I could go anywhere. Once it was confirmed that he lay lifeless in his bed and had probably been there several hours, I had to tell the family I was leaving and that another ambulance or police car was on its way. They looked at me like stunned mullets, but I had to leave. Someone else needed me and I didn't have time to hang around. Thankfully, one of the patient's daughters broke the awkwardness by stepping in and telling me it was okay to leave.

The problem was, though, that when I arrived at the other scene my mind was full of thoughts from what just happened. I was processing walking out on the family and how that must have seemed to them. I couldn't focus on the task at hand. My bandwidth was full and it was affecting my ability to treat the patient who was alive. I had to ask my partner to treat the patient, allowing him to take simple vital signs tests, a task I could usually do without thought.

In Chapters 8–10 you will learn the psychological skills, tools and strategies needed to master your cognitive bandwidth and working memory.

In the *Harry Potter* books, all wizards and witches possess different skills and attributes. Neville Longbottom is highly gifted at herbology, whereas Seamus Finnigan has a particular proclivity for pyrotechnics. All are good at magic in their own way. In this book, you will be able to learn the spells that are best for you. Your unique individual personality and innate abilities will determine which tools to use. There is no three-, five- or eight-step method. Instead you will develop a toolbox of skills that suit you.

INTERVIEW WITH THE AUTHOR
What's it like telling a family member their loved one is dead?

Tough. It's like most things though; the more you do it, the more comfortable it becomes. But it still doesn't make it something you ever hope to do. When I was a student I used to hide and get my mentors to do it. I always admired the paramedics who could do it with great grace and compassion.

I think it's important, when telling someone that their family member has died, to be frank, to be truthful. No one wants or deserves to be lied to, and the last thing you want to do is provide false hope. People always say to me that they wouldn't know what to say, but the thing is, everyone grieves in their own way and there are no perfect words or sentences that will change that. You can certainly make it worse by saying the wrong thing, but don't try and come up with the perfect words. Being genuine is the most important thing.

You have to expect the screaming and yelling, or even blame. Being blamed is hard to take sometimes, but it's important to have the ability to step back and realise that they're experiencing horrific pain and you're just the person telling them the news.

A paramedic once taught me that being with someone at the end of their life, as they die, is a great privilege and we must honour that.

CALL TO ACTION

'You need to over practise, and almost become autonomic in order for you to have mental capacity and cognitive bandwidth, to use your knowledge, to do the best. Master the things that take up a lot of cognitive bandwidth.' – **Aldon Delport, Australian paramedic**

Key Takeaways

- The human survival response is triggered by a release of hormones that prepare the body to either fight, run away or freeze.
- The system is positive until it isn't. This occurs when the response overpowers our thought processes and starts making decisions outside our awareness.
- Seeing goals as a challenge rather than a threat helps the response work in our favour.

Key Tasks

- Identify what triggers your survival response. Determine whether it's activated by a life-threatening source or it's triggered by minor incidents. Is it being triggered when you should be in rest and digest?
- Identify what higher functions (thoughts and abilities) you lose when triggered.

6

Controlling Stress

Personal Experience – Stage for a Shooting

We were called to a double shooting and were trying to weave through traffic well above the speed limit. We didn't know whether we should enter the scene or wait for a police escort. I'm sure my resting heart rate was about 180 beats per minute.

Patients were relying on us to be fast, since we were the closest vehicle to the scene. Unfortunately, we were closer to them than the police were. While we sped to the scene, the call over the radio came that the shooter's location was unknown.

I'd never been dispatched to gunshot victims before. I was also working with a brand-new student. I was responsible for his safety and how he treated the patients. As with anything, though, challenges don't usually come as a single serving.

My mind raced at the thought of what we would find, what we were going to walk into. It was hard not to let images of a bloody scene of carnage and chaos take over. I tried to remember the study I had done in university about gunshot wounds and the ballistics of a projectile, the things to look for when someone is shot. I'd read about it and spoken about it with other paramedics, but now I was about to see it.

Another call over the radio echoed through the ambulance. There were two victims, and they thought the shooter had absconded from the scene. Not having to dodge a crazed gunman was somewhat of a relief, but I still wanted clearer direction on our next steps: was it definitely safe to proceed, and how far out were the police? Our communications centre didn't know the answers. I had to make some decisions.

I decided to tell the student to pull over and be ready, to wait for the police. I figured it was like the aeroplane oxygen scenario: put your own mask on before helping someone else. We still didn't know where the shooter was or the gun. We would be no good if we ended up getting hurt ourselves. This was a very difficult decision to make, knowing that two people lay on the ground, shot.

Fortunately, just as we pulled over, a police car came screaming past. We quickly put our lights and sirens on to follow behind. At least now we had other people with a gun standing next to us.

We arrived on the scene to find a young man sitting in the gutter. Blood was pouring from his mouth and face. He couldn't talk – his jaw was blown away – but he was sitting and breathing. I decided to leave him sitting upright so he wouldn't choke on his own blood and go check on the other victim. This patient was yelling in pain; he was shot in the abdomen and groin. He was yelling out, 'Where's my son? He shot my son.'

The father told me that a random intoxicated person knocked on the wrong house, asking these innocent people for drugs. When they said they didn't have any drugs, the shooter pulled out a sawn-off shotgun and shot both of them.

By this time, I really started to feel the pressure. The police looked at me for directions on how to assist with the patients and the student was asking me what to do. I was asking myself the same questions. I had tunnel vision; it was as if I was becoming blind to the reality around me. I had to do something quickly, because the son was screaming to me that he couldn't see; he was literally blind from his wounds.

It wasn't until I looked up, taking a few seconds to scan my surroundings, that I was able to dial in and offload the negative thoughts in my head. By taking a few seconds to gather my thoughts and look into the distance, I was able to make a definitive decision. Everything suddenly felt clearer.

I decided to treat the son, as he was at the greatest risk of losing his airway (ability to breathe). Being able to make that simple first decision, the first step forward, gave me the clarity and confidence to move with conviction for the rest of the case.

My head was now in the game and my training started to naturally take over. My heart rate began to lower and I no longer felt palpitations in my chest.

The father had no major haemorrhage, which was a miracle given the wound was right next to a major artery in his groin. I directed the student to manage the father and provide some much-needed pain relief. He was still at risk of internal bleeding, so transport to a surgeon was a priority.

I learned a lot from this case. The initial effects of the pressure on my performance were obvious. I realised I could overcome that pressure and develop skills and techniques to control my response to it, in particular my heart rate.

Stress Theories Explained

As we saw in the previous chapter, when we're placed under pressure (stress), our body reacts by activating the fight, flight or freeze response. It's important to understand exactly how this naturally occurring response can affect our performance.

A number of models and theories have been developed to explain how humans react to stress and pressure while performing. In this chapter, I summarise some of these theories and outline why they're relevant to possessing poise. I don't want to get bogged down in the deep theory of the different models for performance under pressure, largely because there seems to be no perfect model. All models have their limitations, and further research is required in the field. In this section, I'll outline the models for possessing poise that I have found helpful as a paramedic.

It's worth noting that a lot of the research in this area is based on the performance of athletes or on conceptualised studies. A few studies have looked at military performance, but again, this does not always correlate directly to the civilian world. What all the research boils down to, though, is that it's not as simple as drawing a few lines on a curve – several factors influence performance. Optimising performance is about developing a toolbox of skills and attributes that we can draw on in the moment.

Over the following pages we'll look at three theories to help explain the science behind the effects of stress on performance. By understanding how you're affected by stress you will be one step closer to implementing skills to counteract it.

The Yerkes-Dodson law

The best way to introduce you to stress theories is through the inverted-U concept – the relationship between performance and stress, also known as the Yerkes-Dodson law. First described in 1908, this law suggests that performance and stress are directly related: increasing stress increases performance to a point, beyond which the physiological or mental arousal of stress reduces performance. In other words, there's an optimal level of arousal for optimal performance. Over- or under-arousal reduces task performance.

The theory arose when US psychologists Robert M. Yerkes and John D. Dodson conducted an experiment. They discovered that rats could be motivated to complete a maze with slight electrical shocks. When they increased the levels of the electric shock given, however, the rats' performance level decreased. The rats responded to the increased levels by attempting to flee, seeking an escape. It was clear from the experiment that the rats' stress levels helped to focus their attention and motivation on the task at hand, but only until an optimum point was reached.

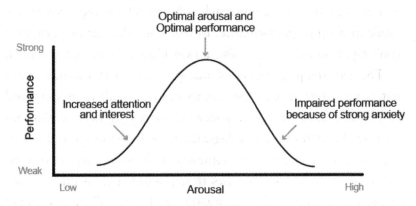

AROUSAL AND PERFORMANCE

Figure 6. The Yerkes-Dodson curve is an inverted U-shape that shows the relationship between arousal and performance. At a moderate level of arousal, performance is best; at other levels of arousal, there may be too little or too much to facilitate peak performance. Source: RM Yerkes & JD Dodson, 'The relation of strength of stimulus to rapidity of habit-formation', *Journal of Comparative Neurology and Psychology*, 1908, vol. 18, no. 5, pp. 459–82.

The idea of the Yerkes-Dodson model is that we need a certain amount of arousal – in other words, a certain amount of stress – or we will lack the motivation and desire to perform at an optimum level. If we have too much stress and are overaroused, however, we will lose performance; our cognitive ability will become impaired and we will lose fine motor skills.

This model provides a good introduction to stress and performance, but given it was developed in 1908, it's overly simplistic. Other authors have since developed more nuanced models of stress and performance.

The Catastrophe Model

The catastrophe model has gained popularity recently within the sporting and athletic world because it links arousal with anxiety.

It suggests that if we're experiencing high levels of cognitive anxiety as arousal increases, we will reach a threshold and then experience a sudden drop in performance. In other words, our performance won't taper off as it does in the Yerkes-Dodson inverted-U model.

The catastrophe model of anxiety and performance states that anxiety has at least two components: cognitive anxiety and the physiological arousal response. Cognitive anxiety determines whether the effect of physiological arousal is smooth and small, large and catastrophic, or somewhere between the two. The catastrophe model hypothesises that physiological arousal is not necessarily detrimental to performance, but it will be associated with catastrophic effects when cognitive anxiety is high.

I like this model because it can be related back to fear. The greater our fear, the more anxiety we will have. Thus, if we fear failure, we will reach a catastrophic level sooner and experience a sudden drop in performance as a result. Seeing tasks in a threat state with a fear of failure will greatly increase anxiety, which will have a detrimental effect on performance.

If you've ever had a bad experience in the past and are now faced with a similar situation, your fear of failure will increase your anxiety, creating doubt and hesitation in your ability to make a clear decision. We know from self-efficacy that our previous experience greatly influences our internal belief to complete tasks. The brain is good at remembering poor performance as it wants to protect us from it happening again. The best example of this effect are boxers.

Ronda Rousey was the greatest female UFC fighter in the world. She then experienced a dramatic defeat, where she was knocked out in the second round, labelled the upset of the year. After that experience Ronda was never the same athlete again. That experience was embedded in her brain, changing her once high self-efficacy and creating a fear of failure. This increased her cognitive anxiety when she stepped into the arena again. She lost her magic as a result. The potential catastrophe of another knockout influenced her performance.

This model has its limitations because it doesn't consider task difficulty or individual competency. Other factors that need to be considered are fatigue and lack of sleep, not to mention an individual's level of physical fitness as well as their level of education and knowledge.

The next model expands even further on the catastrophe theory. It looks at the relationship between stress, anxiety and arousal. It demonstrates how this can impact motivation and the improvement of performance, but also highlights that those optimal levels of performance vary depending on the individual, and on many other variables that impact performance. Despite this model coming from the sporting world, I believe it transitions well to the everyday world because it accounts for individual variables.

Optimal Functioning

The individualised zone of optimal functioning (IZOF), first presented by Finnish sports psychologist Yuri Hanin in 1980, proposed that there's a zone in which an individual can perform at their optimum level. Although this model considers the multiple variables to performance, its limitation is that it was designed for and tested on athletes, not in the emergency medical environment or everyday life. This means it does lack evidence when it comes to other types of fear and arousal scenarios.

The IZOF is defined as 'a narrow range of arousal levels that produces the best performance in a particular activity'. This zone will be different for different activities. For weightlifters, for example, high levels of arousal are best, allowing them to generate maximum power while lifting. In contrast, golfers will benefit from low levels of arousal while putting, as this helps them perform controlled, delicate movements. The zone may also be different for individuals even if they are engaged in the same sporting activity.

Essentially, the IZOF proposes that individuals react to anxiety in different ways. Some tend to succeed when anxiety is low, while others tend to succeed when anxiety is high. In addition, the particular task being completed influences the best possible arousal zone. Each person thus has their own preferred level of arousal that allows them to perform at an optimum level.

This research also indicates that optimum performance will not only require the performer to be within their arousal zone, but within their optimal levels of emotion. For example, if a paramedic is at their optimum arousal level but they lack motivation or are filled with self-doubt, they won't be able to perform at their best.

The zone is composed of emotions and feelings such as excitement, relaxation, liveliness and calm. IZOF emotions are seen as either helpful or unhelpful rather than positive or negative. In IZOF theory, it all depends on whether their effect on your performance is enhancing or debilitating. In other words, if the feeling or emotion helps you perform better, it's helpful. If it makes you perform worse, it's unhelpful. So-called negative emotions can actually improve goal-oriented performance for some people.

When it comes to emotions, the IZOF really becomes individualised, because one person may find nervousness before an event helpful, whereas another may find it very unhelpful. Whether some emotions are helpful or not can also depend on the intensity of the emotion – how extreme the feeling is. A paramedic may find being nervous before attending a car crash helpful, but when the nervousness goes beyond a certain point, it may impact their performance and become unhelpful.

The key message here is for each of us to develop an awareness of the specific level at which we perform best, which emotions inspire you and which emotions hold you back. In sport, some athletes perform better when they have controlled anger, whereas for others anger would hurt their performance. Developing self-awareness is therefore a key component to understanding your best zone of performance.

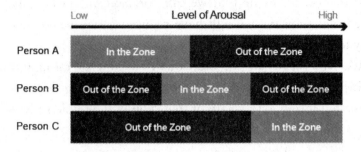

Figure 7. Being 'in the zone' can look different for different people in different circumstances, such as the hypothetical people depicted in this graph.

When we're 'in the zone', we feel in control, things are effortless, we get a sense of enjoyment and satisfaction from the task, and we have great focus and attention to the performance.

The three main areas to consider that impact your individual zone of optimal functioning are your personality, the task being performed and the stage of learning.

If the task being performed requires the use of fine motor skills, then it's better performed at lower arousal. On the other hand, gross motor skills, which do not require fine motor movements, can be performed at higher arousal levels.

Our stage of learning, competency level and ability to perform a task autonomously will impact whether we prefer to be aroused or not. If we have mastered our skills and can perform tasks autonomously, then we can afford to perform at a higher level of arousal than those who haven't. This is why we need to go from simply learning (conscious competence) to mastery (unconscious competence).

The IZOF model also brings us back to perception and self-efficacy. If we can perceive arousal as a positive rather than a negative emotion, we will most likely see the task as a challenge rather than as a threat. If we perceive the arousal as negative, we will see the task as a threat, creating anxiety that will hinder our performance. Believing that we can complete the task at hand – self-efficacy – means we will have reduced arousal and be more likely to succeed at the task.

We will return to the individualised zone of optimal functioning later in this chapter and you can work out where you sit on the scale. Once you're aware of that, you will be able to improve your performance.

Heart Rate and Stress

Dave Grossman is a retired lieutenant colonel from the United States Army. He has conducted a range of studies and written several books for soldiers on performing under combat conditions. His groundbreaking 1997 work, *Psychological Effects of Combat*, identified the key relationships between performance, pressure and heart rate. I highly recommend that you read another of his books, *On Combat*.

Although Grossman's research has focused on the combat world, it can also be applied to performing under pressure. One of his studies, looking at heart rate increases due to a fear response, led him to develop a theory based on heart rate levels.

Grossman's theory describes five conditions warriors can experience during combat. Each condition occurs within a particular heart-rate range and is associated with predictable changes in performance. During a crisis or pressure, it's valuable to know in which condition we're operating. That way we can perform at our best by controlling our physiological responses.

The desired condition for performance optimisation depends on the task at hand. The beauty of this theory, though, is that by becoming aware of our physiological readiness conditions, we can train ourselves to control our physiological state. We can't change our physiology, but we can take advantage of it and use it to our favour.

Grossman's five different conditions are:

- *Condition White:* At rest – normal resting heart rate 60–80 beats per minute.
- *Condition Yellow:* Psychologically alert and prepared for combat – resting heart rate 80–115 beats per minute. At this level, fighter pilots are ready and alert.
- *Condition Red:* Optimal warrior survival – heart rate 115–145 beats per minute. Gross motor skills, visual reaction time and cognitive reaction times peak at the expense of fine motor skills.
- *Condition Grey:* A transitional phase between Conditions Red and Black – heart rate 145–175 beats per minute. Cognitive processing worsens, as do visual and auditory perception, but this may be modified with training. Gross motor skills are still at high levels. Formula One Drivers fit into this category.
- *Condition Black:* Catastrophic breakdown of mental and physical performance – heart rate greater than 175 beats per minute. Irrational or submissive behaviour occurs due to the fight, flight or freeze response.

Grossman identified that, in general, the sweet spot for paramedics is Condition Yellow, where the heart rate is between 80 and 115 beats per minute. At this optimum level for performance we have the highest cognitive reaction times and control in tandem with the ability to maintain our fine motor skills.

Overall the scale applies to when we're feeling the pressure, when our body is in the fight, flight or freeze response, the adrenaline is pumping and the amygdala is working overtime.

We will still be able to operate in Condition Red, but with a heart rate between 115–145 beats per minute we will lose fine motor skills. We need to be aware of this, because if we still want to perform our job at a high level under stress, then we need to prepare for the loss of fine motor skills. Condition Red is the optimal level for combat warriors, but if you need to maintain fine motor control, then aim for mellow yellow.

The best way to counter the loss of motor control is through high-quality, deliberate, self-reflective training and stress inoculation (which we'll get to in Chapter 7). Quality matters. By mastering our fundamental fine motor skills, we drill the procedures into ourselves so much that they become almost automatic. This means that, when we're aroused, your training will compensate for the loss of fine motor skills. By making our fine motor skills autonomous, we will be able to reduce our working memory usage, as discussed earlier. If our working memory is too full of stressful thoughts, then we won't have any capacity to think clearly when performing a task that relies on fine motor skills. Training will allow you to focus your attention on more pressing issues and gain situational awareness.

When we're first learning to drive, our cognitive bandwidth focuses on changing gears, operating the indicators, pressing the brake with the right amount of pressure and so on. We develop tunnel vision, focused on each individual step of driving. Once those skills become autonomous, however, we are better able to consider what's happening on the road and in the world around us. This will help prevent us from crashing into another car if, say, we forgot to indicate at the intersection because we were too focused on changing the gears without stalling.

The goal then is to train our fine motor skills until they become autonomous or almost autonomous. We must train, practise, work hard – assiduousness is required.

When we're faced with pressure or a crisis, we won't just be sitting in one particular state. As with anything, we will fluctuate between various stages, but the trick is knowing our own individual performance preference and matching the task we're trying to complete with the right zone at the right time. If a Formula One driver wanted to relax and sit in Condition White, they would probably miss a corner and crash, due to a lack of alertness. Many paramedics, military and humanitarian personnel have found some real utility in Grossman's heart rate conditions.

There are some variables, however, that can affect the applicability of this scale, such as our level of fitness, our training and our medical history. Although this theory echoes the current understanding of stress science, the heart rate numbers are not always definitive.

You could have a heart rate of 140 and not be experiencing a lot of stress, and conversely, you could have a heart rate of 90 and be totally cognitively overloaded. You may be wondering, in that case, why we would consider heart rate at all. The reason is that it's useful, especially when applied to IZOF.

Formula One drivers are a good example of how someone can maintain a very high heart rate but still have the ability to make split-second decisions, and be calm and composed on the radio with their team, while driving 320 kilometres per hour. Formula One drivers have to maintain a continuously high level of concentration in combination with skill and physical strain. A driver's heart rate would average 140–170 beats per minute throughout an entire race, which takes approximately two hours. It's a remarkable ability to be able to think and perform with such a high heart rate.

Generally, the reason the racing drivers can do this is that they started driving at a young age. They have come up through the ranks, moulding their physical body to cope with the high-stress environment – in other words, through stress inoculation. The fact that Formula One drivers can perform so well with a high heart rate shows there are exceptions to Grossman's theory. While it's not a hard and fast rule, it's a very valuable one. I've found it extremely useful, and I hope you do, too.

You may be thinking that it's impossible to control your heart rate because it's the autonomic (i.e. automatic or involuntary nervous system). Anyone with medical training knows the heart has its own automaticity (it beats to the sound of its own drum), but there are things we can consciously change in order to control our heart rate and, in turn, optimise our performance.

Personal Experience – Burning Heart

I heard the call over the radio; the job sounded terrible, and I could sense the panic in the senior paramedic's voice. He spoke extremely quickly and requested backup immediately to treat a burn victim. I was the closest backup ambulance unit to the patient, so I turned on the siren and started heading towards them.

The patient had been on their moored boat when it caught fire, which ignited the gas bottle within the vessel's cabin and caused a large explosion. The patient was thrown to the ground and was quickly covered in flames. His skin began to melt, the fire burning through the multiple layers of the skin that protects us from the elements. Eighty per cent of his body was burnt.

His skin peeled off like a cooked potato; it had wrinkled away to reveal the layers of the body. The fire had destroyed hair follicles, sweat glands and nerve endings. His burned skin appeared black, white and red, developing a leathery appearance. The largest blisters I had ever seen started to form; they filled with yellow fluid.

When I met up with the crew on the scene, I was shocked to see the senior paramedic driving the ambulance and the student in the back, treating the patient. With next to no experience on the job, the student was doing his best.

My partner and I quickly jumped in the back of the ambulance to take over treatment. We made the student jump out of the way, not realising he would literally jump behind the chair in the back of the ambulance, getting himself caught between the patient's feet and the rear doors.

A quick assessment identified that the patient had received no pain relief: the student and senior paramedic had attempted no medical interventions other than to cool the patient down with water. The patient was clearly in significant pain – yelling, moaning and gritting his teeth.

We quickly established IV access to administer pain relief and fluids and put an oxygen mask on him. We covered the patient in cling wrap to help replace the burned skin. When nerves are exposed to the elements, even the softest blow of air is excruciating.

After the case, I initiated a debrief and asked the senior paramedic why he was driving and not treating the patient. He explained that it was because he thought he could drive faster to the hospital.

The senior paramedic's decision-making was affected because he was in condition black, with a heart rate so high it was almost beating out of his chest. He experienced a catastrophic breakdown of mental and physical performance. Yes, the patient required rapid transport to the hospital, but with a 30-minute drive to the nearest hospital, the patient required life-saving intervention on the way. That intervention must be delivered by the most qualified paramedic. This case starkly illustrated to me the effects of stress on performance.

Discover Your Zone

I encourage you to take the time now to use the following scales to discover your optimal arousal level for improving your performance. Once you know this and develop self-awareness, you will be able to implement strategies and tools to improve your performance so you can operate at your optimal level.

This scale is assessed through recall, which means you will need to reflect on multiple past experiences where you have performed successfully. Don't just rely on one single past performance.

Step 1: Success Emotions

Select four to five positive and four to five negative items from the lists of positive and negative affect emotions below. Choose the items that *best describe how you felt when you performed at your best* (most optimum level).

In some circumstances, we can use negative emotions to our advantage. For example, the energy we gain from anger can be harnessed to motivate us in a positive way, despite anger being perceived as a negative emotion. If we can control the negative emotion, it can have a positive impact.

What you don't want to happen is let your negative emotions control you. That would be like turning to the dark side of the Force in *Star Wars*. When you imagine your previous best performances, it's worth asking yourself whether you harnessed the power of negative emotions for good.

Positive Affect Emotions that Can Improve Performance

Motivated	Willing	Purposeful	Alert	Resolute
Active	Confident	Showing off	Vigorous	Energetic
Charged	Brisk	Certain	Glad	Enthusiastic
Cheerful	Rested	Eager	Easy-going	Brave
Relaxed	Exalted	Peaceful	Fearless	Excited
Satisfied	Stimulated	Calm	Pleasant	Good
Daring	Nice	Happy	Comfortable	Composed
Sleepy	Free	Overjoyed	Animated	Carefree

Negative Affect Emotions that Can Improve Performance

Attacking	Vehement	Intense	Aggressive	In pain
Pressure	Disappointed	Tense	Provoked	Furious
Angry	Irritated	Mad	Nervous	Restless
Concerned	Tired	Tight	Worried	Alarmed
Exhausted	Sluggish	Indignant	Overloaded	Dispirited
Irresolute	Weary	Doubtful	Unhappy	Sorrowful
Sad	Afraid	Distressed	Down	Lazy
Uncertain	Depressed	Unwilling	Strained	Terrified

If there is a word that resonates with you that is *not* on the tables above, you can add your own word.

Step 2: Borg Rating of Perceived Exertion Scale

The Borg rating of perceived exertion (RPE), developed by Swedish researcher Gunnar Borg, is a scale for measuring an individual's effort and exertion, breathlessness and fatigue during performance.

It provides a measure of how hard the physiological response is working in a challenging situation. The RPE is based on the physical sensations we experience during a performance, such as heart rate, breathing rate, level of sweating and muscle fatigue.

Here's how the RPE works:

- Write down each of the five emotions you discovered in the previous step into the corresponding positive or negative table. Then rate the level of exertion your physical body felt when you experienced these emotions – combining all physiological responses from stress and fatigue.
- Disregard any single sensation caused by an emotion, such as muscle pain with no other effects. Focus on the whole feeling of exertion.
- Select a number between 6 and 20 that indicates whether the emotion caused no exertion at all (a score of 6) or high exertion (a score of 20).

From working out my own RPE, I know that when I face confrontation, my exertion level is very high. I am usually a very agreeable person and feel great discomfort when I have to confront people. My muscles start to tighten, I feel restricted, and my hearing almost doubles as I focus on the perceived threat. It's like I can feel the hormones take effect as the heart pumps them around. My exertion is highest when I have to stand against something morally and go against popular opinion.

But because I have identified these feelings, I'm now far better at controlling them when I face confrontation. My self-awareness has improved. I expect to feel those emotions, so I am ready for them. That's the goal of working through these steps.

Positive emotions that improve performance

		Positive Emotion				
		1	2	3	4	5
Score	Level of Exertion					
6	No exertion at all					
7						
7.5	Extremely low					
8						
9	Very low					
10						
11	Mild					
12						
13	Somewhat high					
14						
15	High					
16						
17	Very high					
18						
19	Extremely high					
20	Maximal exertion					

Negative emotions that improve performance

Score	Level of Exertion	Negative Emotion				
		1	2	3	4	5
6	No exertion at all					
7						
7.5	Extremely low					
8						
9	Very low					
10						
11	Mild					
12						
13	Somewhat high					
14						
15	High					
16						
17	Very high					
18						
19	Extremely high					
20	Maximal exertion					

Source: G. Borg, 'Rating scales for perceived physical effort and exertion', in *International Encyclopedia of Ergonomics and Human Factors*, 2nd Edition, Roca Baton, Florida: CRC Press, 2006.

You may be wondering why the scale ranges from 6 to 20 rather than 1 to 15, and there's a unique and simple explanation for that – the scale number corresponds to heart rate. A score of 6 on the Borg RPE scale corresponds to a heart rate of 60 beats per minute in a healthy adult, a score of 11 would equal a heart rate of 110 beats per minute, a score of 14 a heart rate of 140 beats per minute, and so on.

Now, take your results from the Borg RPE scale and find where your individual zone of optimal performance would be. Add up all your scores and divide by the number of emotions you rated to find your average score.

- If your average score was below 11, then you perform better with less arousal.
- If your average score was between 11 and 15, then you perform better with moderate arousal.
- If your average score was above 15, then you perform better with high arousal.

The great thing about this is that you can now overlay the individual zone of optimal functioning and Grossman's heart rate and arousal conditions to discover your individual optimal heart rate when performing under pressure. We will call this the heart rate individualised zone of optimal performance (see page 122).

There will, of course, be some limitations to this, such as the task being performed, but knowing your optimal heart rate is a great tool for improving your performance. If you would like to see my results, and an example of how to fill out the scale, refer to Appendix C (page 310).

You might find it instructive to repeat these steps, but instead of using emotions that have helped you succeed in the past, try emotions that have made you unsuccessful in the past. By reversing the process, you will identify the things that hinder your performance, the emotions that set you up for failure. This might help improve your self-awareness. If, say, you identify that restlessness is an emotion you felt when you performed poorly in the past, and that it was at a very high level of exertion, the next time you sense it you might be able to break the spell by implementing a psychological skill you learn later in this book.

Optimal Heart Rate

Understanding the relationship between the task involved, the skills required to complete that task and your individual zone of optimal functioning is a constant fluctuating battle. Although you may perform better under a particular level of arousal, this may prevent you excelling in other tasks. For example, while a surgeon requires a low level of arousal, as they are using fine motor skills, a baggage handler needs to be constantly alert.

For this reason, it's worth looking at which of your skills require lower levels of arousal and which require higher levels, then try and match your individual arousal preference to those skills to determine what tasks you might be highly successful at.

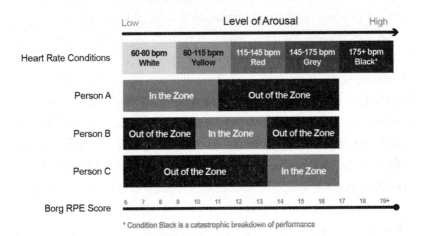

Figure 8. The heart rate individualised zone of optimal performance combines Grossman's work, the Borg RPE Score and the IZOF.

Person A

We can see in the diagram on the previous page that Person A prefers a low arousal with a heart rate between Conditions White and Yellow. This individual would perform a task with very good fine motor skills and wouldn't necessarily need a high level of automatic skills.

If Person A were a paramedic, the general tasks they would excel at would be surgical interventions, gaining IV access, drug calculations and preparing syringes. In everyday life, they might be an electrician, someone who enjoys detail-oriented work in an office, or someone whose side hustle takes advantage of skills such as knitting or embroidery.

Person B

The diagram indicates that Person B prefers a moderate level of arousal with a heart rate between Conditions Yellow and Red. This individual will perform well in most fine motor skills tasks if they have a good level of training and a sound knowledge base – i.e. skills mastery (unconscious competence).

If Person B were a paramedic, the general tasks they would excel at would be applying tourniquets, airway management and CPR.

In everyday life, this person might be a sandwich-maker at Subway who has people queuing out the door. They need a good level of automatic sandwich-making skills to move quickly through the orders and a sense of speed because they have customers waiting. If they go too fast and panic the sandwich will be bad, but if they go too slow the customers will get angry. If there was only one customer in the store at a time, then the sandwich-maker could be Person A.

Person C

The diagram indicates that Person C prefers a high level of arousal with a heart rate between Conditions Red and Grey. This individual would perform well at gross motor skills, and would require a high degree of autonomous skills. This level of arousal is rarer and comes with greater risk of losing control.

If Person C were a paramedic, general tasks they would excel at would be extrication, rescue tasks such as dragging a body out of a burning building, cardiac compressions and largely time-critical tasks. In everyday life, they would perform well in a moment where they were faced with a daunting challenge or a life-or-death situation. Perhaps their car is broken down in the middle of the road and they need to get out of the way quickly before a truck slams into them or they're the auctioneer at a house sale who is trying to get the highest bid and pressure the buyers.

If you would like to see my results and an example of how to fill out the scale, refer to **Appendix D.**

Going through this process, starting with visualising your best performances, will help you improve your self-awareness and outline strategies to improve. You will find this tool an extremely useful way to measure your performance.

INTERVIEW WITH THE AUTHOR
What was it like seeing your first dead body?

Terrible. I was a student but working in a hospital part-time to help put myself through university. I was a wardy. I was pushing a patient on their hospital bed down the long hospital corridors heading towards radiography, where they were due for a CT scan.

As we stopped to wait for the elevator to arrive, the patient started choking vigorously so I sat her up and called for help. Then suddenly the patient coughed up blood and was spitting large amounts of blood everywhere. It was a horrific scene in the middle of the hospital. An emergency team of doctors arrived with the crash cart to treat the patient a few minutes after the call for help.

But they didn't do anything. I was looking around in shock: what were they doing? Why weren't they helping? I asked the nurse and she informed me that the patient was in palliative care for cancer and had a not for resuscitation plan (this was the first time I had come across this). We did nothing, just watched the person die, drowning in her own blood. I had to push the bed back into the patient's room with blood-stained sheets. I was in such a daze that I pushed the bed straight into the wall.

CALL TO ACTION

'For students, it's this whirlwind of heart rate, their own heart rate. And then they'll say things like, "Man, I looked over at my mentor, and they were just casually having a chat about putting in a needle, and I'm like, how do they do that?"' – **Andy Bell, Queensland Ambulance Service**

Key Takeaways

- Stress is not the enemy. It's about taming the stress to work in your favour.
- The Yerkes and Dodson law is a good introductory model of stress but it's limited. We need to look deeper at the other variables involved in stress, such as emotion and physiological responses like heart rate.
- Heart rate plays a big role in managing stress. The majority of breathing techniques are used to control heart rate, in order to place it in the zone of optimal functioning.

Key Tasks

- Discover your zone of optimal functioning by completing the Borg rating of perceived exertion (RPE) scale.
- Read *On Combat* by Lieutenant Colonel Dave Grossman.

7

Preparing for Stress

Personal Experience – Thriving in Extremes

It's hard enough having to perform CPR with a five-person team, let alone solo. I found myself treating a middle-aged woman who was choking and unconscious.

When I arrived at the scene, the family members met me out front. They waved me down in a panic, running in front of the ambulance and yelling at me to hurry up, tears running down their faces. I moved as quickly as I could. I opened the side door, grabbed my bags, put on my gloves and turned on the defibrillator. All of these things take precious time. The wait feels like an age when your loved one is lying on the ground needing immediate care.

I ran into the backyard to find the patient. She was not breathing and had no pulse. She had choked on her dinner, collapsing within minutes. The stress of this moment was high.

I had to remove the foreign body, food, from her throat quickly and commence CPR. Laryngoscopy with Magill's forceps, the task at hand, was the one skill I had practised the most in the training room. I know paramedics who have been on the job for over 30 years who have never had to perform laryngoscopy with Magill's forceps. Choking, especially in adults, is very rare. This procedure requires precision and is almost always performed when time is critical. Speed is of the essence.

Laryngoscopy involves using a blade connected to a handle to elevate the larynx so that you can look into the entrance to the oesophagus, more commonly known as the food pipe. You then place the Magill's forceps – long, bent clamps that look like scissors – into the mouth to extract the foreign body.

I didn't hesitate; I had practised this exact scenario a thousand times before. I removed the food and commenced CPR. The patient still didn't have a pulse. I cut her clothes off and applied the defibrillator pads. She was in a non-shockable rhythm; the defibrillator wouldn't be effective, which dramatically decreased her probability of survival.

Once again, I was relying on the resources available to me. I had to make the most of what I had. I directed volunteers to take turns performing cardiac compressions. As a student, you hear stories about how awful it feels to do compressions: the cracking, snapping and breaking of rib bones as you push down on someone's chest; the noise it makes as the ribcage bounces up and down. But most of all, it's hard physical work. The effectiveness of compressions deteriorates after only two minutes, because you can get tired performing them. That's why setting up a rotation is critical. It was a priority on this day, with me, a single volunteer, and bystanders helping.

The helicopter was on the way, but the patient didn't have the time to wait for more advanced care. I decided to call the local doctor to see if he would attend off-duty. I placed the phone on speaker as I continued to perform CPR. He answered and agreed to attend. The problem with that plan, though, was that he was a locum doctor – a physician working here temporarily – and didn't know where to go. It didn't help that the patient was located in a difficult spot that couldn't be found on Google Maps.

I talked to the doctor on speakerphone as I continued to provide advanced life support to the patient. My priority now was to establish an airway. I had to insert a tube into her throat and windpipe. This was made even more urgent by the fact that the patient had suffered a cardiac arrest through choking. Basically, her heart was fine; it had only stopped because she stopped breathing due to choking.

I can claim that males can multitask after this case, as I simultaneously gave street directions to the doctor on the phone, inserted the tube into the patient's throat and instructed a family member to open the security gate and direct the doctor in from the street. Despite a scenario that should have overwhelmed my cognitive bandwidth and reduced my working memory, the case was flowing well. We were performing tasks at a fast pace. The hours of training and thousands of tubes inserted into a dummy were finally paying off. These skills had become nearly autonomous.

The laryngoscopy worked; the airway was now secure just in time for the doctor to walk into the yard. We continued to perform CPR for 30 more minutes, but unfortunately, this time we weren't able to re-establish a heartbeat and the defibrillator was still unable to do anything. I strangely always get a sense of relief when I can shock someone with electricity, because I know it's their greatest chance of survival. It's a good thing.

I was providing as much support as I could to the family at the time, and rang my communications centre to inform them of the horrible news. But instead, they had some news for me.

The police were delayed for more than an hour and the body obviously couldn't be left alone, so I was going to have to stay. I thought that wasn't too bad until the communications centre told me I had another case pending. They had been holding the job while I worked on this case. It was a two-year-old with severe croup.

The communications centre told me that the police wanted me to remain with the body. As harsh as it sounds, I thought to myself, 'We don't treat the dead, we try to save the living.' I left the scene, leaving the doctor and a security officer with the deceased patient, and travelled to the young patient with croup.

I walked in to find the child severely distressed and gasping for air. The child was sucking in so hard that their rib bones were protruding out of their chest and their throat was being sucked backwards.

There's not much worse than looking at a grey, ashen child struggling for air.

I had to block out the previous patient and the image of her lying dead on the ground if I was going to successfully reverse the child's condition. The ability to focus on the task and my preparedness helped create a state of flow that night.

The crying mother and panicked father didn't distract me from my mission. I was able to block out all external distractions that could deviate me from my goal. All of the hours spent in the training room, taking criticism from mentors, and all the sacrifices were paying off. I will never question the 'unrealistic and extreme' scenarios my mentors would set for me again.

The patient responded well to the medication and I was able to wave them goodbye on the helicopter. The child was laughing and smiling.

I returned to the deceased patient just in time to place her in the body bag for transport to the morgue. As a paramedic, I get to experience both extremes of light and dark: beauty and suffering alike. That night, I experienced both. It's a great privilege to be present when someone takes their last breath, and to hug a mother who thought their beloved child was about to.

Operational Cognitive Readiness

In the moments leading up to being thrust into the pressure cooker, it's essential to have the tools necessary to perform at an optimal level. One day a challenge will strike you; you can expect that unexpected events will occur. Developing strategies such as the ones in this book will help prepare you for that day. If you're not prepared for the unexpected, then a predictable surprise is just around the corner. I know personally that when I was a student and didn't adequately prepare for an exam or scenario-based assessment, I would most likely increase my stress levels (and fail).

According to defence analysts J.D. Fletcher and Alexander P. Wind, 'operational cognitive readiness (OCR) is a state where individuals are ready and prepared for jobs, tasks, and environments that are unexpected – those that cannot be anticipated but central to operations. They are ready to deal with the unforeseen.'

It is a concept used primarily in the military, but it can also be applied to other areas of life. Paramedics work in uncontrolled environments that emphasise the point of the unexpected. Even when we're told over the phone what we're going to encounter, it's quite often utterly different from what you discover when you walk through the door.

OCR is defined as 'the mental preparation (including skills, knowledge, abilities, motivations, and personal dispositions) an individual needs to establish and sustain competent performance in the complex and unpredictable environment'. In other words, it is a state of preparedness.

As a paramedic, you never know what the next call will be. When the pager beeps and alarms you don't know what you will be responding to until you arrive, and so you have to be ready for anything. You need to be trained and equipped to treat an asthma attack, a suicide patient, a pregnancy or a domestic violence patient.

Stress Inoculation Training

We can learn to minimise the adverse effects of stress on performance. One of the best ways to do this is through stress inoculation training (SIT). Through appropriate exposure to stressors and training on ways to deal with stress, we can develop the skills necessary to handle varying levels of stress in the future.

SIT provides people with the opportunity to practise their skills while performing under stressful conditions that approximate the operational environment. In other words, through SIT we can attempt to build our resistance to stress and increase our stress threshold. Then, instead of panicking when you cut your toe, you will gradually increase your threshold to a level that allows you to only panic when you've been decapitated, and, well, it won't matter then. Through being exposed to stressful stimuli in the training environment, we prepare ourselves for the real thing.

Training scenarios need to be as realistic as possible to replicate what we're going to be exposed to. For paramedics, it would be conducting medical scenarios; for a truck driver, it would be driving in the rain at night. The goal is to be as prepared as possible to meet the mission requirements, and this can't be done if we're not exposed to stress before facing it in the real world.

We've established that experiencing stress during performance is linked to altered cognitive processes such as attention, memory and decision-making. Other stressors that cause poor performance include noise, heat and cold stress, fatigue and insufficient physical fitness. All of these things can be minimised or even avoided if we're properly trained and prepared for stress.

SIT is typically organised into three distinct phases:

1. Conceptualisation: understanding the relationship between stress and performance.
2. Skills acquisition and rehearsal.
3. Application and follow-through.

We've already discussed conceptualisation by analysing our individualised zone of optimal performance and the fight, flight or freeze mechanism. Skills acquisition refers to developing the effective coping mechanisms and skills you need to manage stress (i.e. psychological skills training, see Chapter 8). For now, let's focus on the third area: application and follow-through.

Driving to someone who is 80 years old in cardiac arrest at a nursing home is stressful. Driving to someone who is two years old in cardiac arrest in the middle of the night, in the middle of nowhere, by yourself, is very stressful. Driving to a multi-casualty incident with four patients in cardiac arrest is extremely stressful. The fact that your life hangs in the balance as you are driving above the speed limit and running red lights increases the chances of stress overload.

The best way to combat this stress is by systematically exposing yourself to very stressful situations. Being exposed to the fight, flight or freeze response will teach you how your body reacts to stress, help you witness how your decision-making changes, and give you a glimpse into potential pitfalls.

US Air Force Pararescueman Michael Lauria says, 'we trained at 130 per cent so that when our faculties deteriorated under stress, we could still function at 100 per cent. Over time, we each developed skills to work with our natural physiological response, manage it, and even use it to our advantage.'

A good analogy of stress inoculation is the exercise training known as the progressive overload principle, and, in particular, resistance training. Bodybuilders go to the gym to lift weights that cause stress to the muscle group being worked. For example, if their workout includes doing bench presses, they are lifting a bar full of weights to stress the pectoral muscles. The first week they start lifting, they may only lift 80 kilograms for 10 repetitions. Then, the following week, they may be able to increase the weight to 85 kilograms for 10 repetitions. Then the week after that, they can lift 90 kilograms for 10 repetitions, and so on.

Their muscle begins to build strength, and increases its resistance against the previous weight lifted. By placing their body under more stress each time they go to the gym, they'll find it easy to lift the original weight of 80 kilograms for 25 repetitions.

The benefit of SIT is that, by being constantly exposed to high levels of stress in the training environment, we can practise using our psychological skills and different coping strategies. Practising psychological skills helps reduce our heart rate in order to stay in Condition Yellow, and massively improves our cognitive bandwidth. This will eventually allow us to develop an increased stress threshold, or even immunity to a particular stimulus.

An analogous example would be the reason for having a

measles immunisation. Vaccines are a clever way to trick the body and produce an immune response. Certain vaccines use dead or weakened viruses to trick the body into thinking we've already had the disease.

When we get the vaccine, our body will respond by creating antibodies (soldiers) to protect us against future infection. The body's cells remember and recognise the virus, so that when we're exposed to the real thing, our immune system has already been trained to fight against it. Our body rapidly produces more antibodies to destroy the virus. We may still experience some symptoms (Condition Yellow), but we're protected from the most dangerous effects (Condition Red and Black). (Alternatively, if you believe in conspiracy theories, you've just been injected with nanobots and you're waiting for Donald Trump to activate the 5G network.)

By applying stress inoculation training, we're exposing our mind to stress, so that when the real thing happens, our mind will recognise it and protect us from it. We will release the autonomous fine-motor-skill soldiers and psychological skills we need to control our arousal and heart rate so that we can remain in Condition Yellow.

As a trained paramedic who has worked on my mindset, when I see someone with a broken arm, I don't get any signs of physiological arousal; I just go about my business and apply my treatment plan and move on to the next patient. If I'm not careful, I may fall into Condition White, where I lack motivation and empathy. I've had patients ask for a helicopter for a broken arm, only for me to state, 'It's just an arm, you'll be fine' (I still need to work on my empathy).

In order to build your confidence and tolerance to stress, you must practise, test and simulate your knowledge while being exposed to stressful stimuli. Slowly but carefully, raise the bar of your training and make it more challenging. Once you've mastered a skill in a nicely controlled climate with white painted walls and lunch provided – the classroom – you can practise it in reality. Go outside and do it at 3 am, in the rain, or on top of a hill. Then add some actors to distract you, using fake blood and cosmetics to simulate real-life injuries.

The goal here is to gradually increase the stress over time; the last thing we want to do is set ourselves up for failure. If you raise the stress level from 0 to 100 straight away and people start failing, they will just develop self-doubt, shame and a fear of failure: all of the things we are trying to prevent.

It's worth highlighting that stress inoculation training is designed for people who are already in the workforce or for students. Stress inoculation training will not work unless you have the minimum fundamental knowledge necessary for the task, as well as psychological skills training. It's not about being thrown in the deep end and hoping the skills will naturally develop. You need to develop both technical and non-technical skills before stress inoculation training. You then slowly raise the bar of performance.

Getting thrown in the deep end if you can't swim will kill you. Learning to swim is a step-by-step process, from getting comfortable submerging your head, to learning to float, then kicking with a flotation device, then freestyle and its breathing technique. Once one task is completed successfully, raise the bar higher and repeat.

Sometimes it's hard to replicate the real-life scenario or environment, making it difficult to attain stress inoculation, but here are a few suitable methods.

Environment

Get out of the classroom and air conditioning. Do the training when it's raining, when it's dark and when it's cold, because that's when you'll be doing it in the real world. I've only ever been to a single one-car accident with air conditioning and shelter from the sun (they drove into a house), but it still wasn't the same as the classroom. If you only practise in fair weather, then you can only perform in fair weather. If you're an athlete and only train at an indoor sports centre with astroturf, when you have to play outside on grass for your competition, you will be at a disadvantage.

Remember, the more accurate the training environment, the better. Gain your experience of stress through the training environment. Don't wait for 20 years of on-road experience to teach you how to manage stress, because you will experience more failures and have poorer long-term mental health.

Peer Pressure

There's nothing quite like having to perform in front of your classmates or fellow workers. No one wants to be seen as a novice or incompetent among the people they're trying to impress. It doesn't seem to matter when we're practising something on our own; if we fail, there are no consequences as only *we* know, but if we do it in front of our peers the stakes instantly become higher.

This certainly applies to people who have been in the job a long time and who are very experienced. I have found that a lot of veteran paramedics don't perform scenario-based training nearly as much as they should, and I believe a contributing factor to this is peer pressure. An experienced paramedic must continually learn and grow, but they may either believe they already know it all, or their ego won't allow them to make a mistake or error in front of their peers. This fear of failure leads to avoidance behaviour.

Another way to apply this type of pressure is to record your performance. It's amazing how many people fumble and tumble their way through tasks when a camera is placed in front of them.

Exercise

Using exercise to increase our heart rate to induce fatigue and weakness is an excellent technique for practising your skills. By increasing our heart rate through exercise then immediately trying to perform a task, we're pushing our cognitive bandwidth to the limit. The best example of this is when I saw a video of a candidate at the Australian Army's Special Air Service selection course.

The recruit was exhausted from the gruelling tasks demanded of him by the instructors. After completing the physical task, he couldn't perform the simplest maths problem, such as 5 + 13. He was in Condition Black from exercise.

Audience

Performing training tasks in front of an audience is similar to peer pressure. Making a learner do things among a crowd is a great way to place pressure on them. When I first started as a paramedic, I hated doing very public jobs. Walking on a 747 plane caused particular discomfort with a hundred eyes staring and listening to every word. In moments like these, you'd better be on your game.

Auditory

People tend to underestimate how much humans rely on their auditory senses. Playing loud metal music or crowd noises to distract the learner in any way, or to make communication difficult, is a great strategy for inducing stress.

If you can perform optimally in these practise conditions, then you'll have a better chance of succeeding in stressful or unexpected situations. If you train at 110 per cent (let's just say that's possible), when it comes to the real thing you'll be able to perform at 100 per cent.

Use What You Have

You don't need the perfect, the best, or the latest training equipment or facilities to achieve your goal. In fact, only looking to train in the perfect environment can develop negative self-reliance on unrealistic conditions. The ones who can adapt and learn to overcome the limitations placed upon them are the ones most likely to have composure and self-assurance while under stress.

I often see people delaying or putting off training because they don't have enough equipment or the timing isn't right, but when is the timing ever perfect in the real world? I remember an occasion quite vividly when I was on call. The pager went off, making that annoying beeping sound that rings through your spine every time. I was having the most fantastic sex with my wife when this pager decided to beep – what terrible timing that was.

I had a tough decision to make: wait another minute or respond straight away. After a few seconds of thought it was no longer hard. I jumped out of bed and went to work.

You may be the only paramedic without the perfect ambulance that has the most state-of-the-art equipment inside; you may likely be the only person with handed-down equipment from another ambulance service; or you may possess outdated stock and easily the worst working conditions.

But if you hone your skills and apply your craft in that environment with those limited resources and lack of support, then, when things don't go to plan, and the stress builds up, it will seem trivial to you in the future. That's because what you've dealt with before was far worse. If you need the perfect conditions to perform, then when disaster strikes and the pressure is on, you will most likely fail.

The beauty of making the most of what you have is that you develop the ability to improvise and solve problems. You start to be creative and develop skills that can't be taught in the perfect training environment.

Personal Experience – Multiplied by Two

Two vehicles travelling over 100 kilometres per hour crashed head on. Any head-on collision makes the hairs on the back of my neck stand up, as they've always been some of the biggest car crashes I've seen. This call-out was no different. Debris was scattered all over the road, it looked like a bomb went off.

Two tradie utes hit each other and the contents of the trays exploded across the highway. Airbags had deployed and glass was scattered across the bitumen. Crowds of bystanders had already gathered by the time we arrived. Walking towards this chaos always gets the heart rate going. I was going to have to rely on my training to get me through.

The first thing I had to do was take control of the scene and triage the patients. I knew this from many hours in the classroom but also rehearsing multi-casualty scenarios every three months over the previous five years. The most difficult thing at a multi-casualty incident is not stopping to help someone, because you can't get fixated on a single victim, otherwise you'll forget about the rest. Tag and move on. I knew this from talking to my mentors and listening to their previous experiences.

We soon identified that there were only two patients and there were two of us. I still called for backup, as they were both in a critical condition and we only had one ambulance with one stretcher. My patient was trapped inside the vehicle and we couldn't get him out because he had a fractured leg, but he had internal bleeding in the abdomen which required immediate surgery. We couldn't hang around all day.

I was squeezing inside the vehicle trying to put a needle in the patient when a policeman came running over and asked for my help. Another car crash had just occurred 300 metres (330 yards) down the road.

An elderly man hadn't seen that cars had stopped and were backed up on the highway and nor did he see the flashing red and blue lights. He drove at 100 kilometres per hour straight into the back of a parked car. I now had a second crash site with multiple patients.

I reversed my arse out the side of the destroyed ute to scan the area and assess the situation. As I looked around, I saw my partner paramedic's legs hanging out of the other ute down the embankment. He looked busy. Our medical equipment was scattered between the both of us; we only had one cardiac monitor, one drug kit and one oxygen kit. We could only use what we had. Complaining about it wouldn't change the situation.

My training tells me that to achieve the best outcome at a multi-casualty incident, paramedics must fall back on previously drilled systems and plans. The goal is to do the greatest good for the greatest number. I can't allow my emotions to take over. But I'd never experienced this situation before: two separate multi-casualty incidents

300 metres apart. I decided to provide a situation report via radio to my communications centre and request an update on the original backup I'd requested. They were six minutes away.

Realising that by the time I packed up my gear and ran or drove down to the other crash site, it would be roughly six minutes anyway, I redirected the backup to attend the second car crash and returned to treating my original patient. Having the ability to think rationally and make good decisions in this moment of stress was only made possible by my training. All patients that day arrived at hospital alive.

Be a Continual Learner

The most common theme across all high achieving individuals is that they are always looking to grow and develop their skills, knowledge and experiences. They are never satisfied with the status quo or willing to settle for average.

People who flourish are generally very committed to learning and development, and they seek out new challenges. They look for means of continually extending themselves.

Learning doesn't end once you've been given your degree and graduated from university or completed a training course; that's only the beginning. It's a lifelong process. The point here is to make learning a part of your work. If you want to be prepared for the unexpected and ready in times of stress, then you can never rest.

This is only possible if you are willing to learn and have a growth mindset. A fixed mindset will hold you back and prevent you from becoming better and improving every day. Someone with a fixed mindset believes that they have a certain level of intelligence or ability, a bar that cannot be raised no matter how much effort they exert or learning they do. On the other hand, a person with a growth mindset understands and values the ability of the mind to continually grow and expand.

A growth mindset is an important part of possessing poise and the paramedic mindset. If you believe instead that you've already reached your potential, then when you're faced with a situation that exceeds your perceived potential, what can you do to help? Your survival instincts will most likely kick in, and you will start to panic. You will be afraid of taking on challenges and actively shy away from them. You will develop tunnel vision and not see the incident from an objective standpoint, limiting your ability to solve problems, adapt and overcome.

Knowledge is power. The more you know, the more you'll learn, and the more you learn, the more you can do. Having knowledge will give you the reassurance that when you are faced with a challenging situation, you can manage it, you have the ability to respond to it in a positive way. It's the same concept as having to train and develop the fundamental skills to perform your task.

Continual learners see challenges as opportunities to grow and develop, an opportunity to test themselves, to see if they have the ability to take on the challenge and come out the other side. Too many people blame the system, the industry or their employer for their languishing and their career struggles. It's common and easy to blame something else for your lack of growth, but in reality, you control your own decisions and your reactions to disappointment and rejection. Give yourself back the power to control your response to disappointment, and focus on learning rather than resentment.

High-performing people who can operate in stressful situations let go of any resentment and envy; they learn from it. One of Canadian psychologist Dr Jordan Peterson's life rules is, 'Do not allow yourself to become arrogant or resentful . . . Resentment tells you one of two things; one is that you are not standing up for yourself sufficiently and you need to do something about it or that you need to grow the hell up and stop complaining . . . You need to figure it out, because you can harbour resentment for unlived life for a very long period of time. And all it does is corrupt you.' If you're resentful, be introspective and use that feeling to help advance your development.

The other common theme among continual learners is that

they make sacrifices. By making learning a priority, they sacrifice other elements of their lives. They work a second job, go to bed early only to rise before the sun and miss out on social events. I've never heard an athlete who has achieved greatness say that they didn't have to sacrifice something to achieve it. You always have a choice; learning is a choice. The easy option is to sit on the couch, but the harder option is to learn.

Continual learners forgo immediate gratification to achieve something greater in the future. Procrastination is a perfect example of not sacrificing in the short term for long-term gains. I remember procrastinating when I should have been studying for an exam at university; I was too busy hanging out with friends and enjoying my youth at the beach. But when it came to sitting down in the exam room, I was filled with anxiety and negative self-talk. I started to experience the rush of adrenaline. The fight or flight response once again kicked in, and my mind went blank. My palms were sweaty. I felt weak. My cognitive bandwidth was filled with thoughts of failure and worry. The best I could hope for was 51 per cent.

I could have avoided the poor result in my exam had I valued learning. I should have forgone the gratification of the moment to reap the rewards in the future.

Always Challenge Yourself

Challenging ourselves is a way to learn and grow. Yes, we've already talked about the need for continual learning, but I think it's important to highlight the value of challenging ourselves. We want to keep on learning, but we need to make sure we do so in a way that allows us to reach a higher level than we were at yesterday. We need to be challenged.

Being challenged sometimes really sucks, and it generates the same old agitation in our body, tempting us to again run away from it. Without a challenge, though, we won't grow, and if we're not growing, we're becoming stagnant.

Success isn't built on a foundation of continual success, but by learning from failure, reflecting on those lessons and making the required changes. When we're learning, we must set ourselves a task that exceeds our current level of competence. Don't make the challenge so difficult that you reasonably won't be able to succeed at it. You have to set up the challenge in a way such that you have a shot at succeeding. That doesn't mean you will, but it must be at least possible.

Challenging a paramedic to take down a criminal who's pointing a gun at them and expecting them to know the skills of a SAS trooper is unrealistic. It's far better to challenge the paramedic to learn some basic self-defence and survival skills first, before jumping straight into the chokehold.

I was once mowing the lawn and enjoying my day off when the phone rang. It was the boss. I wasn't going to answer because I thought he wanted me to work a night shift to cover someone's sick leave. When I finally answered the phone, to my surprise, he wanted me to come into work straight away. There had been a bus roll-over with potentially 40 patients on board.

I ran inside, put on my uniform and jumped in the car. I arrived on scene 20–30 minutes after the initial accident. It was chaotic; there were so many people everywhere that I didn't know who was a patient and who a bystander. There was no one in charge of the scene, and there were hardly any ambulances because they had all left with other critical patients.

It was utter disorder. It wasn't until an experienced paramedic arrived on scene that things began to come under control. I remember him walking out of the paddock holding an arm; the patient had been transported to hospital before we arrived and obviously had an amputated arm. The look on the police officer's face when he was asked to take the arm to hospital was priceless.

We soon established that there were only 13 patients, not 40. The rest were Good Samaritans. Communication was the first thing that broke down and it snowballed from there. This is an example of a challenge that was too big and too unrealistic for us to have been trained for. Paramedics are used to treating one patient at a time, not 13. We had no stress inoculation against such a challenge. Despite it not running perfectly, we grew from it and now perform regular multi-casualty incident training.

It takes humility to set a task that isn't too challenging and unrealistic. It hurts the ego, because we tend to think we're better than we actually are. If we want a student to develop, we must set them challenges that are incremental in nature. Ask yourself, 'What's the next small step and challenge needed to get to the desired destination?' We have to face our flaws when challenging ourselves, which is very difficult; we need humility and a growth mindset to help us accept those flaws.

Accept that you may need to make small improvements. Remember that small improvements, accumulated over time, become considerable improvements.

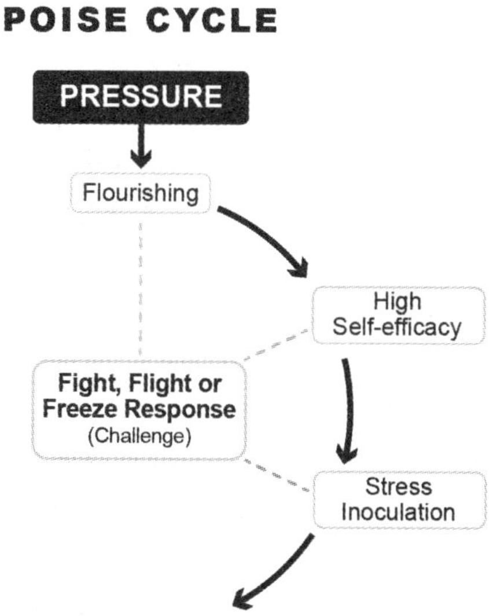

POISE CYCLE

Figure 9. Practise stress inoculation by training in unideal, realistic environments to develop an inoculation against stress and pressure.

INTERVIEW WITH THE AUTHOR
Have you changed as a person
because of the trauma you've seen?

I like to think I've changed for the better. I've become more resilient and grown as a person through my experiences. It does have its side effects though. My wife definitely thinks I'm not very empathetic because I don't care for things I consider minor – I need things to be a crisis to care. For example, if the kids hurt themselves, they have to have a broken arm at the minimum for me to show compassion. Otherwise, they can deal with it themselves.

I try to use the experiences I've been exposed to, to learn and help others avoid them or get through similar circumstances. Overwhelmingly, I believe it has made me a better person. Despite my wife wishing I was better with the minor things, I'm bloody good when the shit hits the fan; in those situations, people actively look to me to fix things.

At the same time, I'm more than happy to provide people with a reality check if they need one. Getting a cappuccino when you ordered a latte isn't worth ruining relationships. Just deal with it.

CALL TO ACTION

'As a Special Operations Paramedic, we'd do all the stress inoculation training, for years leading up to critical incidents. Subsequently, we operated effectively in those environments because we had good stress mitigation techniques in hand.' – **Matt Pepper, Clinical Training Officer for Tactical Medicine, NSW Ambulance Service**

Key Takeaways

- Practise your skills and train under stress. Practise as close to the real thing as possible.
- Train at '110 per cent' so that when you're faced with the real thing it will be easy to operate at 100 per cent.
- Be a continual learner and always challenge yourself.

Key Tasks

- Challenge yourself by training outside your comfort zone: create a stressful environment by adding peer pressure, exercise and auditory barriers to your training.
- What challenges have you been holding back from? Try it now. Climb that mountain, enrol in that class.

8

Your Mental Toolbox

Personal Experience – Jellyfish Alert

Any sting from a marine animal in Australia instantly creates anxiety. At nearly every beach north of Sydney, big warning signs inform swimmers that deadly box jellyfish (Irukandji) lurk throughout the Pacific Ocean. For me, the beaches create even more anxiety when I'm called to a paediatric patient, a child who's been stung.

As I arrived on the scene, a screaming mother rushed to the ambulance with a small boy in her arms. The patient was vomiting uncontrollably. I couldn't believe that a child could have so much in his stomach. It looked like an adult vomiting after a big night out. His face was as red as a lobster, and tears were gushing down his face. If you've ever been stung by a jellyfish that causes Irukandji syndrome, you know that the pain is horrendous and difficult to deal with.

Irukandji syndrome often starts with nothing more than a small sting. Just 30 minutes later though, you will be guarding your lower back as the pain gradually builds and reaches a height of epic proportions. It reminds me of the Cruciatus Curse from *Harry Potter*, causing unbearable pain.

The patient was placed on my stretcher. He rolled around, side to side, unable to stop. He was bending back and forth as if a second body inside him was trying to escape. All of his muscles were cramping at once. His feelings were more than justified. I had to act fast to prevent any life-threatening cardiac complications.

I placed a tourniquet around his arm, aiming to find a vein to administer the needed drugs via an IV. I had treated Irukandji syndrome several times before, but this was my first child afflicted with the condition. For some reason, that subconsciously increased the pressure; maybe it was because he was the same age as my daughters.

Most medical professionals will say that treating a child always brings added pressure. The stakes become higher. I believe it's part of our instincts as human beings. We cherish the innocence of a child and the limited time they have had to experience life.

It was tough to find a vein for the IV. I could only feel one vein on his tiny arms, but it would have to do; I only had one shot and I needed to take it. As I held his arm down, I had the needle in my other hand. I was trembling nervously, like one might in an earthquake.

Despite my feelings, I appeared calm and felt calm, but my hand was shaking a lot. It was not great timing, since I needed to use my hands to put in the IV. I put the needle down and rested my arm on my leg to stop the earthquake. I closed my eyes and focused on my breathing – in for four seconds, hold for four seconds, out for four seconds, hold for four seconds – reassuring myself by reflecting on previous experiences. I'd put in more difficult IVs in worse circumstances before.

It worked. I opened my eyes. The patient's mother was looking at me wide-eyed, like I had decided to start a meditation session mid-treatment. But I stopped shaking and was able to gain IV access.

The next part, though, required a lot more cognitive bandwidth. I had to work out multiple drug calculations for the young patient. The beauty of treating Irukandji syndrome is that we get to play with a lot of medication and use many different skills: infusions, morphine, the famed green whistle (methoxyflurane), glyceryl trinitrate, and magnesium to name a few. Getting the doses right is critical for paediatric patients. The last thing I wanted to do was to overdose or underdose him, rendering the drugs ineffective. I struggle to do mathematics at the best of times, let alone in fight, flight or freeze mode. I revisited my impromptu meditation practice – actually, it was just a box breathing technique.

This time, I had learned from the mother's reaction that I should do it with my eyes open and without making it obvious that I was even doing it. I took out my notepad, and as I worked out the drug dosages and amount to be injected, I thought to myself, 'This hippie stuff really works.'

Training the Mind

Psychological skills training refers to the practice of consistently working on mental skills for the purpose of improving performance. These are skills designed to help us cope with high-stress, high-consequence environments, to bring our heart rate under control, and to control cognitive overload via constructive mental skills.

If we're suffering from fear of failure and self-doubt, scared of the repercussions of that failure, we're more likely to commit errors and perform worse. We won't achieve our mission nearly as efficiently or as quickly as we would hope.

The US Navy Seal selection course is notoriously difficult. Candidates are put through some of the most mentally challenging and physically demanding training in the world. It's designed to find and develop the strongest character who can give everything to the mission.

Out of an average of 140 recruits on the course, only 36 were passing. After a review, those in charge realised that they were losing good recruits through simple and avoidable mental errors. As a result, they decided to implement four simple psychological skills to help increase the pass rate:

1. **Goal setting.** They taught recruits to set extremely small goals and break them down into achievable chunks.
2. **Visualisation.** They instructed recruits to see themselves succeeding.
3. **Positive self-talk.** They encouraged recruits to actively talk to themselves in a positive way to override any fears.
4. **Breathing techniques.** They gave recruits breathing exercises to control their arousal.

When they implemented training in these four simple skills, the pass rate increased from 25 per cent to 33 per cent, a significant number for a gruelling test of character such as Navy Seal selection. This is the idea of psychological skills training, to give us the best chance of succeeding in stressful situations.

The strategies we'll look at in this chapter are paramount for performing well under pressure. The influence of stress on our body can be so profound. Even with all the knowledge and all the training in the world, if our mind isn't clear and focused, none of that knowledge will reach our cognitive bandwidth, and we will respond to the stress by the fight, flight or freeze response. We'll let the reptilian part of our brain control our actions.

Michael J. Lauria is a former Pararescueman in the US Air Force and currently an emergency medicine and flight physician with specialty training in emergency medical services and critical care – so he knows a thing or two about high-pressure moments.

He has drawn from neuroscience, psychology and performance science to help improve medical care in high-stakes situations. He developed the following mnemonic to help elicit psychological skills: BTSF, which stands for 'Beat the Stress, Fool!'

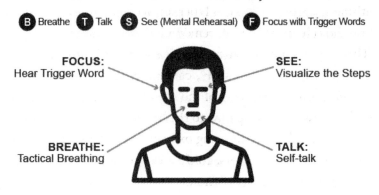

BEAT THE STRESS, FOOL!

B Breathe **T** Talk **S** See (Mental Rehearsal) **F** Focus with Trigger Words

FOCUS:
Hear Trigger Word

SEE:
Visualize the Steps

BREATHE:
Tactical Breathing

TALK:
Self-talk

Figure 10. Michael J. Lauria developed the acronym BTSF or 'Beat the Stress, Fool!' to help develop psychological skills. Adapted from M Lauria, I Gallo, S Rush et al., 'Psychological skills to improve emergency care providers' performance under stress', *Annals of Emergency Medicine*, 2017, vol. 70, no. 6, pp. 884–90.

Let's explore each step of this mnemonic, starting with our breath.

Control Your Breath

Breathing is the only autonomic function that we can control and modify consciously. We can intentionally modify our breathing to help us respond better in high-stress situations, making breathing a powerful weapon in our arsenal. It's well within our control and influence.

Breathing is not only life-sustaining but a critical part of our physiological makeup – influencing hormone release and chemical messengers. When we experience a stressful or emotional situation, our breathing is affected. Someone under stress will typically take smaller and shallower breaths, using their shoulders rather than their diaphragm to move air in and out. This shallow overbreathing, known as hyperventilation, prolongs the feelings of stress.

Our pattern and depth of breathing has a direct physiological impact on our oxygen levels, heart rate, blood pressure, and breathing rate and volume. But the main contributor to stress and breathing is carbon dioxide. Hyperventilation causes low levels of carbon dioxide in the blood, removing it from the body.

This triggers a cascading effect like water flooding over a cliff. It initially alters the body's pH, causing alkalosis, which triggers vasoconstriction (narrowing of the blood vessels, restricting blood flow) that slows the blood flow to the brain, which in turn prevents the red blood cells from carrying oxygen there. This effect explains why we experience dizziness, confusion and anxiety when stress is accompanied by hyperventilation.

The low levels of carbon dioxide also lead to more excited and active muscles, which causes pins and needles in the fingers, numbness and sweaty palms. If we're unable to break the cycle, it will eventually cause us to black out. Once you're passed out on the floor, your unconscious systems take over and bring your breathing back to equilibrium. It's your conscious control that causes hyperventilation. Most people will wake up within 60 seconds when this happens.

There are virtually no mechanisms outside decreasing our respiratory rate (i.e. stopping hyperventilating) that will regulate this loss of carbon dioxide. This is why we need to learn to control our breathing. And thankfully, we can.

Breathing techniques have been widely used in meditation and yoga for centuries, but I'm not going to get you to do a 30-minute meditation before performing a task under stress. The following techniques are designed to reduce short-term stress in real time. When we're under stress, we need a quick breathing technique that will immediately reduce our arousal. If you're in the back of an ambulance, responding to a job for a very, very acutely ill or injured person, you don't have time to call a timeout, hold hands and sing kumbaya.

When we're exposed to a stress response – in the case of a paramedic, a life-threatening emergency – our heart rate increases in order to shunt blood all over the body and increase our ability to respond to the stress. Controlling our heart rate through breathing during these stressful stimuli allows us direct control over our sympathetic and parasympathetic nervous systems.

When we inhale, our diaphragm contracts and moves down, creating more space in the chest cavity. In this process, our heart grows in volume as more space is created for it. This vasodilation (widening of the blood vessels), in turn, slows down blood flow through the heart. A part of the heart called the sinoatrial (SA) node, which controls heart rate, signals to the brain that blood flow in the heart has slowed. The brain sends a message back to the SA node, telling it to increase the heart rate.

Thankfully, the opposite is also true.

When we exhale, the diaphragm expands and curves upwards, making the heart a little more compact and this vasoconstriction (narrowing of the blood vessels) causes blood to flow faster through the heart. The SA node sends the brain a signal that blood flow in the heart has sped up and the brain interprets the message before sending back a signal through the parasympathetic nervous system (namely, the vagus nerve) to slow the heart rate down.

So to calm down quickly, we need to make our exhales longer than our inhales.

The beautiful thing about all of this is that the diaphragm is a skeletal (voluntary) muscle, which means we can contract it consciously, just like doing bicep curls at the gym. This makes it very different from metabolic processes. (We can't ask our liver to speed up the metabolism of alcohol when we have a hangover.)

The Physiological Sigh

Forget about all the times you were told it's rude to sigh in front of other people, because in fact it's a crucial human reflex. Sighing is essential because it helps inflate our alveoli, the balloon-like air sacs in our lungs. Without sighing, alveoli can collapse and struggle to reinflate.

A sigh is a deep breath, but not a voluntary deep breath. It starts out as a normal breath, but before we exhale, we take a second breath on top of it. US neuroscientist Dr Jack Feldman explains that, when alveoli collapse, they compromise the ability of the lungs to exchange oxygen and carbon dioxide. The only way to pop them open again is to sigh, which brings in twice the volume as a normal breath.

When we're confronted with a stressful situation, our alveoli tend to collapse, and carbon dioxide can build up in the bloodstream. We then start to feel agitated due to the increased carbon dioxide. Sighing allows the body to rid itself of carbon dioxide and helps us relax. We sigh naturally throughout the day. It's most notable when we witness someone crying or sobbing, but it can also occur just before sleep or at any time we need to discard carbon dioxide.

US neuroscientist Dr Jack Feldman discovered that one way to induce calm via deliberate breathing is what he calls the 'physiological sigh'. Another US neuroscientist, Dr Andrew Huberman, explains the technique as follows: 'Inhale twice, ideally through the nose, and then you exhale long once through the mouth. So it's inhale then another little inhale, even if you have to sneak in just a tiny bit more air and then a long exhale.'

Perform the psychological sigh every time you need to refocus and engage. But maybe don't do it if you're trying to bluff in a poker game or have a 'serious discussion' with your significant other. I'm speaking from experience.

Researchers have studied the behaviour of soccer players performing penalty kicks. Penalty kicks are high-stress, decisive, game-changing situations where the player performing the kick must score a winning goal or risk losing to the other team. As a result, kickers are under enormous pressure; to them, everything depends on this goal, and it's of incredible importance to them, the team, and their supporters.

The scientists looked at the moments between the referee

blowing the whistle to signify that it's time to take the penalty kick, until the moment just before the player kicks the ball. They found that the players who don't pause, but shoot as soon as they hear the whistle, are much more likely to miss. On the other hand, those players who don't kick immediately are more likely to kick the ball into the net.

The players who pause take three to five seconds to become still in the moment. They take a deep breath (a sigh). These players' likelihood of scoring is much greater than those players who don't take a deep breath. The pause allows the kicker to redirect attention towards the task while diverting attention from the pressure to perform.

More recently, Huberman and his colleagues looked at exactly how effective controlled breathwork practices really are as a tool for managing stress and wellbeing. They found that breathwork, specifically sighing, is more effective than mindfulness meditation in increasing positive impact. This study clearly establishes that breathwork skills improve mood and physiological arousal. In particular, a daily five-minute physiological sigh routine is the most effective stress-management exercise.

The body perceives breathlessness or anticipation of difficulty breathing as a threat, activating the stress hormone cortisol. It creates a downward trajectory, as people who panic become breathless quicker, which causes more stress hormones to be released. Fortunately, the Huberman study identified that the intentional action of controlling the breath is effective in dampening the fight, flight or freeze response.

Through using active breathing skills, we gain a sense of control over the situation. We're actively informing our mind that we have power over the situation. Reducing our breathlessness promotes a sense of calm in our mind.

Box Breathing

Box breathing is another technique used by military and special operations personnel that has been proven to help reduce stress and refocus individuals. Box breathing takes a few more seconds than the physiological sigh but is a very useful tool if you are on the verge of losing control. Combined with the physiological sigh, both breathing exercises are powerful.

Box breathing is a form of diaphragmatic breathing. Diaphragmatic breathing involves contraction of the diaphragm, expansion of the belly, and deepening of inhalation and exhalation, which consequently decreases the respiration frequency and maximises the oxygen and carbon dioxide in the blood.

The best method of box breathing is the four-second respiratory cycle. The technique involves breathing in deeply for four seconds, engaging the diaphragm and attempting to pull the breath down into the abdomen. Then the breath is held for four seconds and exhaled slowly for four seconds, after which the lungs are kept empty for four seconds.

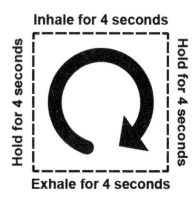

Figure 11. Box breathing is a breathing technique that can help provide a sense of calm in stressful situations and get the heart rate under control.

Physically counting to four is recommended when performing the box breathing technique; this will help calm the stress response even more. This technique helps the body return to a normal breathing rhythm, controlling hyperventilation.

This type of breathing creates an intentional deep breath that activates the parasympathetic nervous system, the opposite system to the fight, flight or freeze response, ultimately reducing heart rate. It helps regulate the involuntary body functions such as the vagus nerve and, in turn, reduces blood pressure, providing a sense of calm.

Door Breathing

Door breathing is similar to the physiological sigh, but instead of taking a second inhale after a normal breath, you take a single, deep, exaggerated breath in, followed by a single exhale, preferably with pursed lips. This is designed to increase the pressure within the thoracic chest, stimulating the vagus nerve to send a signal to the heart to tell it to beat slower. It's a good way to bring down your heart rate if you're verging on stepping into Condition Red or Black (more than 145 beats per minute). Door breathing can be performed in a matter of seconds, thus offering immediate action when time is critical.

It's called door breathing because it gives you a small moment of calm before you open the door and move into a stressful situation. It helps you focus on the task at hand, and what we focus on, we amplify.

Use Positive Self-talk

Positive self-talk is believed to be the key to cognitive control. By employing positive self-talk, we can switch our perception to successfully perform a task.

Dr Ethan Kross, a leading US neuroscientist on mind chatter, states that we can't always control the thoughts that simply pop up into our mind, and they may be negative. What we do have control over is how we engage with those thoughts once they have popped into our mind. We can choose to ignore the thoughts or let them go; we can distance ourselves from them, or even question them within our own mind. We have a range of options when thoughts spontaneously pop up, especially if they are negative; that's how we can gain control over them.

If we let them, thoughts that pop up in our head can control what we do. If they are negative thoughts, then we will act negatively; if they are positive thoughts, then we can act positively. What we should all endeavour to do is allow positive thoughts to define who we are and what we do.

Paramedics are taught many skills in the classroom that they don't perform on a patient regularly, if at all. Practising on a mannikin or dummy is one thing, but doing it in real life is another. In this type of situation, negative self-talk would generate an abundance of self-doubt. What if I miss? What if I puncture a hole in the heart?

A person with positive self-talk, on the other hand, would use phrases that support the task they are about to perform. As they hold the needle before pushing it into the chest, they might be thinking something like: 'I have prepared for this moment. I have the ability to perform this task.'

Self-talk statements come from the individual themselves. The origins of self-talk are consciousness and information processing. In other words, self-talk is an articulation of our internal position. In this case, the internal position is oriented towards success. If we focus our thoughts on positive outcomes and emotions, we will most likely achieve the desired outcome.

Here are a few steps to developing effective self-talk:

- Keep phrases short and specific.
- Use the first-person and present tense.
- Use positive phrases.
- Say it with intention.

- Speak kindly to yourself.
- Repeat the phrases often.

One tool highlighted by Dr Ethan Kross to improve negative chatter is the temporal distancing strategy. Temporal distancing is defined as the amount of time that separates an individual's present time and a target event in the future. Essentially, it's thinking about how you will be affected by a given scenario in the distant future.

You may find yourself kneeling in a pile of human faeces with a patient hanging on for dear life, looking to you to find a solution. A temporal distancing strategy used here to promote positive self-talk would look something like, 'In three months from now, I'm going to be grateful for this experience because it will make similar situations feel easy in comparison. I will grow and become a better paramedic because of this shitty situation I find myself in.' Using temporal distancing to transport myself into the future helps me realise that what I'm going through now might suck, but it's temporary and ultimately positive, giving me an opportunity to grow.

Another way to improve positive self-talk is to give yourself the advice you would give others. It's relatively easy to give other people advice and to help them through their difficult situations. If the problem isn't happening to you, it's a lot easier for you to think objectively and rationally about that experience. Have you ever wished you took your own advice but never actually did?

As good as we are at giving positive advice to others, we're poor when it comes to positive self-talk. Try distancing yourself from the situation and thinking of what positive talk you might give to a friend or family member who found themselves in the same situation. Then repeat that to yourself.

Another small skill that can help increase the effects of positive self-talk is switching to refer to yourself in the second person, using the second-person pronoun 'you' and your name, when talking to yourself. Avoid referring to yourself using first-person pronouns such as 'I' or 'me'. The goal of this is to lead you to think that you're another person – a person who can perform this task. By talking to yourself at a linguistic distance, you're mentally distancing yourself from the negative self-talk – and speaking to yourself as a person who can overcome and achieve.

Using our own name to think about ourselves changes our perspective. It gets us to relate to ourselves as if we're talking to a friend, and that gives us distance. Some example phrases for when you find yourself in a stressful situation:

'[name], you are the right person for this.'
'[name] will overcome this obstacle.'
'[name] is focused on the task.'
'[name] has the ability to do this.'
'[name] has prepared for this moment.'
'[name] will not back away.'
'[name] will win the lotto on Saturday night.' (worth a shot)

Visualise

Visualisation is a purposeful, intense imagination technique that we can use to improve our performance or achieve a goal. Our mind's eye can help us adopt an effective paramedic mindset. What we can see, we can be. If we've already done it in our mind, we've therefore already achieved our desired outcome. This will make it easier to replicate. In fact, our body's physiological response when performing visualisation is the same as if we were completing the task in reality, if done well enough.

The visualisation will help us trust our skills and let the performance flow. Formula One driver and four-time world champion Sebastian Vettel is often found, just before qualifying, sitting in his stationary car with his eyes shut, visualising a lap. He says that 'Qualifying is very raw, so you spend time going through the lap; what are the key points? Where do you have to improve? Once you start the lap, there's no time to think, so you clear your mind, and you have to be in the moment. Even if you make a mistake, it's important not to think about it. You just focus corner by corner; ideally, let it flow.'

Whenever you can find such focus, you will be better able to perform.

Paramedics use visualisation all the time, for performing micro-skills such as intubating a patient or drilling a needle into a patient's bone. But the best example of the power of visualisation is US rock climber Alex Honnold, known for climbing the El Capitan, a 3000-foot vertical wall, free solo (without any ropes). He had to stay calm and perform at his best because any mistake would mean death. This task requires a certain type of mindset.

Alex attributes visualisation with having a profound impact on his ability to complete the climb successfully. He visualised every step, every foothold, and every finger-grab along the entire route. He didn't stop there, though. His visualisation turned to the emotional side of climbing free solo, envisaging what would happen if he got too tired halfway up the cliff, couldn't make the next move and became overwhelmed.

He considered every single possibility on the ground, so when he had to make the ascent without a rope, there was no doubt. He understood that doubt is the precursor to fear and he couldn't risk fear turning into panic. He had to visualise and rehearse until it seemed possible. Through visualisation, combined with mastery of his craft, he knew every hand hold and foothold on the route, a route that would take him three hours and 56 minutes to complete. Visualisation literally saved his life.

Another technique, used in the ancient philosophy of Stoicism, encouraged people to visualise negatively. When we really think about how terrible things could be, we see they're not actually that bad for us right now.

When visualising, it's important to be as detailed and deep-rooted in the moment as possible. Become engrossed in your vision.

Picture each portion of the procedure you're about to perform. Start at the very beginning, with pulling out the equipment from the bag. What noises does the equipment make? What does the equipment smell like?

Feel the actions as if you were present in that moment. Continue this to the end of the procedure, until you have successfully completed the task in your mind. Take a few moments to feel how your body reacted – did your heart rate increase? Did you get nervous? You might even notice your heart rate rise as if you were there in person. This visualisation will help show you the path forward and how to overcome your next stressful encounter.

Use a Focus Word

Develop and use a one-word mantra. Say this word just before starting any procedure or taking any action. This word will bring you to full attention and focus – and snap you out of mindless thought.

As a kid, did your parents ever yell a single word at you to grab your attention and get you to focus? We want to use the same strategy here. A mentor of mine uses this same approach to focus a distracted student.

When confronted with an extremely traumatic or inhumane event, you could be forgiven for becoming distracted for a short period. But it's important for paramedics to learn to re-engage and focus.

When I was working by myself in a remote location, I was confronted with a patient who was held against her will and forcibly raped in a remote campsite. She rode into town on the back of a horse, trying to escape her situation, but was beaten by the perpetrator with a stick that was on fire from the campfire.

This is obviously a traumatic scene, and at first sight I couldn't compute what was happening right in front of me. It was so outside anything I had imagined witnessing that I was disengaged from the reality. I had to use single words other than 'shit' and 'fuck' to help me treat the patient and not become caught up in the obvious emotional side of witnessing such a thing. I used the word 'task' to help me focus on the solution rather than getting absorbed in the victim's suffering.

Come up with a one-word mantra or cue word. Here are some examples: 'focus', 'precision', 'breath', 'pause', 'clarity', 'strength'.

Personal Experience: A Friend with a Fractured Skull

Again, working by myself, I arrived on scene to find a patient lying in the middle of the road next to a pool of blood. There were several people there that I recognised – friends, people with whom I'd had dinner two nights earlier. It was a dark night and there was minimal street lighting, so I couldn't recognise who was lying on the ground in front of me. As I walked closer, I realised that it was a good friend of mine. I immediately became worried.

As I stepped around the blood, he was trying to sit up, forcefully pushing my hands away, but I knew this would make his condition worse. He became aggressive, but he had the gaze of someone looking into another world. He was seriously concussed.

I felt the side of his head. His hair was covered in blood but there was a very soft, tender section of the skull, a boggy mass. He had a skull fracture. That's why he was combative and non-compliant with my assessment – he had a significant traumatic brain injury. There was no way I could 'talk down' this patient; he didn't know which way was up.

The bystanders (my friends) were all crying, anxious, distressed and calling to me to fix the problem. They were trying to help me but realistically were getting in my way. I had to switch into paramedic mode quickly and change my mindset. I had to engage the paramedic mindset and do it quickly.

I wanted to give him the best care possible by laying him on his back and placing a collar around his neck, in case he had a neck fracture. He was intoxicated with alcohol, which made it even harder to distinguish whether he was disagreeable and fighting instructions because of the alcohol or his head injury.

I started to become frustrated because I couldn't gain control, so I took some deep breaths and encouraged myself. The best way to take control of the situation, I thought, was to place him in an environment I could control: inside the ambulance. I managed to get him on the stretcher, not in the most elegant of ways, and got him in the back of the ambulance.

I was then able to shut the doors and block out the anxiety from my friends. His girlfriend wanted to come with me, which of course was appropriate. As we started to drive away, I saw my friend's arms flop to the side and his face roll back. A massive dose of adrenaline was instantly released into my body. He was having a seizure.

His arms were slapping and banging the sides of the ambulance, and his breathing was stressed as he began to hold his breath from the intense muscle contractions. My friend was dying and his girlfriend was going to witness it.

I blocked out any negative self-talk and tried to focus on what I had to do. I had to change my focus before my thoughts paralysed me. His face was starting to change from the bright red of stress to a bluish purple as he became oxygen-deprived. 'You've seen dozens of seizures before,' I told myself. 'You know what to do.'

I was now moving fast, sucking up the medication into a syringe and jabbing him with the needle to inject the medication. A long three minutes later the seizure stopped.

The helicopter retrieval team arrived moments later. They knew the patient's condition was critical, as I noticed the doctor pulling out his cocktail of drugs to paralyse him and insert a tube down his throat – rapid sequence intubation. Since I was sitting in the treatment seat next to the patient in the back of the ambulance, the doctor passed me the drugs to administer.

I pushed the drugs into his veins knowing that I was literally going to stop his breathing, paralyse his muscles and put him in a deep sedative state. Within moments, he was out cold. I watched as the doctor inserted the tube, waiting to see if it was successful and hadn't accidentally gone down the wrong hole into the stomach.

Success, it was in. The doctor then asked me to swap positions with him while he set up the automatic ventilator machine. I did it without hesitation. I had blocked out the fact that he was my friend and I was performing better than I would have normally thought possible: at least until I was in charge of his breathing. I started squeezing the bag, pushing life-sustaining air through the tube, into his lungs.

As I watched his chest rise, I realised I was the only one in the ambulance. The doctor was outside at the helicopter sorting out his equipment. I literally had my friend's life in my hands. If I forgot to squeeze the bag in a calm, methodical and controlled manner, he could die. The fact that he had a head injury made it even more vital to get his breathing rate and volume perfect. The bleeding inside his brain was creating an enormous amount of pressure in his head.

At this moment, I could have easily lost control and become overwhelmed by the pressure and stress placed upon me. But I was able to rely on my previous experience with this kind of injury. I'd been in stressful environments before. I'd practised treating this injury in countless scenarios throughout my training. I recognised my negative thought, took a deep breath, then let it go, re-engaging in the task. I had formed an ability to block out unnecessary thoughts and stress to allow me to focus on the task and act.

Being able to control my body's sympathetic response gave me the power to make clear and rational decisions, without letting my personal relationship with the patient influence my performance. I was able to offload the thoughts of our friendship to keep room in my cognitive bandwidth to correctly apply a plan.

Dark Humour

I've been in hysterics at some of the worst scenes in my career. I've laughed at funerals and cracked jokes at times most people would consider inappropriate. I remember a particular case when we were dispatched to a patient who had potentially been dead for a very long time – no one in his family had heard from him for a couple of weeks.

We could smell his decaying body from outside the house. I looked over at my partner who had walked back to the ambulance. I thought she was ditching me, and was going to make me go in alone. I couldn't believe it. I started heading towards the door, shaking my head. I took a moment to brace myself for what horrors I was about to witness on the other side of that door when my partner suddenly yelled out at me.

I turned to find her standing with a tub of Vicks in her hand. Even better, it was smeared all over her upper lip, like a boxer going into the twelfth round. I immediately started laughing. It looked hilarious.

I tried to compose myself as I stepped through the door, discovering my concerns to be true. I quickly looked to my partner and asked her to pass me the tub of Vicks as I started frantically applying it to my upper lip. The smell was terrible. We both stood there, in front of this poor victim, laughing like a couple of schoolchildren. (For the record, we were the only ones there.)

It sounds like a terrible thing to do, but that laughter helped me cope with a situation that would otherwise have been extremely difficult to deal with. It brought me and my partner together, and it helped us find the resilience to cope with looking at an inhumane scene. The laughter protected us.

Humour, dark humour in particular, has been used by paramedics for as long as they have existed, and is recognised as having therapeutic value. It's a way to deal with traumatic situations and help change our perception of the doom and gloom. Humour is a psychological skill that complements those we've already discussed in this chapter.

Laughter has been shown to reduce the levels of stress hormones in the body such as cortisol, adrenaline and dopamine. It releases endorphins, which is like getting a hit of heroin, creating a sense of euphoria. It increases the number of immune defence cells called T-cells, which protect us from infections, increasing our immunity. It also increases the release of serotonin, a neurotransmitter that affects our mood.

Multiple studies have also confirmed that humour relieves tension and humanises traumatic experiences. It's readily used by emergency service workers to transform the socially unacceptable into a liberating experience. This decreases a paramedic's negative feelings about the traumatic event.

One of humour's main benefits is improving camaraderie among team members. It brings people together and forms a bond between them. This improved camaraderie means the team works better together, which in turn improves their performance. This then improves patient outcomes and clinical care, because the team is performing at a higher standard.

Humour has the added benefit of making people who initiate it appear more attractive, enhancing social bonding with the people around them. If you're ugly, try being funny. Another benefit is that it creates a sense of belonging and social support, reducing loneliness.

Research has found that paramedics use humour to offload their worries and stress. Humour allows them to see the lighter side of trauma and creates an environment where they can reframe and reinterpret a traumatic event.

This all sounds amazing, and it is, but as with most things there are certain caveats. Physiologically, laughing contracts the diaphragm and other respiratory muscles, causing us to breath out. It then increases the capacity of the alveoli to accept more oxygen and increases breathing rate, leading to a decrease in lung volume. It essential mimics hyperventilation, which isn't great in a high-stress situation.

This means that it activates the fight, flight or freeze response, which increases heart rate and blood pressure, so be careful using it if you're already in Condition Black. Having said that, studies have shown that approximately 20 minutes after a good laughing session, the body drops below its normal resting stress levels. But paramedics don't usually have 20 minutes to wait. Other studies have suggested that emergency service workers use humour as a mask, a way to hide their feelings from colleagues. This becomes a social concern.

If you're going to participate in dark humour, then you must be aware of your surroundings. Often, the humour or laughter comes at the expense of someone else. It can be very offensive for others if not interpreted in the correct context. Sometimes it's best to keep the humour as an inside voice, as it's very important to not let your inside voice accidentally become your outside voice. If it does, you might need your inside voice to start helping you write a new résumé.

Some examples of paramedic humour:

What is the most important exercise for being a paramedic? The deadlift.

There's a bloke who just collapsed on the London Eye. Paramedics are on the scene and they say he's coming around slowly.

As a paramedic, I've learned that there is something you can never say with a straight face: I'm having a stroke.

You've probably noticed by now that I've answered some questions throughout the book as an interview with the author. A lot of those answers contain elements of dark humour, my inside voice. Not too much though, because otherwise I would lose my audience and people would think I'd need a visit to the mental asylum.

Grow Your Toolbox

There is no one-size-fits-all solution when it comes to psychological skills. If there is one that's easily identifiable, it's breathing, because its physiological effects are profound, but what I hope to do is give you a complete toolbox full of different strategies. Given that all our personalities are different, what I may find very useful, you may not, and vice versa. In addition, you may find that certain tools work better in specific situations, where others may not work very well.

I'm a paramedic, which generally means I'm pretty useless when it comes to building stuff. I have a very limited toolbox at home of spanners and screwdrivers that are of very low quality. I tried to hang new blinds in our house, and a job that should have taken me 20 minutes took about two hours. What's more, the outcome was far from ideal. The blinds weren't level, and there were a few additional holes in the wall that didn't need to be there.

I had another set of blinds that needed hanging in the kids' room, but my wife insisted that I call my carpenter friend to come over and install them. He turned up with a great set of tools and set them up with no troubles, in no time at all. The next time I had to hang something on the wall I made sure I had the correct tools for the job. There were no extra holes in the wall after that.

Here are a few additional tools you can use to develop poise.

Scanning

One important psychological skill is scanning. Looking up from where your main focus is and scanning your environment will help create a different perspective. It will help you quickly detach from what you're currently focused on. If you need refocusing, this is a great tool to use. Pilots have been using scanning as a way to maintain focus and situational awareness for a long time.

A good technique is to look up and simply scan the room or wherever you are and start naming things you can see, or look into the distance for a few seconds, then open your eyes to the wider world around you, breaking that tunnel vision.

When a patient is suffering from a panic attack, hyperventilating and full of anxiety, we often tell them to use scanning techniques to break the fear that's causing their anxiety. This takes their focus away from their fears, gives them awareness and helps reduce their anxiety.

Cognitive Pause

The idea behind taking a cognitive pause is to disengage your attention and reduce the amount of information you must keep in your mind. Your prefrontal cortex is tasked with keeping information in your memory and directing attention. A cognitive pause helps you unload the contents of your cognitive bandwidth, freeing up your prefrontal cortex to focus on other tasks.

Cognitive pauses are used widely by doctors to prevent medical errors. Our cognitive bandwidth occasionally needs a chance to pause briefly without interruption, even just for a moment, to reflect. It might be as simple as putting down your tools for five seconds, or standing up from your chair. Many times when I've had difficult scenarios or difficult patients, I've had to take a step back and just take a moment to gather myself before I can continue working on or trying to do the best for the patient.

To use a cognitive pause effectively, it's critical that you know when you're becoming task-focused and when you're becoming overwhelmed. At times, it can feel counterintuitive to take a pause or walk away for a few seconds when someone desperately needs your help. But it's worse to stay in an overwhelmed state and make an error. It's much better to pause for a few seconds to be better able to make the right decision.

There's research backing this up. A New Zealand study found that when student and qualified paramedics build an intentional cognitive pause into their systematic approach, it has beneficial effects on the quality of their decision-making.

Drink Water

One straightforward way to improve your ability to deal with stress is to drink water. Staying hydrated is one of the most important things we can do. The brain is about 85 per cent water, and when it and the rest of the body are deprived of an adequate level of water, the body produces the stress hormone cortisol. Even a small amount of dehydration can cause our cortisol levels to increase.

Studies have shown that being dehydrated by just half a litre can increase our cortisol levels. Dietitian Amanda Carlson, who specialises in performance nutrition, says that ensuring we stay hydrated can help maintain low levels of stress: 'When you don't give your body the fluids it needs, you're putting stress on it, and it's going to respond to that.'

In addition, we're more likely to become further dehydrated when placed under stress. In stressful situations, our heart rate increases, we produce more heat and begin to sweat, and your respiratory rate increases, leaking more fluids through every breath. We quickly forget to drink water when we're stressed because that's not a priority; survival is the priority when you're stressed. If we maintain a good level of hydration, then, we can reduce the physiological effects of stress on our mind.

When our body is dehydrated, it's not just our brain that's affected, it's the majority of our body systems. So when we find ourselves in a stressful situation and we're in fight, flight or freeze, our body will react in an even more heightened state. Not only is our mind stressed, but our body's mechanisms for coping with that stress are reduced. As a result, while our heart rate may be 100 beats per minute when we're hydrated, it might be 145 beats per minute when we're dehydrated, in an attempt to compensate for the lack of water.

If you're well-hydrated, your body will be better prepared for when your mind responds negatively to stress. Your brain, when fully hydrated, will be able to better function and produce better thoughts and creative solutions to your problems.

If you're thirsty, it's already too late; you're most likely already dehydrated. You must drink water throughout the day to maintain hydration. The amount of water you need to drink during a day cannot be quantified exactly because there are too many variables. The average is said to be around 2.4 litres a day, but if you've been exercising or you're in the middle of a heatwave, then you probably need more. I've found that the best tool for determining how much water you need to drink is to drink until your urine is clear.

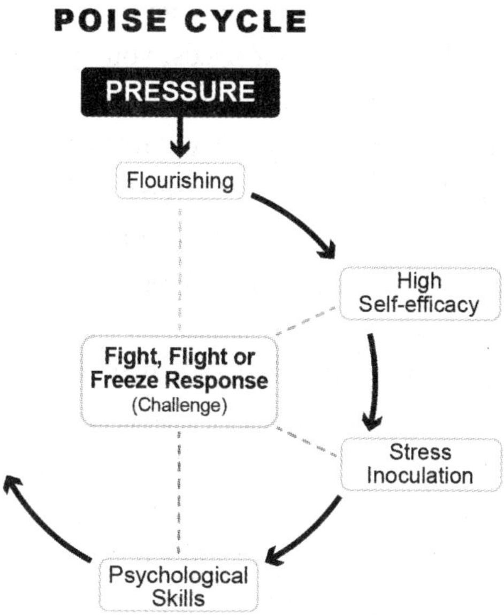

POISE CYCLE

PRESSURE

Flourishing

High
Self-efficacy

**Fight, Flight or
Freeze Response**
(Challenge)

Stress
Inoculation

Psychological
Skills

Figure 12. Paramedics require psychological skills to maintain poise and respond to challenges appropriately and efficiently. Implementing psychological skills can take us from a heightened out-of-control state to one that's composed and self-assured.

INTERVIEW WITH THE AUTHOR
You're used to it, aren't you?

I get asked all the time when someone is sick, particularly by family and friends, to attend to their vomiting and diarrhoea because I'm 'used to it'. It's true that we have to deal with patients who haven't showered in months, wounds covered in maggots and some of the foulest smells on earth, but that doesn't mean I enjoy it. I can't stand vomit but I deal with it.

Generally, because I don't want the patient to vomit on me or even because I'm dealing with bigger problems at the time, such as a dying patient, my focus is off the vomit. When someone vomits in the back of the ambulance at the start of a 12-hour shift it's devastating – it lingers. On a cringing note, I had a patient once faecal vomit – that is spewing poo out of their mouth. It was horrendous and I've never felt so sorry for a patient in my life.

The same applies to death. Just because we see it a lot and we're exposed to death more than the average person doesn't mean it's something we enjoy. It's something we're trained to deal with, so in a way, I guess we do get used to it.

CALL TO ACTION

'I remember a time when I was sent to an eight-week-old baby in cardiac arrest. I sat down and concentrated. I concentrated on my breathing to control my heart rate.' – **Gavin Cousens, head of paramedic science, Central Queensland University**

Key Takeaways

- Beat the Stress, Fool: a useful mnemonic to remember when under pressure.
- Breathing is the most powerful tool to control stress but it's not the only one. Build a toolbox of psychological skills to call upon.
- Humour should not be underestimated as a tool to manage stress.

Key Tasks

- Personalise the psychological skills to suit your needs. Write down what focus words you're going to use under stress. What positive self-talk sentences are you going to implement?

- Develop a strategy to use these skills so they occur naturally in the moment. What scenarios do you expect will come up where these skills will be helpful? How can you remind yourself to use these skills? For example, setting an alarm, leaving yourself a note next to your laptop.

- Spend five minutes every day completing the physiological sigh.

9

Overcoming Fear

Personal Experience – Long Way Down

I had an intense feeling of panic when I was on the balcony with a suicidal patient who was threatening to jump. I was working on an island, by myself again, when I was called to a man threatening suicide in his apartment. I found him smoking on the balcony.

I instantly tried to coax him inside, but he refused to do anything until he finished his cigarette. I stepped out to join him. I'm used to second-hand smoke in the ambulance business; it's amazing how aggressive patients get if they can't have their cigarette.

I was trying my best to establish a rapport with the patient, but he was detached from reality. His mind was somewhere else, certainly not present in the moment. He wouldn't make eye contact with me and avoided conversation. He took another puff as I watched intently, his cigarette slowly burning down. I hoped he would hurry up and finish.

Finally, he pushed the butt into the pot plant beside the balcony. I held out my arm as if to point him inside when my greatest fear happened: he rushed towards the edge of the balcony, grabbing the railing, leaning his head and chest over the edge, looking poised to jump.

Before I knew it, I had my arms wrapped over his shoulders and chest. I squeezed them tightly, trying to rip him away from the edge. I had no time for thought until I stupidly looked down – the drop to the rocky cliff below was at least 50 metres (160 feet).

His grip on the rail wouldn't budge. Suicidal people seem to gain superhuman strength. I spoke calmly into his ear and tried to shove him inside the room. Time seemed to have stopped. I had too much thinking time as we stood there on the edge. I felt an overwhelming need to escape. My heart was pounding as I wondered what to do if he overpowered me. Would I go with him? Could I live with letting him go and falling to his death?

I had a real reason to fear for my life but I couldn't let that fear narrow my decision-making and ability to take in all the information around me. I wasn't sure if I could cope with the consequences of letting go, so I hung on. I secured my footing and began to talk to the patient again. I realised that out of fear I had stopped communicating. Talking helped me look past the blinkers I was wearing and get back on task.

Suddenly, without hesitation, he just let go and casually walked inside. He sat on the lounge as if nothing had even happened. I slammed the door shut and locked it behind me, trying to catch my hyperventilating breath. My hands were shaking and trembling as I took a moment to process what just happened. 'I don't get paid enough to deal with this,' I thought.

Our Relationship with Fear

How we respond to fear will greatly impact our ability to overcome an obstacle and achieve success. Fear is one of our primitive emotions that helps us survive in the wilderness of life, and is closely related to the fight, flight or freeze response. The feeling of impending doom narrows our focus and ability to take on information outside of the perceived threat.

Fear is a normal human process that has evolved to ensure we reduce risk-taking and stay alive, but we shouldn't allow it to have complete control over us. Most negative thoughts result from the initial perception of a threat that never manifests as a physical danger. Fear, like any other emotion or physiological system, is meant to help us and has a purpose. The problem arises when we misinterpret its purpose.

Fear is a necessary system that has evolved to provide optimal physiological and cognitive performance in response to a real threat. But when the system operates outside a real threat, fear narrows our perception and ability to see information outside of that threat. This results in neglect or avoidance behaviour. We become fixated on whatever is stimulating our fear response.

One example is a paramedic who forgot to defibrillate a patient in cardiac arrest because they were so consumed by their fear of the patient dying. They continued to pursue more advanced medical interventions, forgetting about the basics and what has the highest success rate in cardiac arrest – defibrillation. Despite the monitor alarming, making a constant beeping noise and flashing red, the crew failed to recognise this information. Ultimately, their fears came true, just not in the way they imagined.

If we allow fear to take over and control our decisions, we won't absorb the valuable information around us. We will miss information that's critical to our situation, making the fear come true through unseen means. This process will prevent us from making informed decisions. Fear can come in many forms – fear of the unknown, fear of change, fear of pain. In this chapter, we're going to focus on fear of failure.

Understanding the Fear of Failure

To me, the fear of failure is the motivation to shy away from taking action in order to avoid the risk of making a mistake. While fear is a natural instinct that helps us survive, when it occurs outside a life-or-death situation it is often irrational.

Fear limits us from reaching our potential. Our survival

response is ultimately designed to help us survive; it's in the name. We're fortunate enough to live in an era that allows us to live a more comfortable and a less life-threatening existence. Advancements in technology have allowed us to care less about safety and more about self-actualisation.

In mentioning self-actualisation, I'm referring to Maslow's Hierarchy of Needs. Abraham Maslow, a psychologist, developed this pyramid-like hierarchy to explain the ways different human needs – with physiological (health) at the bottom, widest part of the pyramid and moving up through safety, love and belonging, esteem, cognitive (mental) and aesthetic on the way to self-actualisation and ultimately transcendence. Self-actualisation is a state in which we realise our true potential and can achieve our 'ideal self'.

When we experience a fear of failure, we're essentially thinking our survival is threatened. If we recognise that in reality it isn't, then we will be able to take advantage of knowing we're not going to die. The knowledge that we'll survive no matter the outcome will give us the power to overcome our fear and achieve our goal.

Fear is not only a response to immediate and real danger, but also a reaction to perceived danger. Our perception of the threat will determine how we act.

In one instance, I was alone, a single officer in rural Australia, when I was dispatched to a two-year-old with a deadly disease. The bloodstream infection meningococcal septicaemia is a parent's worst nightmare. It's a devastating disease that requires immediate action. Failure to act could result in amputation of the child's limbs, or even worse, death.

The short drive to the scene allowed me time to go through a few strategies we've looked at in this book – and to focus. It gave me an opportunity to prepare mentally and visualise what I was going to do.

But, if I am being honest with you, I was still shitting myself.

What if I missed establishing IV access? What if I gave the wrong drug dose to a two-year-old? How would I be able to answer the desperate parents who were looking to me to save their child?

The familiar, debilitating pattern of negative self-talk kicked in. If I repeated the negative self-talk enough, I might have started to believe it was the truth. I was afraid of failure, and my negative self-talk made that abundantly clear.

Although few of us encounter this level of catastrophe within our daily environments, the same mechanisms threaten to hijack our attention and lead to suboptimal performance.

What if I fail?

Many people struggle with a fear of failure, even if they don't recognise it or admit it. Fortunately, once I arrived on scene and fell back on my training, focusing on my role as a paramedic, I was able to overcome this fear. It took me taking one step forward towards action and completing the task successfully to move on from the fear. It gave me the belief that I was the right person to help this child.

Fear of failure can really limit us and stop us from doing the necessary tasks to achieve our goals and perform with poise. It's easy to go from failing at something to feeling like a failure to even proclaiming oneself a failure.

Here are some of the symptoms of fear.

- An intense feeling of panic or anxiety.
- Increased sensitivity to emotional stimuli.
- An overwhelming need to escape.
- Feeling detached.
- Feeling like you've lost control.
- Tunnel vision.
- Harm-avoidance decision-making.
- Difficulty breathing.
- Chest tightness.
- Increased heart rate.
- Shaking or trembling.

- Feeling faint.
- Digestive distress.
- Sweating.

We can develop fear of failure for a number of reasons, ranging from parental figures to bullying, being exposed to trauma, or previously perceived failures. If we've failed in the past and wound up feeling humiliated, the secondary emotions released from that failure can stay with us and prevent us from taking future positive action.

The Opposite of Fear

Fear creates an obstacle to possessing poise because our mind subconsciously tries to avoid the challenge at all costs. We can find safety in the status quo and actively avoid situations that make us feel vulnerable or involve perceived failure. For this reason, we must work on ways to reframe the fear of failure and let go of any self-doubt.

The fear of failure is the opposite of what we're trying to achieve – self-assurance. This means having an unwavering belief in yourself, knowing that you've done everything within your capability to succeed. Self-assurance is a by-product of all the work and foundational knowledge you've developed.

High-performing people fail all the time – it's human nature to make mistakes – but they don't fear it. The difference is that they know within themselves that they performed at their best when they failed. This means they learn from their mistake and turn it into a positive. When we learn from it, it's no longer a failure, it's a lesson.

You won't be able to get everything right every single time, no matter how great you are. The key here is to make sure that, when failures occur, they don't happen as a result of negligence, complacency or poor preparation.

The only times I've experienced the fear of failure is when I've felt unprepared, and I was only unprepared because I didn't put enough effort in learning the fundamental skills. Failure is rarely a result of inability to complete the task or lack of intelligence. It comes down to individual accountability and motivation to work hard – discipline.

Personal Experience – Complaint Email

Night after night, paramedics travel the streets, a beacon of hope in a sea of darkness, answering the calls of those in need. I was one of them, ready to be called to action. I remember one ordinary night, as my shift began, it seemed like the city was pulsing with a frenetic energy, and I felt excitement about the fact that anything could happen in the next twelve hours.

What I didn't expect was that 'anything' would be receiving an email on my phone with the subject line: 'Formal Complaint Review'.

After the familiar chime of the notification, seeing the word 'complaint' sent a chill down my spine, and I felt my heart sink. My heart started to pound and my body felt tense. I struggled to read the words on the screen; it was as if I forgot the English language. At first, I had no idea what case they were referring to. With a paramedic's caseload, it's easy to forget what you've done and whom you've treated. But as I read, it all came back to me.

The complaint detailed an incident that had occurred several months earlier, during a particularly chaotic call involving several critically injured patients. I had made some tough decisions in a complex situation, but a complaint had now been lodged against me for my actions that day.

Initially, as I read through the details of the complaint, I felt a surge of anger and frustration welling up inside. I wanted to go straight to my boss to share my side of the story, take responsibility and do whatever was needed to resolve the complaint quickly. I knew I had done the right thing for my patients, and they had all had good outcomes in the end. To receive a complaint in this situation was infuriating.

In the days that followed, though, I also found myself consumed by a sense of injustice. After all my years of dedicated service to the community, I couldn't shake the feeling that I had been betrayed. I had always prided myself on my professional abilities, and I had treated thousands of patients without any issues, which made it all the harder to accept this complaint. My hard work, my integrity and my commitment to my job had been called into question.

What hurt most of all was the inability to share this burden with anyone. Bound by confidentiality and legal restrictions, I found myself unable to discuss the details of the case with my closest confidants or even my professional mentors. The sense of isolation gnawed at me, exacerbating my anxiety and leaving me feeling adrift.

As the investigation into the complaint progressed, dragging on for days, weeks and eventually months, I was cut off from the camaraderie of my colleagues and the support of my friends. I started to isolate myself even further, retreating from social situations. The weight of the accusation hung heavy on my shoulders, casting a shadow over every aspect of my life.

Sleepless nights and restless days became the norm as I grappled with the uncertainty of my future and various worst-case scenarios. What if I lost my job? How would I provide for my young family? The prospect of facing unemployment and reputational disgrace loomed large, threatening to upend the stability I had fought so hard to achieve.

Despite my best efforts to pretend everything was normal and maintain a facade of toughness, I felt myself unravelling under the emotional strain of the complaint process. Once a fearless and confident paramedic, I now felt like a shadow of my former self, plagued by self-doubt.

When I had time to think, I spent it rehashing cases I hadn't thought about for years. Patients I'd treated – cases where I'd made mistakes or didn't perform to my own standard – haunted my thoughts. It felt like I was walking on ice – I didn't want to go to work, in case I made another mistake. Remember, in the medical world, mistakes have the potential to kill. Was another complaint inevitable? Could I even continue in this job?

A simple complaint had completely eroded my confidence, and I couldn't understand why I felt so destroyed by it.

In the depths of that difficult time, I found myself rereading Viktor Frankl's *Man's Search for Meaning*, a book that has long held a revered place on my bookshelf. Frankl had been a concentration camp prisoner during World War II, but he wrote movingly of the possibility and importance of finding meaning in the face of adversity. Being reminded of Frankl's message had a big impact on my mindset.

I began to see that the struggle and suffering I had endured, while painful and challenging, was ultimately going to be a blessing in disguise. Through adversity, I had been forced to confront my deepest fears and insecurities around my identity, my purpose and my work, and in doing so, I had discovered reservoirs of strength and resilience I never knew I possessed.

As I continued to navigate the complaints process, I couldn't help but grapple with the fear of tarnishing my reputation. I was so worried about how I would be perceived by my family, my colleagues, my superiors and the broader community once the complaint became public knowledge. Would they trust me again? As someone researching and writing a book about mindset based on my experiences as a paramedic, I was also acutely aware of the weight that a complaint could carry in the eyes of the public. My reputation was definitely on the line.

However, amidst all the uncertainty, I came to a profound realisation: a good character is far more important than reputation.

While reputation may open doors and garner accolades, it is one's character that serves as the true measure of a person. Character, I discovered, is the essence of who you are as an individual. It is rooted in your most fundamental values, beliefs and principles. It is the compass that guides your actions and decisions, especially in the face of adversity.

As I reflected on the circumstances of the complaint, I found solace in the alignment of my actions with my core values. I had done the right thing for my patients in the difficult circumstances. In doing so, while my reputation may have been called into question, my character remained steadfast and true. It was this realisation that gave me the confidence to stand by my decisions, knowing that they were grounded in the bedrock of my values, and to remember that I was still a good paramedic. While reputation may ebb and flow with the tides of public opinion, character endures.

With a changed mindset, I now allowed myself the chance to reflect with greater consideration. Instead of beating myself up or spiralling into anxiety, I approached my thoughts with the same compassion and empathy I offered to my patients. I began to grant myself the forgiveness and understanding that I so readily extend to others in need.

In acknowledging my role and accepting responsibility for the complaint, which I had already done as part of the investigation process, I had taken the initial steps – but it wasn't yet enough. What I had failed to do was to assess the circumstances with fairness. It became clear that in order to truly move forward, I needed to cultivate a sense of understanding and kindness toward myself instead of feeling betrayed or ashamed.

By embracing self-compassion, I allowed myself the space to acknowledge my humanity and imperfections. I had caused no harm to my patients; in fact, I had alleviated their pain and improved their condition. But mistakes do happen – making mistakes is an inherent part of the human experience, and it is through these mistakes that we can learn and grow.

The complaint was an opportunity to think about things deeply and reflect, and I could choose to do that with a positive or negative mindset. I could choose to dwell on feelings of blame and judgement. Or I could choose to be positive, dig deeper and approach the situation with a sense of curiosity and openness, seeking to understand the complexities and nuances at play.

At various stages throughout the process, I felt like I had been emotionally stripped bare. Yet, in that vulnerability, I found an unexpected source of power – the power to rise above the challenges that threatened to overwhelm me.

After the fraught complaints process, which took many months, meetings and phone calls to resolve, I was issued with a caution. My career as a paramedic – which I had been so afraid I would lose – was safe, and I was able to return to work with a clear head and renewed commitment to doing the best for my patients.

All journeys worth traveling are marked by challenges and obstacles, and it is how we navigate through them that defines our character. My journey of self-discovery has been fraught with uncertainty and doubt, but through it all, I came to understand even more deeply that true strength lies not in the absence of suffering, but in the ability to find meaning and purpose from it.

In the end, by embracing uncertainty and doubt and changing my perspective, I discovered a reservoir of inner resilience and determination that I never knew existed. This helps give me the confidence to embrace the uncertainties of the future. Whatever obstacles lay ahead, I know they will ultimately make me stronger.

Self-doubt

Self-doubt – feeling of uncertainty and of losing self-assurance – is the greatest barrier to success. Self-doubt is a self-defeating belief that one is not good enough or that you can't succeed. It's the feeling of having no confidence in your abilities and uncertainty regarding your capacity to make decisions and perform. It prevents us from doing our best to help ourselves and others.

Psychologist Dr Tchiki Davis has defined self-doubt as 'a state of uncertainty about the truth of anything'. It influences everything from our beliefs and emotions to our opinions, the decisions we make, and how we see ourselves and reality. More specifically, self-doubt makes us question our competence.

Self-doubt can significantly impact our ability to perform under pressure. It can make us respond to our doubts in a negative way. A common consequence of self-doubt is self-handicap – finding ways to sabotage ourselves so that we can blame other factors for our failure rather than laziness, or a lack of ability.

For example, the student who worries about missing a vein with a needle will blame the patient's veins for being too hard to find rather than their lack of ability. Or a ballerina might deliberately tie their pointe shoes incorrectly at rehearsals so they have an excuse for failure when it inevitably comes.

Imposter syndrome is a psychological term often used in the paramedic world. It refers to the phenomenon of doubting our achievements and fearing exposure as a fraud. It can manifest as doubts about our ability and status, whether we're worthy of being a part of the team or of receiving accolades for our efforts.

Imposter syndrome reflects the belief that we're inadequate and incompetent, despite evidence indicating that we're skilled and quite successful. Imposter syndrome may make us avoid taking action out of fear of being seen to claim abilities we don't have.

I understand that everyone, including successful people, has doubts. No one should be upset if doubt creeps into their mind on occasion. But if we want to have poise, we must learn to overcome this doubt and be optimistic. Some doubt can be good because it gets us questioning our decisions, but not the doubt that cripples our decision-making, because then we believe that none of our answers will help.

People who have self-doubt expect poor performance. They cannot confidently state that they will achieve a particular goal or outcome, because they believe they will perform incompetently. They're generally uncertain that they can achieve a desired outcome, no matter their ability or knowledge.

Comparing ourselves with others is one way to foster self-doubt. We live in a competitive world, and we often compare ourselves to the people around us, telling ourselves they're better than us and how much we lack compared to them.

If we don't feel confident, we're likely to fail. Indeed, much of what we do comes down to confidence. If a surgeon is about to operate on someone's heart but isn't confident in their ability, and doesn't believe their technique or talent is sufficient for a successful outcome, then they will fail. It doesn't matter how brilliant they are – no one performs well in a state of doubt and fear.

When we doubt ourselves, we second-guess ourselves, delaying action and taking longer to perform tasks. We're unable to make decisions, or we change our mind and we're indecisive.

While fear creates self-doubt, self-doubt also creates fear. This leads to stress and anxiety, triggering our fight, flight or freeze response. Things around us become uncertain; we believe we're no longer in control of the outcome and begin to fear making mistakes.

If we want to perform under pressure – if we want to have poise – we must change the way we see ourselves. A common cause of self-doubt is our past experiences, which can change our beliefs about ourselves. Think of past events that have caused you doubt. You must acknowledge these experiences so that you can learn from them and grow, rather than letting them fester in the background. This process will help build your self-efficacy.

Shame

Many psychologists have identified that the underlying cause of fear of failure is fear of the resulting shame. One of our most primitive emotions, shame is an important factor in the formation of our identity. Two hallmarks of shame are to make ourselves small and unremarkable, or to diminish others.

We want to avoid the painful experience of shame at all costs, so we self-sabotage by not acting. Our shame-filled self-talk plays an endless loop that keeps us stuck in doubt, blame and criticism.

Brené Brown, a leading researcher in the field of shame, defines it as 'the intensely painful feeling or experience of believing that we're flawed and therefore unworthy'. In her research, she found that when people don't recognise their shame, they put up screens –defence mechanisms to protect themselves. Shame activates our primal fight, flight or freeze response, which means we're either:

- Moving against shame by trying to gain control or power over others or being aggressive.
- Moving away from shame by withdrawing, hiding, keeping secrets or staying silent.
- Moving towards shame by seeking approval and belonging.

By identifying your reactions, you can work towards making alternative choices when faced with shame. One strategy to overcome shame is to recognise and acknowledge your body's reaction to fear. You may exhibit anger and narcissistic behaviour, and/or humiliate others. You may engage in avoidant behaviour and self-harm by not taking opportunities to connect or grow. You may be overly focused on having people like you or on pleasing authority figures in your life.

Helping yourself recognise and then address your fear is vital to overcoming shame and feeling worthy. Shame is not helpful or productive, so make a conscious effort now to face your fears just as the Spartans did, and take small steps towards acquiring poise.

Accept It

It's completely normal to be nervous when you're faced with a challenge and put under pressure. Our normal human reaction to fear is stress.

Accept the challenge as if you've chosen it.

These days, we try to diagnose human emotions at every opportunity – if you're afraid, then something must be wrong. But this is not the case – we all get anxious at times. Remind yourself that you're not mentally ill simply because you're afraid. Instead, ask yourself whether the emotion was expected or unexpected given the circumstances.

For a paramedic, accepting the reality that you're in is a crucial element to a successful outcome. You will find yourself in many situations you don't want to be in.

I remember waking up at two in the morning for a call-out to a male in his 20s who had fallen off the edge of an infinity pool, on a house that overlooked a cliff. I was already cranky because of the time, but when I opened the door of my house to be greeted by strong winds and sideways rain drops the size of small golf balls, I was even more annoyed.

I drove to the scene to find the patient lying unconscious on the side of the now-muddy cliff, with ten drunk friends gathered around in boardshorts. The patient had been sitting on the edge of the infinity pool when he leaned backwards, falling off. He had landed on the bottom edge of the water catchment below, opening up a gash on his forehead the size of a dinner plate. His skin was flapping in the breeze. The most frightening thing, however, was that when he breathed out his eyelids would inflate like a puffer-fish. He had fractured his face, which directed the flow of air up and behind his eye.

It was dark, I was tired, I was the only sober one there, and I had no idea how I was going to get the patient to the ambulance – but it was my situation and I had to accept it or fail. I stood up and took a moment, looking at my surroundings, and started to smile. It was a really shit situation but I realised that I was privileged to be here. Being out in the elements is what makes a paramedic unique compared to other medical professionals, and if I survived, it was going to be one hell of a story.

Wearing my baseball cap at night to keep the rain out of my eyes, I managed to recruit some sober volunteer firefighters to come help carry the patient out. It was a relief to close the back of the ambulance doors after pushing the stretcher inside, as it meant things were now controlled. What got me through and changed my perspective was accepting the situation as if I had chosen it. I actually ended up enjoying it.

When we acknowledge our fear, we bring it into our conscious awareness, which weakens our physical reactions to the thoughts that are making us anxious and nervous. This prepares us to conquer our fear and be courageous. If we choose to suppress or ignore our anxiety, fear will control us and spread through our body like a virus. We will be in no state of poise.

Self-reflection

The ability to engage in self-reflection in an open and honest way can be the difference between learning and growing, and avoiding and declining. Self-reflection is the ability to look at yourself and say, 'I've lost, but I've learned something.'

We must accept criticism and perceived failure in order to grow. I remember when I was a student paramedic being constantly harassed, during practical placements and in the classroom, while running scenario-based training. As a student, I welcomed the criticism; it helped me learn and improve. As the years rolled on and I became more qualified and more experienced, my ability to self-reflect and accept criticism decreased. This meant that I had to work consciously on self-reflection and using constructive feedback to grow and improve.

Reflective practice pioneer Donald Schön defined reflective learners as people who analyse and question their learning experiences in order to understand how they learn, and this helps to improve the way they learn in the future.

Reflecting on your practice will enable you to identify any barriers to your performance and to develop strategies to overcome those barriers. Self-reflection will help you solve problems and avoid making the same mistake again in the future. It will even help you appreciate what you've accomplished already and how far you've grown, inspiring you to continue moving forward.

Reflective practice ensures that you're taking responsibility for yourself and your actions. Through assessing your shortcomings and strengths, you will develop a greater awareness of the factors you can control that improve your learning. It may even help you answer questions like, 'Why are you a paramedic or emergency service worker? What motivates you to do the job?'

Schön defines reflective practice as 'the practice by which professionals become aware of their implicit knowledge base and learn from their experience'. He talks about two main reflective practice strategies to help us develop and improve:

1. **Reflection-in-action.** This involves taking a pause during the event and reflecting on what is occurring in real time. It's about reflecting on the incident when you still have the ability to change the course of your actions and impact the outcome. It gives you the opportunity to be innovative and resourceful, allowing you to apply your knowledge to a new experience.
2. **Reflection-on-action.** This is reflecting on your action after the event. It's essential for understanding how our actions contributed to the outcome of the event and to develop learning takeaways to improve our performance in the future.

By following Schön's model of reflection, you will develop a questioning approach to whatever area in which you wish to succeed. You will consider why things are as they are and how they could be. This will help in overcoming fear.

As in life, work of a paramedic is unpredictable, and no two situations offer the same experiences. In such situations, reflection is very important in developing new ways of thinking and innovations in treatment.

PANIC CYCLE

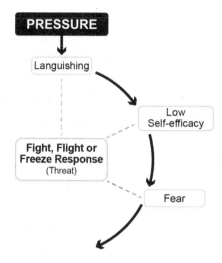

Figure 13. Panic under pressure leads to languishing, low self-efficacy, and a fear of failure. If we wish to develop poise, we must make a conscious effort to face our fears and be assiduous in improving our psychological skills, mindset and training. Having courage to push against the agitation of fear is critical.

INTERVIEW WITH THE AUTHOR
Are you an alcoholic?

According to the definition of alcoholism, no. I definitely have had periods of overindulgence. From my personal experience, it's not chronic alcoholism that has been my problem so much as bingeing. Going on big benders is worse than having a couple of beers a day, and recent research has found that bingeing's negative impact on the brain is profound.

Paramedics tend to do extreme things, which means that when they drink alcohol they go hard – and I'm no exception. A fellow paramedic told me a story that whenever he goes to a paramedic wedding and all of the paramedics are placed at the same table, it's always the drunkest table at the wedding. You could generalise and say this is a result of the trauma we've seen. While this certainly plays a part, I like to think of it in other ways.

We like to live life to the fullest. Another paramedic I know loves to binge and told me that throughout his career he's seen people die in all sorts of ways – the movie *A Million Ways to Die in the West* has some truth to it. As a result, he lives life to the fullest and is a lover of life, so he often verges on the extreme, pushing the boundaries.

I think I fit into a similar category. Life's too short to muck around with it. Put yourself in the arena.

CALL TO ACTION

'It doesn't matter where the threat of making a mistake comes from, if you have the fear of failure, you are now going to avoid it. The repercussion of the threat becomes your fear and it becomes the dominant thought. You protect yourself by inaction. You won't make decisions because it's easy to justify not doing anything compared to doing the wrong thing.' – **Daniel Cooper, SAS Regiment, Australian Army**

Key Takeaways

- The fear of failure is a debilitating and negative pattern that can lead to self-destruction.
- A fear of failure will stop you from achieving your goals and dreams. It will make you not attempt any challenges because of the shame associated with potential failure.
- Self-doubt is the precursor to fear of failure; it creates a sense of negative uncertainty that can spiral out of control.
- Self-reflection is critical if you want to perform at a high level. Accepting what happened and learning from your mistakes will prevent it from happening again.

Key Tasks

- Do you recognise any reactions to fear and shame in yourself? Take the time now to reflect on how you acted the last time you were put under pressure. Did you move against, away from or towards shame?
- Write down past experiences that have caused you self-doubt.
- Read Brené Brown's books and research on shame and vulnerability.

10

Pushing Beyond Discomfort

Personal Experience – Mind Bog

I was excited when I received the call informing me to change vehicles and take the four-wheel drive to respond to a patient on a remote farming property.

Getting to do challenging things is something I really enjoy about being a paramedic. It's even better when you're driving a government vehicle and don't have to pay for any damage. I would be attending a man who had fallen off his horse – and been kicked in the head on the way down for good measure.

As I was driving to the scene, I could see that the road had flooded recently. Grass, plants and branches covered the road. The roads were wet and muddy from the terrible storms a couple of days before. The dirt had turned to mud, and the water had created numerous potholes throughout the journey. I remember arriving at a particularly nasty section of the road that required me to build up speed and maintain the momentum to get through a bog. The car was slipping and sliding, and I was bouncing over the holes and bumps in the ground. I watched mud flick up into the air – it soon covered the vehicle, too.

Despite the bumpy, muddy drive, I was able to get through. When

I arrived on the scene, I found the patient lying on his back in a state of altered consciousness. I was not only concerned about an internal head injury – he was also a high risk for spinal injury. Like most cowboys, he wasn't wearing any protective gear or helmet while riding the horse. The other stockman on the scene told me that they were out rounding up cattle when the patient's horse bucked, causing him to fall.

The patient's vital signs were normal, and he was relatively stable given the incident, but he did have some numbness down his left arm and had lost some feeling and sensation in his fingers and forearm. This made me very concerned about a potential spinal cord injury.

I took every precaution to stabilise his spine. Research shows that movement can exacerbate spinal injury by creating damage secondary to the initial incident. The solution is to avoid moving the spine around too much. It was therefore vital that I took great care.

The helicopter wasn't available, so it was up to me to transport the patient to the hospital. It was something I really didn't want to do on that road; it had already given me so much trouble on the drive in. It was a very slow and easygoing drive back until I came to the infamous rough section that had given me trouble on the way. Now it would prove challenging again. I felt agitated about what to do. Friction was building up inside me. I wanted to floor it to get through the bog, but that would risk causing life-altering spinal injury to the patient. Clearly, I didn't want him to end up in a wheelchair for the rest of his life.

I couldn't sit there all day, though, and do nothing. I started to drive – overcompensating and driving slowly – when the inevitable happened. Within 10 metres (30 feet), I bogged the ambulance. I was stuck in the middle of nowhere and wasn't moving anytime soon. What the hell was I going to do?

I thought I would have to wait for my boss to drive another four-wheel drive ambulance to pull me out. That option would take several hours: precious time that the patient couldn't afford. I was embarrassed and now my body's agitation was at full throttle. I didn't want to accept my predicament. I got out of the vehicle thinking I could dig a few holes around the tyres, let some air out, and I'd be on my way – but that didn't work. My wheels were glued to the road.

I needed to reframe the situation. I started to look at the positive, examining my predicament from multiple perspectives. At least I didn't cause more spinal damage by going rogue and flying through the dangerous road. The patient was stable and I could still provide advanced medical care. And there were people in a house nearby who could assist me. How hadn't I seen that before?

The farmer near where we were stuck happened to have a tractor, obviously. He was more than willing to assist me and drove the tractor down to the road to pull the ambulance out. We hitched the ambulance up to the tow rope and he started to drive. It worked.

After accepting my situation and reframing my personal, biased point of view, I was able to overcome agitation to come up with a solution. In fact, it was a better solution than my original option to drive through the mud. The tractor was slow and smooth. It pulled the ambulance through the roughest parts of the road with ease, and the bumps weren't as exaggerated.

Limbic Friction

Medical emergencies provide a great opportunity to experience the emotion of stress and to turn that stress into an extremely rewarding and positive experience. Most people typically don't walk towards stress by choice, but in the medical world, you often find yourself walking deliberately and directly to it.

Faced with stress, and fear of failure and the unknown, our body sends hormones through the bloodstream to make us feel on edge or agitated. Friction is this sense of inner tension and rest-lessness. It not only affects our capacity to make sound decisions and maintain conscious awareness, but results in many physical symptoms, including tingling, nausea, faintness and shaking. It's created by the fight, flight or freeze response. When this feeling occurs, we feel uneasy and tense, and often cannot sit still.

The agitated, uncomfortable feeling is our subconscious telling us, 'This isn't your "normal", so I'll make your body feel extremely uncomfortable to bring you back into your "normal", no matter what that normal is.' If your 'normal' were, say, sitting with your phone, browsing social media, I wouldn't be surprised if, when you're faced with this friction during a crisis, you started looking at Facebook.

Neuroscientist Dr Andrew Huberman calls this 'limbic friction', which he describes as the gap between the brain's cerebral cortex, which is logical, and its limbic system, which is emotional. It's the difference between wanting to do a task and actually doing it. Limbic friction is the urge trying to pull us back to our reflexive behaviour, back to our 'normal'. To keep you safe, the limbic system wants to pull you into a direction against your willpower, and generally, the direction it takes you in is a reflexive one – whatever your habits are.

For example, when my alarm goes off in the early hours of the morning, signalling that I need to wake up and go to the gym, I feel immediate friction. My brain is making my body feel as uncomfortable as possible to ensure that I stay lying on my nice and warm therapeutic mattress. I must overcome the pull of my brain's desire to stay comfortable and relaxed in bed. My brain is predicting the future and knows that I will feel pain and suffering at the gym. It's the brain's natural survival response to try to protect my body from pain. The brain doesn't care whether it's pain from a crocodile attack or pain from exercising – pain is pain. So my brain makes me feel as uncomfortable as possible. If I want to achieve my fitness goals, I must have the mental strength to overcome this friction.

This friction is also what we sense when faced with fear. All of these systems are linked – it's how we're controlled through our human physiology – but we do have the ability to overcome it, as we are more than just skin and bones. We have consciousness.

Huberman describes limbic friction as the strain that's required to overcome one of two states in our body. The first state is one of anxiousness; the other is feeling lazy or tired. Limbic friction sets out how much active energy or motivation we need to overcome those urges that are preventing us from getting up and going.

To counteract this friction, you first need to gather awareness of the individual emotional and physical warning signs your body goes through. Do you experience tension, heart palpitations, fear, anxiety? Next, look at your behaviour – what are you saying in that moment of friction, and what are you doing?

It's normal to have friction, so don't fight it. Rather, learn to recognise it. Become aware of its presence, feel it in your body and veins as the hormones are pumped in your bloodstream. The goal here is to develop self-awareness regarding limbic friction, learning to recognise when you're going through it, and trying to figure out how it's influencing your actions and behaviour.

In a medical emergency, it's the fear of the unknown that will generally trigger friction – will this person live or die? If I provide this intervention, will it help or make it worse? I always feel agitated in the moments before I must inform a family member that their loved one is dead.

One particular case sticks with me. I went to a middle-aged man suffering a cardiac arrest from an asthma attack. We arrived and started CPR. This time we had plenty of resources on scene and were working well together. We had trouble gaining IV access in the patient's arm, but after several attempts we found a vein in his foot instead. Around the 30-minute mark, we still hadn't detected any shockable rhythm, which meant we were unable to use a defibrillator, and the patient started to feel cold and lifeless.

As the senior paramedic on scene, I told the team to continue CPR as I went to talk to the family, to tell them that we'd done everything possible to save him and that we were about to stop CPR and declare a time of death. As I approached the family, I could feel the friction in my body trying to pull me back. Limbic friction is normal and expected in this situation but if I want to perform well in my chosen profession, I need to overcome it and step forward. If I didn't overcome the friction now, then who would tell the family?

I started to speak to the family, telling them there was nothing more to do, then I turned around to see that the team had stopped compressions. Thinking that it was over, a family member began to cry. I made eye contact with my partner as he stood up from doing compressions; he said they got a heartbeat. I nearly fell over.

I'd just told the family the man was dead. How was this possible? They said it just miraculously started. My friction quickly turned to extreme embarrassment and I wanted to crawl into the foetal position, but the family didn't seem to mind – we had a pulse.

This is an extreme example of friction, of course, but whatever its cause we can take advantage of our fear and the stress response and use it to give us the courage to step forward and act. The friction we feel under stress – the awkwardness and uneasiness – is specifically designed to get us up and moving. It's a system that has developed in humans over millions of years. This is the fight, flight or freeze process working in our favour, encouraging us to be courageous.

The Courage Circuit

The forward movement towards fear is the point of highest anxiety, and the highest arousal response of the body. Yet taking that step forward, being courageous, triggers activation of the neurotransmitter dopamine, which you may be familiar with for its role in the reward system. Dopamine is also associated with motivation and reaching our goals. If our goal is to have poise, then having the ability to step forward and be courageous is extremely important.

This is called the courage circuit.

If we act with courage, dopamine will help reinforce our actions, helping to change our future perception of stress. It makes us more likely to engage in courageous behaviour the next time we're confronted with a similar situation, thereby making the behaviour feel more like a habit to us. If we show courage and take action, that behaviour will become second nature and we will no longer need courage to overcome the obstacle causing us friction – it will happen naturally.

As an example, the first time I had to insert a large needle through the gap between the patient's ribs into their chest to help decompress their collapsed lung, I felt great friction. I didn't know if I was capable of performing the task on a real patient. I had to have the courage to perform the procedure, despite feeling like someone was holding my arm back. I kept checking the chest for where the needle must be placed. I knew anatomically where the placement was because I had practised it a hundred times, but I still had doubts. I had to make quadruply sure I wasn't going to puncture the heart. The friction was delaying the procedure. It didn't want me to do it.

As I forced my eyes to stay open, I pushed the needle through the skin, then through the lung cavity, then felt the pressure ease and a sound of air rushing out of the needle. The procedure was successful and now, as a result of me showing courage and acting against the friction that day, I no longer associate the procedure with fear and doubt. Doing it successfully with courage reinforced my ability to do it again. The next time, I did it without hesitation.

This is like the scene in *Pulp Fiction*, when John Travolta's character is trying to stab one of the biggest needles I've ever seen directly into the heart of Uma Thurman's character. As friction builds up, they start arguing among themselves. 'Find her heart.' 'Does it have to be exact?' 'Yeah it has to be exact, it's a shot in her heart, I guess it's gotta be fucking exact.' 'I don't exactly know where her heart is.'

After fighting over who's going to do it, they stab the patient, and she miraculously came back to life. The next time Travolta has to do it, it'll be much easier. Except there won't be a next time, because Bruce Willis shoots him shortly after. (Sorry, spoiler alert.)

By acting and decompressing the patient's lung, I overcame the feeling of friction in my body – my racing heart, sweating and awkwardness went away. The fight, flight or freeze response was removed – I'd dispelled the stress.

South African neuroscientist Caroline Leaf explains that anxiety and friction are 'a signal we need to listen to, not an illness we need to manage. [They are] a reaction to life's challenges, not a biological disease to be treated.'

Friction can be one of our greatest teachers.

Cognitive Offloading

You may remember our discussion in Chapter 6 about cognitive bandwidth, where I mentioned the importance of ensuring our mind is free and clear while attending to situations. Cognitive offloading is a strategy for improving our cognitive bandwidth and leaving more space for the knowledge we need in the moment to complete the mission.

The term cognitive offloading refers to the practice of using physical aids to reduce the cognitive demand for tasks. If you've used a to-do list to remember something, then you have used cognitive offloading. Offloading can lead to improved performance on tasks in progress that have high cognitive demand, especially those where we need to keep several pieces of information in our brain at once.

In the past, we were heavily reliant on memory and the ability to embed information in our brain for use in the moment. For paramedics, this is still the case. It's expected that we will know drug therapy protocols and clinical procedures by heart, but under stress, this information may not appear to us in our working memory. That's why it's important to offload some of the stress, and the best way to do that is through checklists.

There may have been a time when it was frowned upon to pull out a checklist and read something when you were treating a patient, or when we might have let our ego got the better of us out of fear of judgement for using checklists. These days, though, checklists are recognised as an effective tool for improving reliability of care by promoting cognitive offloading. Having checklists to hand, such as a quick reference guide to drug protocols, helps reduce the cognitive load, and thus the chance of making mistakes.

As technology and medicine advance, paramedicine becomes ever more complex, creating a real need for cognitive offloading techniques. We often live in a world that provides too much information too fast. Paramedics now need to develop the skill of determining what information is relevant, offloading what isn't in order to free up cognitive bandwidth and prevent distraction.

When metronomes were first introduced to our treatment of cardiac arrests, I took little notice of their importance. A metronome is a timer invented for musicians to practise playing pieces at the right speed and rhythm. In paramedicine we use it as an indicator of when to apply cardiac compressions; a small beep noise is amplified from the defibrillator, indicating when to push down on the patient's chest. I thought it would be a handy tool if I ever remembered to turn it on, but I was ignorant of the benefits that such a small, somewhat innocuous tool could provide.

It turns out that subconsciously reacting to the noise a small beep sound telling me when to compress a patient's chest allowed me to offload the thought of timing. This enabled me to improve my situational awareness, and to focus on other areas of cardiac arrest. The beep helped me slow down my compressions and push in time, preventing the adrenaline rush from taking over, and helping control my fight response. Most bystanders who perform cardiac compressions will be going way too fast – that's the stress response. It's amazing how a small beeping noise can do all that and improve patient outcomes.

Reframing

Reframing is a very useful tool when we're confronted with limbic friction, allowing us to shift our mindset so we can look at the same situation from a different perspective. You can also use reframing any time you experience self-doubt and shame. Psychologists often use reframing when their clients are stuck in a negative thought pattern that keeps on repeating.

The essential idea behind reframing is that the frame through which we view a situation determines our reality. When we shift that frame, the way we see the situation changes, which can alter the way we think about and react to it.

A lot of comedy is reframing. Comedians share their own traumatic experiences and the laughs help them reframe those experiences. This also helps the audience reframe their own trauma if they've had similar experiences.

It's easy to get caught up and believe that there's only one point of view and outlook for the situation you find yourself in. You need to reframe to change your point of view. Ask yourself, 'Is there another way to look at this situation?' For example, you could reframe a perceived failure as an opportunity to learn and gather the information you didn't possess before. Thomas Edison once said, 'I have not failed. I've just found 10,000 ways that won't work.' Don't confuse this quote with making 10,000 of the same mistakes; repeating the same mistake continuously would be unacceptable.

Another good reframing tool, taught by Australian executive coach Carol Fox, is to stop and ask yourself, 'What are seven good things about this situation?' This will quickly help you change your perception of failure. By focusing on the positive, you will essentially be telling yourself, 'How could you be failing if there are seven good things?'

Reframing will allow you to view the world more clearly and open yourself up to accept other information you had previously discarded, information that you neglected or didn't even consider.

With the new information, you'll be able to make decisions with confidence.

Savouring

Similar to reframing, savouring is our capacity to appreciate and enhance the positive experiences in our life. Savouring is the opposite of simply coping with a situation. Instead of just getting by and dealing with the crap, you take a cognitive pause and savour the positive aspects. To do this, you need to intentionally search for the positive aspects of the predicament you find yourself in.

Savouring is something we need to actively work towards. It doesn't tend to happen naturally, it's something we have to do. We can savour the moment by looking inwards and reflecting on what's special about it, what we can take away from the challenge in order to grow from it.

A paramedic once told me that whenever he goes to a horrific incident, he consciously tells himself that he's grateful to be there, that he's glad it's him witnessing the trauma, because he has the training and skills to manage it. He savours the moment and is thankful that it's him. By expressing gratitude, we too can be thankful for our situation and realise that we're the best person to deal with it.

Learn to Prioritise

Multitasking doesn't work, kind of. The reality is that we can't have multiple thoughts at the same time, only a lot of thoughts very quickly. If we try to do multiple things at the same time that require simultaneous thoughts, we will either fail or won't do any of them very well, and sometimes the frustration of trying to multitask will create friction. The term multitasking was first coined to describe the ability of a computer to complete a lot of tasks quickly. Humans aren't computers, and we can't do multiple tasks simultaneously.

You may be able to do several things at the same time, like listen to classical music while reading a book and eating your favourite potato chips. What you can't do is focus very well on any of those tasks. Our attention will oscillate between all of them. A perfect example of this would be driving a car and talking on the phone at the same time. It's illegal to hold the device because so many people become distracted from the task of driving (which in itself requires multiple tasks), which can be fatal for themselves or someone they crash into.

We can 'multitask', though, if we've mastered the skills and they're in a state of unconscious competence (also known as mastery; see page 47). If the task we're completing requires little to no thought, then we can perform another task that does require thought at the same time. That's why when we're driving, we can indicate, turn the wheel, push the accelerator and look for oncoming traffic at the same time – we've mastered those skills. That's why a learner driver struggles to check their mirrors when they're just starting out – it's too much cognitive load.

US entrepreneur Gary Keller, the author of *The One Thing* wrote, 'It's not that we have too little time to do all the things we need to do, it's that we feel the need to do too many things in the time we have.'

If you haven't mastered the skills and what's required of you is taking up a lot of cognitive bandwidth, focus on prioritising tasks. If a patient is on the ground after being shot and is bleeding out, the paramedic's priority is to stop the bleeding, so I'd first put on a tourniquet. Then I'd think about gaining IV access and only getting IV access. Once that's done, I'd think about providing pain relief. When that's done, I'd focus on what's next on my priority checklist.

Using checklists is a great way to help prioritise tasks and direct our focus. For example, if you've ever completed a first-aid training course, you would have been taught the mnemonic (checklist) DRABC – danger, response, airway, breathing and circulation.

Prioritise danger first, because if you injure yourself or others, how are you ever going to help the patient? Next on the list is response. Determining the patients' consciousness level will help you quickly ascertain the severity of their condition. Next is the airway. Is the patient's airway clear and patent (open and working)? If it's not, they won't be able to breathe. Then there's breathing. Is the patient breathing? If they're not, then it won't be long before their heart stops. Finally, consider the circulatory and cardiac aspects. Does the patient have a heartbeat? Because if they don't, they will probably need CPR.

You can see how prioritising these tasks and using a checklist makes the job easier by clearly identifying what you need to focus on. When this strategy is combined with operational cognitive readiness, stress inoculation and having trained your fine motor skills to be almost autonomous, your speed and ability to complete multiple tasks become very close to a flow state.

The key to all of this is, again, high-quality training that is self-reflective and deliberate.

Personal Experience – Please Don't Die

I arrived on scene and gathered as much information as I could before entering the building and assessing the patient. Two large dogs approached me, barking and proudly showing their large teeth. The dogs looked very aggressive and ready to pounce on any unexpected guests. The house was a small, dilapidated shack. There were broken-down cars in the driveway and rubbish all over the ground. This was not a friendly place.

I was called because the patient had chest pain radiating down his left arm, which he described as a crushing pain, associated with shortness of breath: the classic symptoms of a male heart attack. But what was I to do? Exit the vehicle and be eaten by dogs, or stay in the ambulance and ask the patient to walk to me, knowing full well that walking could cause him to go into cardiac arrest? I decided to get the patient to walk to me so I could avoid the dogs. I'd treated enough dog-attack victims to know that it's not a friendly experience.

The patient walked towards the ambulance, and I was praying that he wouldn't collapse halfway across the driveway. I was confident that the dogs most definitely would attack me if I was approaching their owner lying dead on the ground. I watched as he took every single step. Inside, I wanted him to run to lessen the agony I felt watching his slow journey, but running would most definitely have killed him.

After what felt like an eternity, he made it to the ambulance. I completed a full assessment and confirmed that he was suffering a heart attack. Fortunately, we carry a life-saving drug called tenecteplase. It's like Drano for the arteries: it comes in and blasts away the clot that has blocked the blood flow to the heart.

I went through the checklist, making sure the patient met the proper criteria for the medication. Luckily, he ticked all the right boxes. In this situation, the checklist is critical: if the medication is given to the wrong person – about one in every 100 patients – it can cause a stroke.

We gave the medication, monitoring the patient's heart rhythm as it began to change. Unfortunately, the change was not for the good. I looked back at the patient to find that he had fallen unconscious. Sometimes, tenecteplase can cause arrhythmias, so we waited a few seconds to see if he was going to come around.

I thought I'd just killed the patient. I'd been trying to save his life by administering an amazing drug that I'd seen work several times before without any complications. That was in the past, though. Now, I watched as the patient's heart stopped as a result of my actions.

I had to focus on a new solution to save him. I didn't have a lot of time to think; I needed to take action. Thankfully, we had thought ahead and, anticipating cardiac arrest, we had placed the defibrillation pads on his chest. I just didn't think the cardiac arrest would happen after we gave the drug; I thought it would be because we made him walk to the car.

I hit the button on the defibrillator to charge the batteries so it would be ready to send an electric shock through his heart. Nothing happened; the machine wouldn't charge. I couldn't believe it. 'What the hell is going on?' I thought to myself. I looked at my partner; the panic on his face said a thousand words.

What had happened, had happened. I needed to control what I could at that moment and let go of the rest. My partner looked at the pads and followed the cord back to the machine. A sudden yell of 'fuck' came from his mouth as he realised that, in his panic, he'd attached the spare pads to the patient's chest – not the ones connected to the machine.

We quickly swapped them over, voiced the 'all clear' warning and pressed the shock button. The defibrillator worked, and a single shock restored the patient's pulse. He was alive. By the time we arrived at the hospital, the patient was sitting up, talking to us and wondering why his chest was so painful. The drug had done its job to resolve the heart attack.

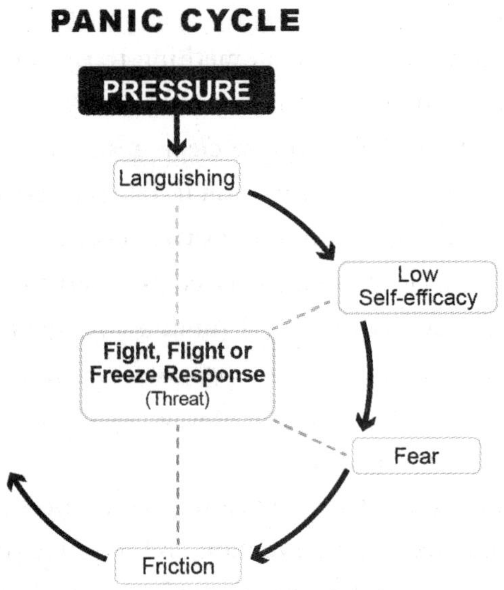

PANIC CYCLE

Figure 14. Friction is a normal part of facing pressure. It occurs when the fight, flight or freeze response is activated. To develop poise, it's important to recognise friction and work to accept it. Reframe and learn about ways to use cognitive offloading to perform better under pressure. If the agitation controls your actions, it will lead to panic.

The Real Secret

The law of attraction was made famous through the book and film *The Secret*. The author, Rhonda Byrne, argues that positive thoughts will bring positive things into our life. In a way that's true: but it's not just positive and negative thoughts, it's whatever we focus on.

When you arrive on a high-stress, high-consequence scene as a paramedic, you know what to focus on clinically, and that's of critical importance. But we never arrive at a job independent of our own human factors – personality, bias, fatigue, adrenaline and others. If you're only attending to the clinical picture (using only your fundamental skills), you will miss the human-factors part of the puzzle, and that will negatively impact your performance and your health.

You cannot attend to something that's out of your awareness. In other words, you can't act on something that you don't even know is there. When you're clear about what to focus on, both clinically and personally, you'll be able to execute competent decision-making that has a positive result.

Dr Michael Yapko introduced an important concept: what you focus on, you amplify. It's a fundamental principle of perception. If we focus on negative feelings and thoughts that don't enhance our ability to perform, then that negative focus will determine the quality of our experience.

For example, if you're dealing with a person who is in need of immediate medical intervention and requires you to insert a needle into their vein, but you're fixated on the chance that you might miss the vein, then that will determine the outcome. You will miss, and your greatest fear will come true.

If you're on a first date at the cinema and all you focus on is trying to hold their hand, you'll forget to watch the film or eat the popcorn, and you'll lose your bearings. You'll overproduce sweat and your hands will become clammy, making the situation even more embarrassing, then panic will start to build. Your date will catch you as you nervously shuffle back into your chair, getting ready to make the move. You'll go in for the grab but miss their hand and knock over the iced coke instead. Your greatest fear is coming true.

The skill we need to develop, therefore, is the ability to direct our own focus. People who panic under pressure quite often focus on what is wrong, on the worst possible outcome, on their own flaws, and these thoughts generate anxiety. All this does is amplify panic, which is defined as 'a sudden overwhelming fear, with or without cause, that produces hysterical or irrational behaviour, and that often spreads quickly through a group of people.'

What we engage with mentally will determine a lot about how we feel, both physically and emotionally. What you're trying to do is to engage with, and focus on, what will help you create positive outcomes when placed under pressure. This way, you can amplify your strengths, and generate poise in the face of high stress – to remain calm.

Poise lies in focusing on the objective through challenging times, turning those emotions off, engaging the logical decision-making process, and knowing that you can turn your emotions on at another time.

Focus on Action

Imagine a robber walks up to the bank counter and points a gun at the teller. The robber demands, 'Give me all the money, or I'll shoot!'

The teller with the gun to their head has the ability to act. Despite their fear for their life, they have the option to give the robber the money or not. They see handing over the money as being part of the solution for removing the robber from the bank, eliminating the threat.

Despite how frightening and nerve-racking the situation is, after it, it will be the person who took action who will be less likely to develop long-term mental effects. The teller watching on from the next window had no ability to be part of the solution and act, unlike the teller who was held up, who could influence the outcome. The observer would have felt helpless, detached and stranded, having witnessed the event without any ability to influence it. The observer is more likely to suffer anxiety and panic as a result.

A study of paramedics and their behavioural responses in critical incidents revealed that those who had cognitive and functional control of the situation reported a positive and empowering experience. Those who experienced a lack of control experienced difficult and negative emotions.

Which brings us back to the secret: what we focus on we amplify. If we focus on what's outside our influence we'll become disempowered. Focusing on the correct action is paramount. Marcus Aurelius, the great Stoic, wrote: 'The impediment to action advances action. What stands in the way becomes the way.'

The most influential theory of stress and coping was developed by US psychologists Richard Lazarus and Susan Folkman. They defined stress as resulting 'from an imbalance, both between perceived external or internal demands, and between the perceived personal and social resources needed to deal with them'. In other words, the resources you have to manage a situation aren't adequate, so you are overwhelmed. They described two coping strategies for stress: adaptive and maladaptive. Adaptive coping is an action we take to help us return to feelings of safety. In contrast, we use maladaptive coping strategies to distract, avoid and deny, often leading to suppression or inaction.

Adaptive coping strategies operate as a protective shield that limits the adverse effects of traumatic and stressful experiences. Adaptive coping ultimately reduces the likelihood of stress even occurring. This shows that any approach that involves confronting the problem directly and taking action is the best strategy for eliminating the stressor.

Let's say a paramedic student and their mentor are dispatched to a 24-year-old's suicide by hanging. Both paramedics are exposed to exactly the same stress and pressure to perform. The mentor deals with the stress by using adaptive coping mechanisms, reading the guidelines for dealing with hanging before arriving on scene. Being prepared helps her focus her mind on the task, and focuses her energy on solving the problem.

When the mentor arrives at the scene, she jumps straight into action, cutting the rope and freeing the patient from the noose, laying them on the ground and commencing lifesaving treatment.

The student, on the other hand, in dealing with the same situation, decides to disassociate from reality. They look at social media on the way to the scene and they avoid conversation, withdrawing from the situation. Though the student may feel a sense of relief at that moment, their limbic friction builds over time until it turns into shame and negative self-talk, which further compounds their stress. The student arrives on the scene and freezes. He delays treatment by opening equipment that isn't needed, and by completing tasks unrelated to the situation facing him.

These maladaptive coping strategies of avoidance have evolved to allow us to escape fear, delay immediate pain, or provide some form of instant gratification. But eventually this will come back to bite us, increasing future stress. It's a loop that keeps repeating. As a consequence of using maladaptive coping mechanisms, the student is more likely to reach for alcohol and engage in other substance abuse. People who don't have suitable coping mechanisms tend to turn to addictive avoidance behaviours, such as gambling and a diet that includes a lot of sugar and carbohydrates.

Examples of adaptive coping strategies include:

- being task-oriented: engaging in an activity that directly impacts the situation
- mindfulness: letting go of what you cannot control
- being solutions-focused

- using humour
- accessing social support
- employing a systematic, repeatable approach
- exercise
- eating healthily
- sleep
- releasing built-up emotion through journalling (see page 230) or talk.

Focus on Control

Control what you can and let go of the rest. This is probably the best lesson I've learned in recent times. It's allowed me to recognise what I can't control and let go of it, accepting that I can't control everything. It's fruitless to think that you can control it all – or worse, attempting to.

US neuroscientist Amy Arnsten specialises in the limbic system and stress. She has said that 'the loss of prefrontal function only occurs when we feel out of control. It's the prefrontal cortex itself that is determining if we are in control or not. Even if we have the illusion that we are in control, our cognitive functions are preserved.'

Once you focus on the things you can control, it will influence what actions you take to respond to the events that occur in your life or at work. In addition, you will be more motivated to take action. You will want to step forward with courage because you know you have control over the outcome; you won't worry about things outside your sphere of influence. If you focus too much time and energy on things you can't control, it will only increase your stress response and create frustration.

If I choose to focus on things that are outside my control, then I will have no positive impact on the outcome; I won't be able to be a part of the solution. Focusing on things you can control is a choice, and we all have it.

Setting unrealistic goals that rely on chance, luck or a miracle will only help set us up for failure and disappointment. Remember, the thoughts we focus on lead to our actions, so by focusing on what we can control, we can take achievable, realistic action.

Imagine the following scene – a true story. A cyclone is overhead, creating winds above 150 kilometres per hour, wreaking havoc across the town, bringing with it a deluge of rain and flying objects. A patient calls the emergency line requesting assistance during this cyclonic event. The patient is alone and stuck: their legs are trapped under a collapsed wall within their home.

You are informed of the case, but what can you do? The weather is not in your control. If you choose to leave the safety of the ambulance station and drive out in the middle of a fierce storm, I'm sure the outcome won't be what you want. Most likely, the vehicle will be damaged by a flying object, flooded by the rain – or worse, you will be injured yourself. If you let what isn't within your control dictate your actions, you'll only set yourself up for failure and increased anxiety.

By accepting that you can't assist this patient in the immediate term, you focus on what you can control. You have the patient's phone number, so you can call them and reassure them, giving medical advice over the phone for them to help themselves. You then wait for the eye of the storm – a short window to rescue the patient.

If you try to achieve your goals by controlling things you can't, you will only increase your anxiety and stress. When you inevitably fail to achieve a goal you were unable to control, your mind will reinforce this failure. You will feel hopeless, or begin to resent others, blaming external factors. Unfortunately, this can lead to chronic mental health issues.

Focus on the Process

Focus on the process, not the outcome. This is where passion comes into play – loving what you do makes the process enjoyable. When paramedics first join, they're excited by the challenge. They enjoy the unexpected nature of the job and the exhilaration that comes with influencing another person's life, especially under pressure.

Somewhere along the way, though, the passion for the job may have given way to the pressure, expectations, desires and fear of failure. Now the paramedic may be working simply to achieve outcomes. Maybe those outcomes aren't patient-related: it could be just to get a paycheque at the end of the week.

You've probably experienced your mind drifting off the task and focusing on potential negative outcomes from time to time. These thoughts make the body feel more tense and anxious. Not only will you not achieve the outcome you wanted, but it will probably be way off target. Remember the 3-to-1 ratio.

Playing golf is a perfect example of this. Golf is all about results, but when you only worry about the results, your anxiety to achieve will affect your performance. The only way to get optimal results is to focus on what you're doing: focus on the process. Following a routine and not being distracted by thinking about an outcome that you cannot control will ultimately give you better results. Golfers focus on walking up to the tee, how they place their hands on the club, how their feet are positioned, how their knees are bent, their breathing and their swing.

If all they were focused on was getting the ball in the hole, they would forget how to hit the ball in the best possible way, using the best process. Focusing on sinking the ball creates pressure, because what's going to happen if they miss? They won't win, and if they don't win, they must be a loser. The key here is to develop a passion for the job and a focus on enjoying it, accepting potential poor outcomes knowing that you did everything within your capability to achieve a positive result.

American college basketball coach John Wooden had the opportunity, as a young player, to shoot the winning free throw. There was only a second left on the clock to win his team the state championship. Everything was on the line, and he missed.

His opponents, catching the basketball on the rebound, scored a three-pointer at the last minute to seal Wooden's team's defeat.

What's extraordinary about this story is that he wasn't disappointed or depressed over missing. He went back into the locker room to find all of his teammates crying and emotional, but he wasn't. He said he wasn't upset because he knew he did everything within his power to get the shot in, but he missed on this occasion. He focused on the process, not the outcome. He did all the hard work, put in the training and effort, everything within his capability, leading up to that shot but missed. He knew within himself that there was nothing more he could have done, so he wasn't upset with the result. He had earned the right to say, shit happens.

Focus on Solutions

Most of us have heard the quote or been told by our boss that we need to be part of the solution, not part of the problem. We've likely frowned or scowled in response, but this statement has a lot of merit when responding to an emergency.

If you feel like you're part of the solution, you've seen yourself as a fixer, not a destroyer. Rather than standing idly by, you helped. By constructing solutions rather than fixating on a situation's problems, you will be more likely to act and have a positive impact. For example, if a patient is stuck under a car, the problem is obvious, but if you focus on the problem – the car is too heavy, they will probably lose their legs and never walk again, they will most likely bleed to death, and so on – there's nothing positive to focus on there.

Instead, if you maintain a solution-focused mindset – thinking about what medication the patient will need, how to cut the car to access the patient and free them from the wreckage, and what resources you will need – you will set clear, concrete, specific, and measurable goals that will create steps towards solving the problem.

Focus on the Task

One of the benefits of being a paramedic is that we're task-oriented when we arrive at an emergency. We have a clear focus on what needs to be done and how to get it done.

It's very typical for paramedics to forget patient names and even what patients look like, but they will never forget the injury or illness the person had. People have walked up to me on the street to thank me for helping them, but I had no idea who they were. If instead they told me, 'I was the guy with the broken leg from a cricket bat,' it would all come back to me.

Paramedics are focused on the task. Completing that task directly addresses the situation and provides a result in stressful, performance-based settings such as medicine. The task-oriented strategy involves taking direct action to alter the situation itself and thus reduce the amount of stress it evokes.

Task-orientedness is a proactive way for the paramedic to reframe the emergency situation they're exposed to. With a task-oriented reframing, the situation no longer evokes a negative response.

The benefit of being task-oriented extends to coping with the traumatic event: blocking out the emotional stress of the situation and focusing on what needs to be done to resolve the issue.

The Power of Routine

Having routines makes things familiar and expected. Paramedics should have a system in place for checking their medical equipment, running tests and conducting training. They should have a process for assessing a patient. The trauma response method MARCH (massive bleeding, airway, respiration, circulation, hypothermia/head) is a routine – a system to follow that ensures focus on limiting errors, and enhances decision-making.

A paramedic has a routine for every patient they attend. For me, it starts with an introduction, and then I feel the patient's radial (wrist) pulse. I then go through a step-by-step systematic assessment. I like to go one step further and use my vehicle and equipment check at the start of each shift as a way to get my mind ready for the day ahead. My morning and evening shift routine prepares my mind: I check whether the ambulance oxygen cylinders are full and the vehicle is stocked correctly. Professional athletes use pre-game rituals and routines all the time to help prepare their mind for a big game or event.

Throughout their training, a paramedic is exposed to scenarios they're likely to face in the real world. The routines they develop through these simulations will prepare them for facing the unexpected and allow them to prepare mentally and visualise the impending emergency.

Patient assessment is one of the most critical parts of the job. The assessment combines a number of important steps: assessing the scene, establishing the main complaint, fixing acute life-threatening conditions, taking a medical history, and doing a physical examination. All paramedics should be using a system-atic, routine approach to patient assessment. Otherwise, you may miss a step that could lead to negative consequences.

In general life, we're all governed by our routines, from brushing our teeth to cooking dinner. When we're stressed, we fall back on these unconscious routines. I, for example, will procras-tinate on my tasks and watch another episode of my favourite show – instead, I should be building better routines.

Know Your Goal

My goal: help people flourish under stress.

Your goal identifies what you want to achieve, which must always be your point of focus. You only feel stress because you have a goal. My wife doesn't get stressed when we watch the State of Origin, but I freak out because my goal is for Queensland to win. For the paramedic, most medical situations will be uncertain, and so while they should obviously try to find out as much information as possible, they shouldn't be distracted from what really matters: saving a life. The mission and the situation lead to a decision. That decision should pursue the goal using all available resources. The paramedic's resolve is what helps the decision-making carry forward into problem-solving.

This idea applies to any goal you might have. For example, I'm travelling to Ecuador soon and hope to climb the mountain Cotopaxi. If this is my goal, then I have to make decisions with this in mind. I might skip having an ice cream for dessert; I'll have to say no to my friends when they want to go out late and drink alcohol, because I need to get up early and go to the gym. All my decisions should be based on achieving the goal, even the smallest of choices.

This also comes back to suffering and having a goal great enough to endure the pain. I have great fear and apprehension about sharing a lot of my personal experiences within this book, but I have to constantly remind myself that I'm doing it for a greater purpose – to help others flourish. This can't be done without making decisions that have potential negative consequences for me.

Stick to the mission, no matter what.

INTERVIEW WITH THE AUTHOR
Why do you always cut people's clothes off?

We don't do it for fun! Cutting off people's clothes is something we have to do for patients with traumatic injuries. Exposing the patient is a critical part of our assessment of someone who has injured themselves, particularly in major traumatic events such as car accidents. We must be able to find and discover any potential wounds or injuries that we would otherwise miss if we left their clothes on. Trust me, I don't want to see your grandpa's crown jewels, but if the situation calls for it, out come the scissors.

For example, a patient who has been shot must be exposed to see if there's an exit wound or where the bullet has caused the damage, and to identify any serious bleeding, fractures or organ damage. The last thing a paramedic wants is to miss a potential life-threatening wound because they're too timid to expose the patient. If you arrive at the emergency department with a clothed trauma patient, the doctor will be more than happy to yell at you for not cutting their clothes off.

Having said that, the paramedic should always show the greatest respect and dignity for the patient throughout the process. It's surprising how quickly people forget all of the fear of and embarrassment about the naked body once they're in a critical condition.

CALL TO ACTION

'It's the dialogue you have with yourself that is very important. When you tend to focus on positive outcomes, you tend to be more successful. Your brain, instead of being focused on – oh my gosh, what happens if this person dies? – it is about generating goal-directed behaviours by focusing on specific steps.' – **Dr Michael Lauria**

Key Takeaways

- Limbic friction is your mind's attempt to pull you into comfort and away from adversity, but without adversity there's no growth.
- The courage circuit reinforces courage and will help you overcome future challenges. Step forward and take action.
- What you focus on, you amplify. Amplify positive action by first focusing on what you can control and letting go of the rest. Athletes do this really well – they focus on the process, not the outcome. Trust that the outcome will take care of itself.
- By focusing your attention on the task, you will feel a part of the solution and do the deeds that need to be done.

Key Tasks

- Reframe your situation by thinking of seven good things about it. Create an alternative perspective.

- What can you do right now to offload your stress? Can you create a checklist or give the task to someone else? If it's appropriate, delegate it to your spouse, colleague or friend.
- What are your routines like? Reflect on the habits you've formed and how they can be improved.
- What is your mission?

11

Resilience

Personal Experience – *The Matrix*

We arrived at the skyscraper expecting to see a body splattered all over the road, but we couldn't find anything. Falling five stories – approximately 22 metres or 75 feet – onto concrete could not bode well for sustaining life. We looked around for the patient, but couldn't find him. People were yelling that he landed in the pool area of one of the ground-floor apartments' private pools. There was a 2.5-metre (8-foot) brick wall around the apartment block; we couldn't find a way over it.

I pulled the ambulance to the front of the building and turned the siren off. We couldn't access the private apartment to treat the patient; it was unoccupied at the time. We had to break in. While we were strategising our next moves, another crew from a different ambulance service arrived. I'd never worked with an interstate service before. Team integration is pivotal when managing a critically ill patient.

The private apartment had its own elevator, which required a keycard to stop at the ground level. We took the stairs down to the apartment. The other crew remained in the elevator as they tried to find the manager or another resident. We discovered that some of the fancier apartments had their own private elevator that acted as the apartment's front door.

I ran down to the fire door entrance to the apartment and kicked down the door, which felt cool, like a Hollywood scene. Most things in Hollywood are fake, but this happened. I stepped through into the apartment to be greeted by shattered glass all over the building, everywhere. The apartment had floor-to-ceiling glass walls overlooking its private pool.

My first thought was that the patient somehow bounced off the ground like a tennis ball and ricocheted, smashing through the panoramic glass into the apartment. Thankfully, I was wrong. Bystanders had arrived before us and they had smashed the glass to be able to get to the outside pool. At that moment, I also realised I probably kicked open an already kicked open door. Again, I wasn't as cool as I thought.

We stepped over the razor-sharp broken glass to find a young male patient lying on his side with his back facing me. Blood was covering the ground. I immediately went to the patient's head to see if he was breathing. As I got a closer look, I saw that the skin had peeled off half of his face, his nose was broken, and his mouth was no longer attached to his jaw. The patient had an obvious Le Fort fracture, which is a fracture to the midface that involves the separation of all or a portion of the midface from the skull base. He looked like Two-Face from *Batman*.

As my partner exposed the patient by cutting off his clothes, we found that his pelvis was shattered, and multiple fractures to his hips were causing major internal bleeding. He also had open fractures in both legs. I could see the white polished-looking bones in his legs pointing out, staring back at me.

The patient needed all hands on deck, and we needed to quickly establish a working relationship with the interstate ambulance service. There was no time for introductions. I took management of the airway, which meant I was in the best position to manage the scene, because it gave me a complete view of the patient and the scene.

The equipment bags placed next to me belonged to the interstate services, not us. It was different equipment from what I was used to, but it was all I had at that moment. I asked the other paramedic to set up the suction so I could clear the airway. Right then, the patient projectile-vomited copious amounts of blood. The fractures to his face were filling his stomach with blood. I'd never seen someone vomit so much blood before. It was imperative that I gain control of the airway or the patient would stop breathing.

My paramedic partner was able to gain IV access, a life-saving procedure since we could now administer blood through the line to replace the ridiculous amounts of blood he had already lost. This IV was precious because we weren't able to find another vein, despite multiple attempts from highly skilled paramedics. We doubled down on securing the IV to the patient so it couldn't accidentally be pulled out (it's happened before).

The patient's jaw and face were coming apart, So I tried to grab hold of his mouth and keep his airway open for air to move in and out. It was crucial that I try to suck out as much blood from his airway as possible. Suction again, unblock the suction, then suction again and again was the procedure. He continued to vomit, projecting more and more blood across the floor and onto my legs. It felt like someone was pointing a hose at me, turning the tap on and off, but instead of water pouring out, it was blood.

We all jolted in surprise when the patient replied to me calling his name. I was looking for a response, pushing on his fingernails and yelling his name but I expected him to be unconscious. His words were tangled together like a drunk's, but he had enough brain function to speak through the confusion. He was in a state of stupor – needing vigorous and repeated stimuli to be stirred. If left alone, he would immediately lapse into coldness.

We wanted to sedate the patient so we could perform a procedure called rapid sequence intubation, an airway-management technique that involves administering drugs to paralyse the patient and make them unconscious as we take control of their airway. Rapid sequence intubation comes at great risk, because we are essentially choosing to stop the patient's breathing. If we failed to insert the airway tube, or otherwise breathe for him, he would die.

To perform this procedure in the out-of-hospital environment – out on the streets, not in the hospital – we required a doctor's approval. Unfortunately, the doctor didn't approve the procedure because the patient was still in a state of stupor, somewhat conscious but obtunded (out of it), but most importantly he was able to maintain his own breathing despite all the trauma. We were going to have to manage the airway as best we could all the way to the hospital.

We extricated the patient and loaded him into the back of the ambulance and had a brief moment to talk to his friends. They told us he'd taken some illicit drugs just after watching the latest instalment of *The Matrix*. The patient's friends watched him as he thought he could fly like Mr Anderson. It turns out that the Matrix isn't real – and, suffice to say, don't try illicit drugs.

I'd been a qualified paramedic for more than 10 years by then. Over that time, I'd overcome much worse and felt confident in my ability to lead. I'd grown from previous traumatic events leading up to this situation. The trauma of the patient, despite being grossly disturbing, didn't affect me. In fact, I had a runner's high following the case, knowing we had saved the patient's life. I had the resilience to protect myself against the trauma. I went home that night and fell straight to sleep.

Bouncing Back

Resilience is the ability to overcome adverse events. It has been defined as 'a dynamic process encompassing positive adaptation within the context of significant adversity'.

The nature of being human suggests that at some stage during our life, we will experience a traumatic event. This will require us to be resilient. We need to be able to cope with unexpected challenges and harness our inner strength to rebound from setbacks. If we lack resilience, we may dwell on problems, become overwhelmed, feel victimised or even turn to unhealthy coping mechanisms, such as substance abuse.

If an individual's core beliefs are challenged, an experience is considered traumatic. In this case, resilience is necessary to overcome the imbalance between our beliefs and what we have witnessed. This is why people who have high self-efficacy tend to have higher resilience: their belief in their ability to overcome difficult challenges helps them cope with the situation. In some cases a highly resilient person will savour the struggle.

Researchers at the University of Aberdeen have developed a series of behavioural marker systems for helicopter crews based on research into non-technical skills (human factors) used for offshore transport, and search and rescue. The systems are called Helicopter Non-technical Skills or HeliNOTS for short.

The HeliNOTS organisation has completed a large amount of research on cognitive readiness, specifically for helicopter search and rescue. After surveying several experienced clinicians, they were able to define resilience as the ability to maintain performance and follow standard operating procedures despite exposure to highly stressful circumstances. In other words, resilience involves being able to effectively manage our reactions to stress.

HeliNOTS identified positive and negative markers for maintaining resilience. These are behaviours that contribute to superior or substandard performance. People who maintain resilience and effectively manage their reactions to unforeseen or stressful circumstances possess the positive behavioural markers.

Review the markers below and see if you can identify any in yourself.

Positive behavioural markers	Negative behavioural markers
• Stays composed when surprised or startled	• Appears stressed and/or distressed when surprised or startled
• Can quickly respond to unexpected situations by adapting, changing tasks, and maintaining flexibility	• Notices changes in the rescue situation slowly, and reacts slowly too

Positive behavioural markers	Negative behavioural markers
• Responds in a steady, effective way when the required task changes suddenly	• Responds to unfamiliar or intense rescues with hurried, disordered or inappropriate actions
• Stays focused and carries on with what's needed despite adverse conditions	• Responds in a negative, defeatist way to bad conditions
• Responds rapidly to new information by changing priorities for rescue	• Carries on with original task even when new information arises

Build Your Shield

The most comprehensive text I've read about resilience is *The Resilience Shield* by Dr Dan Pronk, Ben Pronk DSC and Tim Curtis. They articulated clearly that resilience is dynamic, multifactorial and modifiable. If you identified some negative behavioural markers just now, then the Resilience Shield will help you build your armour against adversity.

Pronk, Pronk and Curtis grouped multiple dimensions of resilience into layers of a shield – the more layers, the stronger your shield and the better you'll bounce back from hardship. They give the example of a woven rug to demonstrate the interconnectedness of the layers in the shield: the tighter the weave, the stronger the carpet.

The six layers of their shield are innate (genetics), mind (psychological and spiritual factors), body (physiological factors), social (support from others), professional (vocational factors) and adaptation (transferability). They also identified two important things that we know for certain regarding resilience: 'Firstly, for resilience to exist, there needs to be some form of stress. And secondly, you need to come out the other side of the stress event in one piece.' Luckily, you're reading a book about dealing with stress.

The reason the Resilience Shield model is more beneficial than others is because it takes a holistic approach. It identifies that resilience has a range of contributing elements. In this model, the layers of the shield interact with each other to form resilience. It's putting everything together that builds your resistance to stress – to bend but not break, to flourish through stress.

Pronk, Pronk and Curtis concluded that the mind overwhelmingly has the greatest impact on resilience. In this book I've focused heavily on the mind and developing psychological tools to use in times of stress, and we've naturally covered a lot of topics that help build resilience. Without even knowing it, you've built up your resilience by coming this far. There are, however, some areas that we haven't covered.

Social Engagement

To flourish in life we must have a strong social network and a high degree of engagement. Researchers report that social support greatly improves resilience to trauma. Social support has been defined as 'support accessible to an individual through social ties to other individuals, groups, and the larger community'.

Sociologist and psychologist Dr Corey Keyes, who we met earlier as the creator of the Mental Health Continuum Short Form, has identified that social involvement is critical to flourishing in life. He states that people who flourish have especially good social wellbeing. Such people are part of their community and derive comfort from it. They have a sense of belonging and feel valued by those around them. And finally, flourishing people are socially tolerant, accepting those around them, and allowing them to express their opinion, whether they agree with it or not. (Tolerance is putting up with things that annoy you, like having to watch *Bluey* with the kids rather than football. It only rubs salt in the wound knowing that Bluey's dad is a far better dad than I am. But they're my kids so I accept it.)

Humans who flourish believe not only in self-actualisation, but also, as Keyes puts it, in social actualisation. He describes social actualisation as society's potential for growth, development and change. Flourishing people see the value in doing something bigger than themselves, in helping others rather than themselves. They understand that it's better to help people rather than pursue selfish gain and self-promotion.

Resilient people can use a strong social network as part of their adaptive coping mechanism when confronted with trauma. When dealing with stressful situations, someone with social support is less likely to engage in risk-taking or reflecting negatively on the situation, and more likely to face the trauma. They know that despite the difficulties, the people around them will still love them for who they are and they are not alone.

Social isolation has been strongly associated with depression. It can result in poor physical health and exaggerated responses to pressure. American adventurer Christopher McCandless one day decided to cut up his ID and credit cards and head into the Alaskan wilderness alone. You may know the story from the film *Into the Wild*. He found an abandoned bus and lived completely alone and isolated for 113 days before he died of starvation. McCandless had a long time to think and contemplate before his death and highlighted the following paragraph from Boris Pasternak's 1957 book *Dr Zhivago*, perhaps illustrating what he learned:

> And so it turned out that only a life similar to the life of those around us, merging with it without a ripple, is genuine life, and that an unshared happiness is not happiness . . . And this was most vexing of all.

The film ends with Chris annotating within the book: 'Happiness is only real when shared.' Despite feeling a great sense of connected-ness to the earth, away from unwanted distractions and the stress of the daily living in a modern society, he came to the realisation that he needed social connectedness to be happy.

As we discussed when talking about flourishing, psychologist Dr Barbara Fredrickson wrote an article with Lahnna Catalino called 'A Tuesday in the life of a flourisher'. All the activities they identified as improving positive mental health are usually done socially – helping, playing, interacting, learning and spiritual activity. By far the most beneficial activity was helping others.

When you're going through something tough and you're struggling to get through it, turn to your social network for help. Let them in and watch them help you build your resilience. I encourage everyone to join a local sporting club or book club, or create a games night – any activity that you enjoy. Fifty year olds who participate in Masters sporting activities don't do it in pursuit of Olympic glory, but for the social aspects: feeling part of a group, feeling needed and cared for.

Journalling

The first time I realised the power of journalling was when I heard the story of Shaka Senghor. In 2010, Senghor was released from prison after serving a 19-year sentence for second-degree murder that included seven years in solitary. While in prison, Senghor used reading and writing as inspiration for self-reflection, coming to terms with the past, coping with the present and planning his future.

In his memoir, *Writing My Wrongs*, he recalls the moment he fired the gun killing his victim: 'I didn't know where the shots I fired had landed. But something in my soul told me that a terrible thing had happened. In that moment, I knew the guy had died. I had shot several people before, but only to scare them off. This time was different; this time, I had shot to kill.'

During his time in prison he became terrified by the depth of his own negative thoughts. Solitary confinement made him feel disconnected from the deepest part of his own psyche. He was spiralling out of control mentally, riddled with guilt, shame and unworthiness. This led to suicidal ideation, but he hid his shame by expressing it in other forms, such as anger and rage.

Every day challenged his humanity. He couldn't escape the thoughts and regrets that had plagued him since committing his crime. In a rare moment of calm he sat back and listened to the chaos around him and, feeling like he had nowhere to turn, started keeping a journal.

He wrote about his thoughts and feelings. Surprisingly, what had the greatest impact for him was when reading back what he had written a few days earlier. It profoundly disturbed him.

He started to recognise that self-examination through journalling was changing his mental state. Within the lines of his notepad, he got in touch with a part of himself that no longer felt fear and was able to feel compassion. For the first time, he began to recognise his true self.

He continued to journal, and with each day that passed he felt himself growing stronger. Through journalling, he realised that his actions were a result of years of child abuse, drug use and exposure to violence. He took ownership for his actions and eventually had the courage to write a letter to the person he'd killed.

Now he works to help others overcome their past through hope and forgiveness. Through no longer defining himself by his past, he became a voice for second chances. All thanks to the power of journalling and writing.

Keeping a journal, writing down his thoughts and feelings changed Senghor's trajectory. He had shot someone dead but could still find a way to flourish, despite all of his mistakes and fears. No matter what you've done, you can come through it.

Journalling is a powerful tool that can help you get through some of your more difficult thoughts. One of the benefits of journalling is that you are taking your thoughts and storing them on paper instead of in your brain. Once you realise that the thought is stored forever on paper, you no longer have a need for it to stay in your mind.

We think in narrative, by telling ourselves stories. It's how we speak to other people and how we conceptualise the world. Writing is the greatest form of thinking; it makes us think in a deeper and more thoughtful way. That's why journalling can help get you through some of your deeper secrets.

Exercise

Unfortunately, the general decline in physical activity is resulting in huge increases in physical disability and disease, and a rising number of cases of mental ill health. Almost 60 per cent of the Western world's adult population is classified as overweight, and 10 per cent have type 2 diabetes, which can be largely prevented through diet and exercise.

A growing body of research suggests that exercise improves not only our physiological health, but our psychological wellbeing as well. A lot of the high-performing people I've had the privilege of speaking to on my podcast all focused heavily on exercise. Many of them not only exercised, but participated in outdoor activities for enjoyment or fun that provided a form of cardiovascular training. Researchers in Japan have found that as little as 20–30 minutes' daily exposure to nature can significantly reduce cortisol (stress hormone) levels.

For 99 per cent of human history, we've lived off the land and looked to nature not only for basic survival needs and health, but also for pleasure and physical activity. If you put the entire human existence into 24 hours, then only in the last few seconds have humans not had enough exercise.

I think it's obvious why it's important for paramedics and other emergency service workers to maintain a certain level of physical fitness to perform their job. Being physically fit and healthy will provide endurance and help them respond to the physical demands of certain cases, from lifting patients to carrying equipment or hiking up a walking trail. I've heard of horror stories of paramedics standing on a patient's chest, using their boot to perform compressions instead of their hand because they were too obese to kneel.

We've already talked about the importance of controlling heart rate to maintain an optimal range of alertness and cognitive readiness (see Chapters 7 and 8). If a paramedic who's physically unfit arrives at a scene after walking up three flights of stairs carrying their medical equipment, their heart rate will already be nearing the optimal range and getting closer to Condition Black. This is before adding any other external pressure of having to perform life-saving interventions and prevent death. Topping up their lack of physical fitness with the pressure of the job only exacerbates the situation. It's very difficult to possess poise when you're hyperventilating because you're unfit.

What I want to focus on here are the mental benefits of exercise, and how it can lead to better decision-making. The effects of exercise on our physical body are obvious: our muscles get bigger and our lung capacity increases. What's more fascinating, though, is how it improves brain function.

A breakthrough study completed by US neuroscientist Carl Cotman discovered that when we exercise, there is a surge in brain-derived neurotrophic factor (BDNF) in the brain. BDNF, which has been described as fertiliser for our brains, is a protein that nourishes neurons (in this case, brain cells) and prevents them from dying, and even triggers the growth of brand-new neurons. This is important because the survival and growth of brain neurons leads to learning.

Research has established that people learn vocabulary words 20 per cent faster following a healthy amount of exercise than before exercise, and that this rate of learning correlates directly with levels of BDNF.

Drs John Ratey and Eric Hagerman, in their book *Spark: The Revolutionary New Science of Exercise and the Brain*, say that exercise improves learning on three levels:

1. mindset – improving alertness, attention and motivation
2. encouraging nerve cells to bind together to log new information
3. the development of new nerve cells from stem cells in the part of the brain called the hippocampus.

Ratey and Hagerman also highlight the importance of stress and how challenges allow us to strive, grow and learn – as long as the stress is not too severe and the neurons are given time to recover. The brain activity as a result of exercise creates molecules that can damage cells, but under normal circumstances, the neurons begin to repair themselves, which leaves them stronger and better prepared for future challenges.

It's like the tree that goes through a storm after being torn apart and damaged in a cyclone; if it's given time, the tree will grow back stronger and be better prepared for the next storm. This is what happens to our brain cells when they are placed under stress, including the stress exercise causes in the brain.

I personally enjoy going for hikes, getting out in the elements, seeing a bit of nature and walking through a few annoying spider webs. I love sailing and being on the water. I can't really describe kicking back on a sailboat as exercise, but it's great for clearing the mind. When I've been exposed to a particularly stressful or traumatic case, I also use exercise as a way of reducing the built-up tension and agitation in my body.

Meditation

Recent research has proven that resilience is more pronounced in people who meditate. According to Dr Richard Davidson, a mind-fulness researcher, meditation allows us to experience our negative emotions as they arise, and then let them go. Meditation reduces our tendency to ruminate (stew) on our negative emotions, and this has been associated with positive changes in the brain. 'When adversity happens,' Davidson says, 'it's appropriate and adaptive to experience whatever negative emotions may arise, but then to let them go when they're no longer useful. Meditation can help to facilitate that.'

By practising mindfulness and awareness through meditation, we can move beyond our daily-grind patterns of behaviour and take a pause to listen to our thoughts and understand our distractions. Mindfulness involves training our mind to come back to the present and stop perpetual self-indulgence or pity.

It is human to be distracted and get caught up in our own self-negative talk. Taking time out of our day to practise meditation helps us appreciate what we have. It gives us an opportunity to recognise our thoughts without judgement and without reacting to them. A lot of the fundamental teachings in this book rely upon recognising your own behaviour. Suppose you can't recognise it; how will you ever be able to change it? Meditation really helps build resilience by allowing us to let go of whatever tension or feelings we're caught up in.

Another interesting form of meditation is yoga nidra, which means yogic sleep. It tries to place the body in the moment between consciousness and sleep. Recent research has shown that its benefits are quite profound. It promotes the parasympathetic nervous system, putting us in a state of rest and digest. A study in Denmark revealed that 10–30 minutes of this practice restored levels of dopamine within the basal ganglia. This part of the brain controls behaviours and emotions, and also – via its connection with the cerebral cortex, our 'rational brain' – helps us make decisions. Yoga nidra can thus reset the brain, helping us get ready to go back into action.

Dr Andrew Huberman explains that as most people are too often on high alert and under stress, yoga nidra could help them return their body to homeostasis, a state of balance, after a stressful day. It helps the body go into deep relaxation. Huberman also recognises that people who work in high-risk, high-consequence environments, such as emergency workers, find it difficult to meditate because we are always in a state of high situational awareness. They want to know what's going on in their environment, which makes meditating difficult.

The power of yoga nidra is that you are in control; you are teaching your body to go into deep relaxation deliberately. You are using your body to control your mind. Another significant aspect of yoga nidra is that it helps people fall to sleep or stay in a deeper state of sleep. It helps us get better at sleeping.

Sleep

You can die from the lack of sleep faster than from a lack of food.

Lieutenant Colonel Dave Grossman makes this point quite emphatically by condensing human history into 24 hours (as we did earlier with exercise). Until the last 15 minutes we were hunter-gatherers, he says, and until the last five seconds we've had enough sleep. In those last five seconds came electricity and television and video games and the internet, all those distractions that prevent us from getting enough sleep. This lack of sleep affects a range of brain functions, including judgement, information processing, motivation, vigilance and reaction time – all important aspects of performing a task under pressure.

Sleep contributes to the restoration of vital body functions, so not getting enough sleep increases the level of stress hormones, not allowing the body to replenish. Poor sleep is reported by 40 per cent of the population; I shudder to think what the percentage for paramedics would be.

I'm no sleep expert, and I won't delve into the science of sleep, but it's an essential aspect of any discussion of the paramedic mindset. Lack of sleep will significantly affect performance, especially under pressure. You won't be able to possess poise if you don't have enough sleep.

Sleep dramatically affects our resilience. Dr Dan Pronk,

co-author of *The Resilience Shield*, writes that sleep is exponentially more important than other aspects of our physical health, like diet, exercise and body mass index.

Improving your sleep will give you better cognitive awareness and function, which in turn puts you in a better position to face uncertain circumstances and stress. Facing stress when your decision-making is impaired and you're unable to make logical arguments puts you in a place of vulnerability. With a lack of sleep, we find it harder to interpret others' emotions and have empathy; we're more likely to argue than find solutions.

Get enough sleep!

Personal Experience – Your Best is Not Always Enough

It was the early hours of the morning, still dark when I was sent to a high-speed car crash. I could tell immediately from the tone of voice used by the call taker that it was a big one.

Driving along in the dark with no one else on the road, knowing you are creeping closer every second to trauma and chaos, is like the moments before an athlete runs onto the field or springs out of the starting blocks. There's an unknown future ahead of you and a sense of great anticipation and apprehension. I still remember watching the blue and red lights reflect off the damp road and nearby buildings as I tried to fit my fingers into my blue gloves and take off my seatbelt to put on my high-visibility jacket, hoping my partner wouldn't crash as I did it.

The engine was screaming as we revved up the hill. We could see a crowd of people gathered around a wrecked car wrapped around a street-light pole, the front of the vehicle kissing the back. I jumped out of the door, took a deep breath, then slid open the side of the ambulance to grab my bags, taking a short pause before turning and entering the carnage.

I was instantly met by a bystander and crying loved ones. They led me to the first patient, who had been ejected from the vehicle and was lying in the gutter unconscious, not responding but with a pulse.

The patient had significant head, abdomen and pelvic injuries. It was difficult to see due to the lack of lighting; but it was obvious that time was critical if this patient was going to survive.

We began treating him, stopping any life-threatening bleeding, cutting his clothes off, straightening his broken legs with no thought of his pain. IV access was crucial if we were to administer life-saving drugs. My partner didn't hesitate. It was dark, with flashing lights, fearful bystanders, screaming noises and a rapidly dying patient in front of him, but he nailed it first go.

I was at the head and started to do a complete assessment after securing his airway. I noticed that he was suffering from a tension pneumothorax (a collapsed lung). At this time paramedics had the authority to stick a large needle into the patient's chest, to decompress the build-up of air in his lung cavity, but I needed approval from a doctor to perform it if the patient still had a heartbeat.

I rang the doctor and put him on speakerphone as I tried to place a cervical collar around the patient's neck, suspecting a spinal injury, then moved on to putting on a pelvic binder (a tight and wide belt around his hips to help control internal pelvic bleeding).

I had to sell the patient's symptoms to the doctor as if I were the best second-hand car salesman in Australia. Asking permission to perform a procedure that, done incorrectly, could have devastating effects is always difficult over the phone. The doctor needs to trust me and I need to paint a good picture of the patient's condition. I had to give the best elevator pitch I could, because the patient's life depended on it.

I sold it the best I could, but the doctor wasn't convinced and said no. I couldn't believe it. He was asking more questions to fill in any gaps I may have missed, but I had to throw the phone in my front shirt pocket as the patient groaned then went into a seizure. We started to treat him for the seizure. We managed to stop it after a few minutes, but the patient's heart stopped with it.

Before beginning CPR, I pulled the phone out of my pocket and said, 'The patient is now in cardiac arrest and I'm going to decompress,' then hung up the phone. I pulled the needle out of my medical kit, found the correct location on the patient's chest, looked at my partner as our eyes fixed as if to say, 'Are we really doing this?' His nod of approval was enough, and I got him to check where I wanted to stab the patient in the chest. It was the first time I'd performed the procedure on a real patient.

The needle went in and the sound of the released air was the most beautiful thing I'd ever heard. We were working extremely hard and fast, doing our utmost to save the patient's life. There was blood every-where. Sweat was pouring off my forehead. I tried to wipe it off, only to cover my head with blood, forgetting I had gloves on.

The hospital was a 20-minute drive away. We were going lights and sirens all the way, with a police officer driving, but it didn't help. I called the time of death just as the ambulance was being reversed into the hospital. Not being able to save a patient and having them die in front of you is a tremendously tear-jerking situation.

The screams echoing through the hospital hallways when the patient's daughter found out her father had just died are still with me today. After the case, I kept thinking of things we could have done differently. I thought that maybe my actions caused the patient to die. That night I was second-guessing everything I did and going through an endless cycle of 'what if'.

I could feel friction building up inside me, knowing my resilience was being tested. I knew this image would be with me for the rest of my life, but I wasn't sure if I would be able to bounce back after witnessing such suffering and being unable to save the man's life. Despite my best efforts in the moment, the patient still died. 'Was I enough?' became a question I asked myself.

Then I spoke to Gavin Cousens, my mentor at the time, who gave me invaluable advice: we can only control what we can control. It wasn't in my control that the patient crashed their car because they were drink-driving and speeding. It wasn't in my control that the patient wasn't wearing a seatbelt. There was no way I could have prevented his injuries from occurring. What I could and did do was to control the situation I was given.

We can't save them all, and learning this was a difficult reality to accept at the time.

Post-traumatic Growth

Psychologists have learned that negative experiences can spur positive change, including recognition of personal strength, a greater appreciation for life and the exploration of new possibilities.

The concept of post-traumatic growth was developed by psychologists Richard Tedeschi and Lawrence Calhoun, who stated that people who endure psychological struggle following adversity could often experience positive growth afterwards. Post-traumatic growth and resilience can often be confused with each other. Resilience is the ability to bounce back. Post-traumatic growth, however, only occurs when someone has difficulty bouncing back and the traumatic event challenges their belief system, and as a result they endure some sort of psychological struggle.

If we're already resilient when we experience trauma, Tedeschi says, we can't undergo post-traumatic growth because the traumatic event doesn't shake our belief system and send us in search of a new one. Despite the misery of a life-threatening, grotesque medical emergency, most paramedics develop healthy post-traumatic growth in its aftermath. They cultivate inner strength through the knowledge that they've overcome tremendous hardship. In fact, post-traumatic growth results in a widened sense of wisdom about the world, as you've come through something significant and survived.

To determine the extent of growth after trauma, Tedeschi and Calhoun developed a self-report scale called the Post-Traumatic Growth Inventory. Those completing the scale give responses in five areas:

1. appreciation of life
2. relationships with others
3. new possibilities in life
4. personal strength
5. spiritual change.

Positive responses in this area mean you have an opportunity to grow and become resilient after a traumatic experience. It's not all doom and gloom.

POISE CYCLE

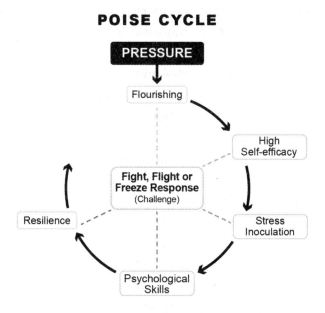

Figure 15. Psychological skills can help build resilience and promote post-traumatic growth to support poise. With resilience you can cope with not only traumatic events but any event that's perceived as negative. Overcoming adversity is a key component of poise.

INTERVIEW WITH THE AUTHOR
What's the most embarrassing thing you've seen?

A lot of people consider things paramedics see as embarrassing, but in reality, a lot of what we see is normal human behaviour. Humans are just really good at hiding it from each other. We all go through embarrassing moments in life that we try to hide from others, not realising that the person we're hiding it from has probably experienced something very similar.

One of the most disturbing things I've had to treat was a patient who had snapped his penis (penile fracture). It hurts me just saying it now. It occurs when the muscular fibres of the penis rupture.

We arrived on scene to find the patient walking around the bedroom holding his penis, which was bent in half like a broken arm with blood pouring out of it. He told us that he was engaged in sexual intercourse at the time of the incident and, to make it worse, it was with his ex-wife. It was the first time since the divorce.

Despite this, I think the ex-wife was more embarrassed than the patient because she was good friends with one of our colleagues. Luckily, we are bound by confidentiality.

CALL TO ACTION

'I want people to know that if you're going through trauma, if you act, you'll come out of it. In the end, you will grow from it, and be better than you were before the impairment happened.' – **Daniel Sundahl, firefighter, paramedic and artist**

Key Takeaways

- There are a number of definitions for resilience, but essentially it's the ability to bounce back from adversity. When you are knocked down, you can get back up and keep going without any injuries from the fall.
- Resilience is dynamic, multifactorial and modifiable.
- Social support is not only important for resilience but also plays a key role in flourishing.

Key Tasks

- Identify the behavioural markers that are triggered when you're becoming overwhelmed.
- How well are you integrated into your community? Are you a member of any social clubs? If not, what club have you been

thinking about joining for years but never taken that step forward to join? Do it now.

- Keep a journal. There are many ways to journal. Experiment with different techniques and find the one that suits you.
- Take the Resilience Shield survey online and read the book *The Resilience Shield*. I cannot recommend it highly enough.

12

Preventing Predictable Surprises

Personal Experience – Roo Run

'You need to do a "roo run",' came a voice blaring over the radio. At first I didn't know what that meant. Did I have to get out of the ambulance and jump around like a kangaroo or try to outrun a kangaroo? Or maybe I had to box one of them? Instead of asking these questions over the radio, I made the wise choice to ring them instead.

I discovered that it had nothing to do with hopping around. The Royal Flying Doctor Service (RFDS) pilot had requested that I clear the remote grass runway of kangaroos. There was no policy or guideline for this, just a verbal instruction that it was something we did.

The first time I did it, I loved it. Flicking on the blue and red lights I roared down the airstrip, dodging a hundred kangaroos as they hopped frantically around me. Turning the vehicle around at the end to come back was the best part. By now the runway was free of the bouncing missiles. Time to see how fast the ambulance could go.

A roo run made sense; the last thing you would want is an RFDS plane crashing because kangaroos managed to jump over the so-called kangaroo-proof fence. It was always a good sight to see the plane land, because you knew they were about to take your patient and you could go back to bed. But one incident occurred that made me stay wide awake for several hours afterward.

By now, I'd done the 'procedure' multiple times and I recognised its value. I'd almost crashed into more than 60 kangaroos the night before – they were everywhere. As usual, after receiving the usual call from the communications centre requesting a roo run, I started to drive forward onto the runway. It had become a normal procedure and a lot of the initial enjoyment had gone; it was simply part of the job now.

I hadn't slept in more than 30 hours, so I was looking forward to getting the job done. I radioed the communications centre informing them that I was entering the runway and commencing my roo run. 'Copy that, proceed' was the message in reply. I was staring down the kilometre-long runway, slowly pulling forward, when suddenly the plane rocketed over the top of me, its wheels right before my eyes. I thought it was the end – the RFDS plane was about to crash straight into me.

Some news headline that would have made: 'Four Dead, RFDS Plane and Ambulance Engulfed in Flames'.

I was shaking as the plane door opened. I wasn't sure if my tremors were from the adrenaline rush of the near miss or because I thought the pilot was going to kill me. Either way, it was bad. First the nurse walked down the small steps of the plane, then the pilot. They were smiling and happy to see me, saying the general greetings. They had no idea how close we were to crashing. They didn't see me. I couldn't believe it; the blue and red flashy lights are very visible at night-time, or so I thought.

I later spoke to my boss and a few other experienced paramedics about my death-defying incident. To my astonishment, none of them seemed concerned. It had happened before and it was almost accepted. It had become normalised.

The greatest tragedy, though, is when we don't reflect on and learn from our mistakes, but instead repeat them. When someone else has already paid the price of a near miss, injury or death, we must learn from it so that it doesn't happen again. We must archive and review disasters. In this circumstance, there was a history of near misses but no tragedy, therefore we hadn't properly learned from the shortcuts taken when conducting roo runs. I needed to break this cycle or have it end in catastrophe.

When Wrong Feels Right

I first learned about the normalisation of deviance from retired astronaut Mike Mullane. According to him, normalisation of deviance is getting away with short-cutting safety practices until that 'deviance' becomes your 'normal'. These practices not only become your normal, but you are oblivious to the fact that they happened. We're generally driven into these shortcuts because of the pressures on us.

When pressure causes us to take shortcuts from best practice, there's usually no disaster – we get away with it. This is called false feedback. The favourable outcome of the shortcut provides us with validation that we can 'manage' a risk we previously defined as 'absolute'. The absence of something bad happening suggests to us that the risk of doing it is manageable.

Paramedicine, and life, involves decision-making amidst complexity and uncertainty; there is a great risk of deviance in practice. In fact, a large number of medical guidelines and protocols have been written in blood – after disaster and tragedy – the lessons learned from death. Those lessons are written into the guidelines.

Normalisation of deviance was coined by American sociologist Diane Vaughan when reviewing the Space Shuttle *Challenger* disaster. In 1986, the *Challenger*'s right-hand solid rocket booster exploded into a thousand tiny pieces 73 seconds after launch, killing all seven astronauts on board, including the first ever civilian space traveller, school teacher Christa McAuliffe.

The *New York Times* headline was: 'The Shuttle Explodes, Crew and High-School Teacher Are Killed 73 Seconds After Liftoff'.

Thousands watched as a rain of debris plummeted to earth, and Christa's parents were caught on camera as they witnessed their daughter's death.

Vaughan noted that the root cause of the *Challenger* disaster was related to the repeated choice of NASA officials to fly the space shuttle despite a dangerous and obvious design flaw with the O-rings and circular gaskets that sealed the rocket boosters. The tragedy was a predictable surprise, a disaster that shouldn't have been surprising when it occurred.

The solid rocket fuel boosters had to be manufactured in separate parts because they were 45 metres (150 feet) tall. The four segments were put together with fireproof putty before being bolted together. When the rockets were lit, they burned at about 2760 degrees Celsius and at a pressure of 1000 pounds per square inch. The steel that made the shell of the rockets melted at around 2760 degrees Celsius, so it could never touch the fire it contained.

They coated the interior with insulating material to prevent this from happening, but the obvious weak point of the design was where the segments were bolted together, which was a path for the pressure to escape. To prevent this, they engineered an O-ring to seal the gap. Two sets of O-rings ran across the entire diameter of the rocket shell to form a seal preventing any flames from touching the steel. At the *Challenger* launch, the O-rings failed, causing the catastrophic explosion.

The *Challenger* mission was the 25th mission of the space shuttle fleet. No previous disaster had ever occurred, but the design flaw of the O-rings was known. NASA was able to recover the previous 24 solid rocket boosters, which had parachuted into the ocean after separating from the space shuttle. Of the recovered rockets, 12 of 24 revealed hot-gas O-ring erosion and damage. They were being touched by fire. In fact, the first occurrence of damage was from the second ever flight.

The NASA engineers documented their findings and concerns.

Six months before the *Challenger* disaster, one wrote: 'It is my honest and very real fear that if we do not take immediate action to dedicate a team to solve the O-ring problem having the number one priority, then we stand in jeopardy of losing a flight, and all the launch pad facilities.'

In fact, the NASA policy if the O-rings showed damage was to give a criticality category of 1, meaning that, if there was any risk of damage, NASA must ground the fleet and stop any launches. So why didn't they stop?

NASA performed ground-level testing on the O-rings and no damage was ever found, giving them a false sense of security. In addition, despite having damage on 12 previous missions, none of those missions had ever ended in disaster. This rationalised the belief that a little bit of damage was acceptable. They created their own belief system. Ultimately, though, it was the pressure to continue the program that made the engineers find shortcuts.

NASA was under a huge amount of political pressure, spending billions of dollars, and not being able to meet its own promises of making space travel as easy as commercial airliners was unthinkable. It had declared that the space shuttles had aircraft-like qualities of safety, maintainability and reliability. This overwhelming pressure led to further rationalisation. People wouldn't speak up out of fear of failure. It was a pressure-driven predictable surprise.

This divergence occurs when people within an organisation become so inured to deviating from standard practice that it doesn't feel wrong anymore. In other words, the unacceptable becomes acceptable. Wrong feels right and you don't even know it.

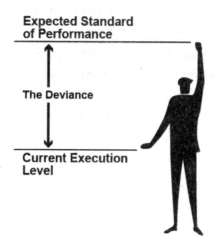

**Expected Standard
of Performance**

The Deviance

**Current Execution
Level**

Figure 16. Normalisation of deviance refers to taking shortcuts to make the unacceptable acceptable. Unfortunately, the deviance from the expected standard of performance creates dangerously high-risk situations.

The Disaster Process

Here's a typical process for normalisation of deviance, using the example of drug doses:

- When placed under pressure, the human desire to take shortcuts is activated by our fight, flight, or freeze response.
- Negative self-talk says, 'I need to take a shortcut because I cannot meet the standard.'
- The mind then tries to rationalise the shortcut: 'If I follow the drug protocols, the procedure will take too long, and I don't have time to waste. So I'd better not follow the protocol.'
- You take the shortcut. Guess what happens?
- Nothing. There are no bad consequences. You are successful; the shortcut worked despite you giving the incorrect drug dose.

- This reinforces your decision to take the shortcut again. 'I was right,' you think.
- The next time you find yourself in the same circumstances, you're tempted to do the same thing again because there were no consequences. You tell yourself, 'It worked before, so it will work again.'
- You follow this loop enough times that the shortcut has now become the norm. **The shortcut is your protocol.**

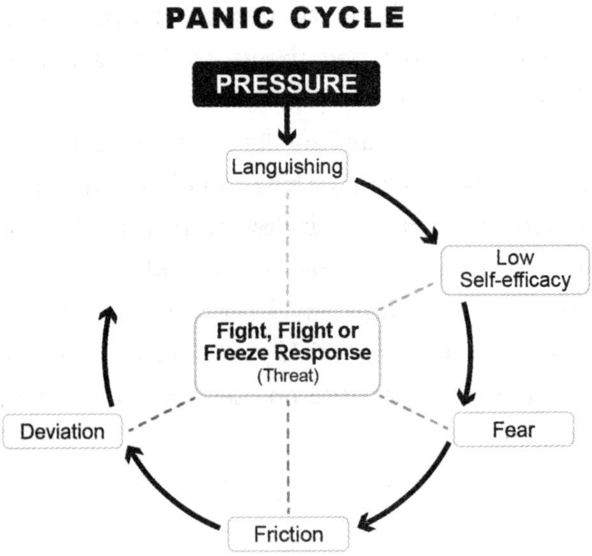

PANIC CYCLE

Figure 17. In the panic cycle, taking shortcuts under pressure leads to deviation from the norm. Over time, the deviation becomes the new norm. This sets us up for high-risk situations and, ultimately, a reduced standard of performance, leading to poor and even dangerous outcomes.

Predictable Surprises

Predictable surprises are the disasters we should have seen coming, any circumstance or disaster that could have been avoided.

The surprise has been bottled up through the normalisation of deviance.

Predictable surprises require a sacrifice in the short term to achieve the greater goal and prevent disaster. Make it a priority to prevent predictable surprises, and do not remain oblivious – ignorance is not bliss.

Hurricane Katrina is a perfect example of a predictable surprise. A large review completed after the major natural disaster concluded that the threats posed by the hurricane, and the likely aftermath, were all well known and unsurprising to most who'd thought about the hurricane threat to New Orleans. In other words, the outcome was expected.

If you're a paramedic and you know a hurricane is on the way, and that you should check your first-aid kit for adequate supplies – then do it. Do not put it off in the hope that you will avoid disaster. Think of all the things you know you should be doing but have put off. When was the last time, say, that you checked the expiration dates of your first-aid supplies? If you're about to go bushwalking in summer, are you up to date on the latest snakebite protocols? Don't put it off.

Rationalisation

The human decision-making process is heavily influenced by outside pressures – the burden to meet deadlines, problems we face and targets we must achieve. As a consequence, we try to rationalise shortcuts to overcome the pressures and achieve the outcome. In essence, we're satisfying, rather than optimising, results.

Something that was once intolerable becomes acceptable through rationalisation. We try to justify our actions in our mind, and come up with excuses for our decision as to why it was the best choice. By doing this, we gain a sense of satisfaction, believing we made the right decision.

Have you ever found yourself saying, 'It does not matter if I do this, because . . .'? To help prevent rationalisation, you must take accountability and responsibility for your actions. I know from experience that we don't set out intending to make choices that cascade towards disaster and harm. Deviation occurs because of barriers that prevent us from following the correct procedure – usually, that barrier is pressure.

Take a moment to write a list of times you've taken shortcuts and rationalised your behaviour. Here are some common ones that would apply to paramedics:

- Because I worked in the same ambulance yesterday, I don't need to complete a vehicle check or make sure I have all the equipment.
- I don't need to check the expiration date of the drug before giving it to the patient because I checked it three days ago, and I've never made the mistake of giving expired medications before.
- I'll restock the medical kit later; we probably won't need it anyway. It's rare that I'll need it, and I've got by in the past without it.

Personal Experience – The Lucky Escape

At the start of every shift, I take the drug kit from the vehicle and place it inside the station to sign out drugs from the safe into the kit. This is something I've done a thousand times before, without any thought, in autopilot mode. During this time, I generally talk to my colleagues about their shifts. We catch up and I ask if they've had any interesting cases.

I was dispatched to a job not long after I logged on into the ambulance. I was sent to a middle-aged woman who had fallen and potentially broken her arm – a straightforward case for a paramedic.

I arrived on the scene, put my gloves on, walked around the side of the ambulance, and opened the side door to grab my medical kits.

My jaw dropped. I think my heart skipped several beats before stopping for a few seconds. I'd left the drug kit on the table back at the station.

Here I was, attending to someone who had broken their arm, but I had no means of providing pain relief because I'd forgotten to put an essential bag in the car. That was a normalisation of deviance.

When I first started the job, the standard that I followed was different. I would sign out the drugs and walk immediately to the vehicle without distraction. But over the years this process fell into automatic pilot, creating complacency. I would walk away and put my lunch in the fridge, get into a conversation about the weekend or something else. Over time, I deviated, which resulted in a predictable surprise.

I've heard similar stories from other paramedics who have turned up to a job without a defibrillator because they took it out of the ambulance to run training scenarios at the station instead of using the provided training monitor. Any deviance from the standard without clear justification will eventually lead to a disaster.

Preventing Normalisation of Deviance

Mike Mullane is a retired USAF officer and a former NASA astronaut who successfully executed three space shuttle missions. He is a passionate activist for the teachings of normalisation of deviance. Mullane offers the following five suggestions to prevent it: recognise your vulnerability, execute to meet standards, battle complacency, trust your instincts and learn continually.

Recognise Your Vulnerability

Vulnerability has been described as 'uncertainty, risk, and emotional exposure'. It's that agitation we get when we step out of our comfort zone.

Accepting our vulnerability opens our eyes to the signs of risk and engages our curiosity. In challenging situations, this allows us a more comprehensive idea of the circumstances. We must also apply that curiosity to our own weaknesses. Even though they make us feel uncomfortable, accepting that discomfort allows the awareness that we are fallible. This in turn means that we can develop ways to combat these weaknesses before they lead us into a predictable surprise. Suppressing your vulnerabilities will only delay disaster for a moment.

We all know that humans are imperfect beings. The imperfections of the human mind can easily leave us vulnerable to disaster. The following vulnerabilities have been identified as the main causes of deviance:

- Lending greater weight to evidence that supports the status quo, and ignoring anything that brings that status quo into jeopardy (also called confirmation bias).
- Thinking only of the present and lacking the courage to consider the future, avoiding what's hard now because it's easier than preventing hardship later.
- Only acting on things we've already experienced and lacking the imagination to foresee danger that doesn't affect us personally.

Writing this book has made me extremely uncomfortable. Every time I go to write about a personal experience, I feel great agitation. I've had to become vulnerable throughout this manuscript. Without vulnerability, I would be concealing reality and limiting the opportunity for progress. I feel the agitation of shame when I think about a lot of the cases I've shared with you. But without accepting my vulnerabilities, I wouldn't have been able to grow and learn from my failures. I'm now a better paramedic because of it.

Everyone has failures and vulnerabilities, but we rarely speak about them. My hope is that this book will help give you the courage to identify your own vulnerabilities.

Execute to Meet Standards

When we take action, we need to ensure that our action meets the standards required. In paramedicine, there is a vast archive of medical errors, mistakes and blunders that have prompted the creation of our medical standards. People have literally died for them. That knowledge is now used to protect lives, both ours and those of the people we treat.

The failure to comply with professional standards is a fundamental cause of disaster in the medical industry, and no doubt many others.

Battle Complacency

Complacency will give us a false sense of security. Don't approach a challenging situation in autopilot mode and stop paying attention to what you're doing; this can lead to taking shortcuts, which creates risks. Whenever you start to feel 'comfortable', use it as a warning sign to review and refocus.

Don't become arrogant. It will lead you to believe that you're above making errors. I've learned from paramedics who have been in the job for more than 30 years that no matter how long you've been doing the job, there will always be something you haven't seen before, or something that will surprise you. Don't let arrogance stunt your growth and willingness to let vulnerability in. Showing vulnerability is not only courageous, but an essential way to learn and prevent complacency.

Trust Your Instincts

Don't dismiss your concerns. If you have a feeling something is wrong or a bit off, trust your instincts and speak up. Take a timeout and reassess. Your brain has recognised that things are different from your normal patterns of experience, and that requires further investigation.

Investigate to try to discover why your spider senses are tingling or what your instincts are trying to tell you. This can be hard if you have an abundance of outside pressure weighing you down. Recognise your bias and look inwards as to why you're not trusting your instincts at that moment. Identify whether it's justified or you're trying to rationalise avoiding a decision you truly don't want to make.

Learn Continually

Learn from previous failures and near misses. Archive and review all cases, not just the failures but the successes too. We can learn more from our success than our failures. Identify how things went well, how you managed to overcome seemingly insurmountable odds and succeed. Make sure you document that as well.

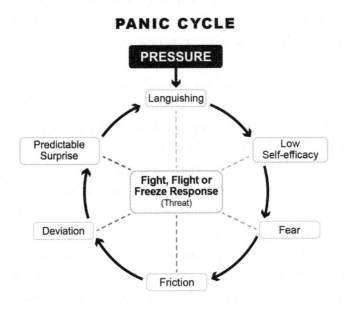

PANIC CYCLE

Figure 18. Deviation from established standards creates predictable surprises, which can be dangerous. This further contributes to languishing under pressure.

The Positive Deviance Theory

Positive deviance is the idea that in every large group of people working in the same environment on the same problem, all with access to the same resources, a few people will find unusual strategies that yield better solutions to the problem at hand.

Back in the 1990s, the Save the Children fund decided that its programs for reducing the numbers of malnourished children in impoverished Vietnamese villages were failing. Pouring resources into trying to change the villagers' behaviour in order to ensure better outcomes was a losing strategy.

They changed tack and asked the villagers themselves what was working and whose children were the best fed. This approach – asking which villagers were breaking from convention in order to feed their children – cost them virtually nothing. By learning how those people were bucking the trend, they were able to implement changes that reduced malnutrition dramatically within two years.

The main lesson here is that people need to build on the capabilities they already have in order to achieve results. It's less useful to simply tell people how they must change; we need to give them tried-and-true knowledge for them to do so.

If you believe that you can't perform under pressure in a pressure situation, then you need to find the people in your industry, profession or environment who've done it successfully already – and learn from them. What makes these people successful where others have failed? Why don't they panic? How can they perform under pressure with the same skills and training as you?

Who among those around you acts and remains calm in a crisis? Identify those people's behaviours – and mimic them. This will help you build a higher level of self-efficacy as you seek to emulate what has worked for them.

INTERVIEW WITH THE AUTHOR
Have you ever treated an animal?

People call the ambulance all the time for their pets, but I haven't personally treated an animal. I've heard stories of some old-school ambos performing CPR on their neighbour's dog. The vet does it, but we definitely treat humans, not animals.

I have, however, experienced a lot of cases that involved animals, such as shark attacks, snakebites and a woman having her breast bitten off by a dog. One case among these is particularly memorable.

We were called to a car versus a horse scene. As we arrived, I found a horse lying in the middle of the road with an obvious fracture to his hind leg. He was trying to stand up, but we had to ignore that and treat the humans who were in the car.

The RSPCA arrived on scene and decided to euthanise the horse as he was so badly injured. They pulled out the biggest gun I've ever seen – it looked like a sniper's rifle. Unfortunately, just as the vet decided to pull the trigger, I lifted my head out of the car and witnessed the entire thing. I've always had poor timing.

After treating the humans I decided to put a sheet over the horse so the bystanders didn't have to stare at the corpse. Just as I did that, the owners of the horse arrived on scene and were obviously distressed. They ran down just in time for a big gust of wind to blow the sheet off the horse.

As we were driving back from the case, we witnessed a car accident in front of us and, to our astonishment, it was a car versus two dogs. Two runaway dogs had run out in front of a car, kilometres away from their home. One was killed instantly while the other was barely alive. He had a pneumothorax (collapsed lung) and was breathing heavily. My partner and I knew how to fix that, and for a moment half-jokingly thought of doing it.

I remember vividly a bystander becoming irate because we wouldn't put the dead dog in a body bag. For one, we don't carry body bags in the city and even if we did, where would I take it? I always think of the future patient. Try explaining to a loved one that the ambulance was delayed and their mother died because it was tied up transporting a dead dog to the local dump (where most city roadkill sadly ends up).

CALL TO ACTION

'Normalisation of deviance in a sentence – it's the pressure-driven shortcutting of best practices and getting away with it until you don't.'– **Mike Mullane, retired US Air Force officer, former NASA astronaut and safety activist**

Key Takeaways

- Normalisation of deviance describes the deviation away from the expected standard of performance. If not corrected, it will lead to a disaster that could have been prevented.
- Predictable surprises are the disasters that you should have seen coming.
- We rationalise our deviance from the norm by any means necessary. We actively search for ways to support our new position.

Key Tasks

- Do you recognise your vulnerability? Are you currently executing at a level to meet standards, or have you deviated?
- Watch the documentary *Challenger: The Final Flight.*

13

Courageous Self-leadership

Andrew's Experience – Rarer than Bravery in Battle

I first met former aid worker Andrew MacLeod when he was the keynote speaker at an ambulance conference. As he spoke, I sat on the edge of my seat and listened intently to every word. I was amazed at how much he had achieved and the courageous self-leadership he had shown throughout his career as a humanitarian. The first thing I did when I left the conference was order his book, *A Life Half Lived*, and read it from cover to cover.

He's the best example I know of someone who has courageous self-leadership. A quote from Robert F. Kennedy at the start of *A Life Half Lived* sums up the daring of Andrew Macleod:

> Few are willing to brave the disapproval of their fellows, the censure of their colleagues, the wrath of their society. Moral courage is a rarer commodity than bravery in battle or great intelligence. Yet, it is the one essential, vital quality for those who seek to change a world that yields most painfully to change.

MacLeod's previous humanitarian work included deployments to

Rwanda and former Yugoslavia for the International Committee of the Red Cross, and multiple deployments for the United Nations, including as chief of operations of the UN's Emergency Coordination Centre in Pakistan.

MacLeod gives a long list of personal examples demonstrating moral courage: from speaking out and raising awareness of the atrocious sexual abuse against women and children by aid workers themselves, to raising funds to improve the mental health of aid workers transitioning back home.

He would find one huge moral test in October 2005 in Pakistan. A 7.6 magnitude earthquake struck at 8.30 am at the point where the mighty mountains of the Hindu Kush, the Karakoram Range and the Himalayas converge to create the Indus River. The quake shook for about a minute, causing unthinkable damage. More than 5000 homes, 307 health facilities, 3994 water-supply facilities and 715 government buildings were destroyed.

Three and a half million people were made homeless, and about 75,000 were killed. Horrifically, nearly half the dead were children, as 5348 education facilities were wiped out.

At the time of MacLeod's deployment to the Pakistan response, the international relief community was halfway through a review process. The review was happening because of previous poor responses to natural disasters and duplication of aid. The report's recommendations were complete but had not received final approval. This left the disaster community in limbo. MacLeod writes that no one knew which system to use: the old discredited one or the new unendorsed one. The UN decided to stick with the old system.

MacLeod knew that the lives of 3.5 million homeless people were at stake and the Himalayan winter was fast approaching. Keeping them alive meant negotiating with people on the ground and making the right decisions, regardless of protocols. He wanted to avoid the bureaucracy's aim of 'doing nothing wrong' by doing nothing.

After negotiations, Pakistan's government green-lighted the new unendorsed cluster approach, where the humanitarian response is divided into a number of sectors. MacLeod's nerve in taking this step, knowing it was the right thing to do despite it being against current UN policy, was courageous self-leadership in action.

He believes that just because nobody else is doing anything about a problem doesn't mean it's okay not to act. The decision not to act is also a decision. Worse, a decision not to act is a decision to allow wrongs to continue. MacLeod argues that inaction in the face of injustice is complicity. Say, for example, you see a man committing a crime in the street. Yes, he's the criminal, but if you've done nothing to intervene to stop it, aren't you partly responsible as well?

Back in Pakistan, during the negotiations, MacLeod found himself in awe of the courageous self-leadership shown by Pakistan's Director-General of Military Operations, Major General Mohamed Yousaf. In MacLeod's view, Yousaf did the bravest thing he'd ever seen an army general do in any country, at any time. He simply said, 'Honestly, we do not know what to do.'

In most countries, an army general would never admit to a foreigner that he didn't know how to handle a problem in his country. It takes enormous strength, confidence, self-awareness and selflessness to realise that your people's needs are greater than your organisation's pride.

MacLeod also believes that we can judge a person's moral character by the number of times they break the rule that says 'never burn bridges'. When MacLeod had just joined the Melbourne Scots association, for example, and attended his first ever meeting with his father, someone stood up and asked why the club didn't admit women. The chairman quickly shut down the questioner and the question wasn't answered.

MacLeod saw this as wrong and told his father that he would say something about it. His father, embarrassed, begged him to say nothing. MacLeod wouldn't have it. He wanted to know why women couldn't join, and he didn't want to be a part of a club where someone in power shuts down debate and won't answer questions. MacLeod didn't want to be part of an organisation that wouldn't answer legitimate questions.

He raised his hand and said to the president, 'Look, I'm just new here. I've been a member for about 20 minutes. That question to me is a really important question. Why aren't women allowed to join?' His dad was now cringing and hiding behind the table. The president answered by saying, 'We will not discuss it.'

MacLeod replied to the entire room, 'If you're not prepared to discuss it, I've got to tell you I'm not prepared to be a member of this club.' He would have to be the shortest-term member of the Melbourne Scots.

At the end of his speech at the ambulance conference, MacLeod made the powerful statement that we must set moral and ethical boundaries and stand by them. Sometimes you might fail at this – we all do. But if you want to not only advocate for change, but actually make change, you don't just work with good people doing good. You make the world better by working with bad people and making them less bad.

You get more positive change and more improvement by dealing with some of the worst people and situations in the world. The only way to do that is within an ethical framework that guides your own self-leadership.

Self-leadership

Austrian American management consultant and educator Peter Drucker described being a self-leader as 'serving as chief, captain or CEO of one's own life'. Self-leadership is having the strength and dedication to steer your own life in the best way for you. It's taking action to make things happen *for* us rather than letting them happen *to* us. It's the process of learning from our mistakes and constantly taking small steps to improve. It's about owning our own actions, whatever the consequences, rather than blaming those around us. Self-leaders transform adversity into resilience.

A courageous self-leader is, to paraphrase William Ernest Henley's poem 'Invictus', 'the master of their fate and the captain of their soul'. Courageous self-leaders understand what it takes to possess poise. They appreciate that it's the small steps, the small 1 per cent gains they make every day, accumulated over time, that make the difference. They do the hard work by themselves, when no one is looking. They don't take shortcuts. They hold fast to their beliefs when there's nothing there to keep them accountable. They keep themselves accountable by letting their moral compass guide their decisions.

As I noted earlier, the highest point of anxiety and arousal comes right at that moment before you decide to step forward and be courageous. The sense of dread and terror of something bad happening can be overwhelming, and your body will feel extremely agitated. At this moment, you're on the cusp of making a decision. It doesn't matter whether you're running away from a lion or talking to your spouse about your relationship, or having that meeting with your boss, you will experience the arousal of fight, flight or freeze in your mind and body.

If there are things that frighten you – the chaos and suffering of life certainly generates plenty to be afraid of – the best thing to do is to open your eyes to it and confront the thing you're most reluctant to face. The alternative would be to sit back and wait, letting your fears find you. You're much better off finding the self-courage to confront it head on.

This doesn't mean facing the fear blindly, though. The key is to break your fears up into little pieces and encounter them one by one through controlled exposure. Mastering this process will get you through the chaos.

Many situations we find ourselves in are beyond our control. While we can't control all external forces, we must do all things possible to control our response to them. Paramedics need to look at medical emergencies as an opportunity to make them stronger, smarter and better. We all need to remind ourselves that worthwhile results come from adversity.

Don't look for an out or an alternative. Your situation is your situation. Play the hand you're dealt, especially if it seems unfair. You may be faced with atrocious problems of great human suffering. In such situations, courageous self-leadership is vital. In most other circumstances, you may remove yourself from the disaster, but when someone's life is on the line, it's not an option. You must step forward and mitigate the risk as best you can. This can only be done through courageous self-leadership.

Captain Chesley 'Sully' Sullenberger showed extreme courage and leadership when he was placed under great pressure and stress. He was the pilot of an Airbus A320 when it suddenly struck a flock of birds three minutes into the flight. This caused both of the plane's engines to fail. With 155 people on board, he had to make a quick decision to save lives. Listening to the calm sound of his voice over the radio when this emergency was occurring demonstrates a perfect example of poise when he was dealt an unfair serve.

Sully decided to ditch the aircraft into New York's Hudson River. His example shows us the power of taking action, meeting standards and facing fear. But what could perhaps be considered even greater is his leadership after the incident. He took complete accountability for his actions.

Everything we've spoken about so far in this book has led to this point – learning to lead yourself. Self-leadership is about:

- conquering your fears
- recognising your fight, flight or freeze response
- having the courage to take action
- being resilient.

Nancy Koehn, whose research at the Harvard Business School focuses on crisis leadership and how leaders and their teams rise to the challenges of high-stakes situations, wrote that most of our lives, we're beset by crises. 'Courageous leaders are not cowed or intimidated. They realise that, in the midst of turbulence, there lies an extraordinary opportunity to grow and rise.'

Be Accountable

You're the right person to do something about your situation, regardless of what it is and who is to blame. No one else can do that for you.

Canadian businessman and author John Izzo is an expert on responsibility. He has said that taking responsibility is 'about doing what you can in your sphere of influence to create change, and not looking to anyone else'.

These days, there's a lot of finger-pointing and blame-shifting. It's always someone or something else's fault. By being accountable, you're giving yourself the opportunity to learn from your mistakes and successes. A paramedic who blames and makes excuses is not someone people will follow. Admitting fault and taking responsibility shows excellent character. People will be drawn to your courage and are more likely to trust your decisions.

When we make excuses, our body creates the same discomfort and agitation as described earlier. Our body fears that we're self-sabotaging by admitting fault and taking the blame. Luckily though, the sensation of taking accountability is just as powerful and reinforcing.

Be Honest

Speak the truth in spite of possible negative consequences.

There are many reasons why we don't want to tell the truth, the most common being that we believe we're helping or protecting the other person. In reality, though, we're putting up a false shield.

A key skill for a paramedic is the ability to tell family members or a victim the truth with empathy. It's critical, when telling a family member that their loved one has died, to not make false promises or give false hope. You will only increase their suffering. It might provide short-term relief, but in the long run it can have catastrophic consequences.

Telling the truth can cause the same resistance and limbic friction in your mind and body as any other stress. It especially takes great courage to tell the truth when you know it will have short-term negative outcomes for your own life and wellbeing, but I see no other alternative if you want to perform well under stress.

I've had student paramedics lie to me about their ability to perform a task because they feared being judged or deemed incompetent. One time a brand-new student told me they knew how to operate the stretcher and didn't need further training. As a result, I naturally trusted the student. Later that shift, we were treating a patient who was suffering from a heart attack up two flights of stairs. Not wanting to leave the patient, I asked the student to get the stretcher out of the ambulance and set it up at the bottom of the stairs.

The student wasn't honest with me and as a result our extrication from the patient's house was delayed and I had to remove myself from the patient to complete the task. This seemingly simple lie at the time had a profound impact later. The student was not courageous enough to reveal to me that they were not competent and needed extra support.

Admittedly, this is a much easier challenge if you don't put yourself in a situation where someone you love might ask you, 'Do these pants make me look fat?' All jokes aside, don't put yourself in a situation where you feel you need to lie. Don't attempt the task or challenge if you think you'll have to lie to get through. Even if you do manage to achieve it and survive, you won't have learned the lesson needed to perform under stress.

Imagine this: you go to see your doctor, and they lie to you about your diagnosis. The doctor withholds the fact that you have high blood pressure because they don't want to increase your stress levels, given you're already suffering from anxiety. The doctor tries to protect you, but in a few years' time, your heart fails, and you end up on the heart transplant list. No matter how hard it is, paramedics must tell the patient and family members the truth of the situation and its severity.

There is, however, a correct way to express the truth – and that is with empathy.

Personal Experience – Being Courageous Can Suck

Working by myself, I responded to a child in cardiac arrest who was clinically dead. When I arrived on the scene, I found the patient lying on the side of the road. A bystander was performing cardiac compressions in an attempt to save him. They were surrounded by people yelling, screaming and crying, looking to me to save the child, and begging me to bring him back to life.

The child's father had run off, just up from the road, to stand near the railway lines. He was contemplating committing suicide if the resuscitation was unsuccessful. He blamed himself and felt he couldn't live with that blame.

I decided to get a bystander to restrain the father so I could commence CPR to revive the child. I followed my training and the CPR protocol, but after about 30 minutes of effort and my best attempts, I was unsuccessful. I informed the parents of the time of death and asked the police to assist with restraining the father.

When I was back at the station and reviewing my paperwork, I realised I'd defibrillated a patient who had no heartbeat, which was a mistake. In the heat of the battle, I mistook the electrocardiogram wave from effective compressions as a shockable rhythm, when in reality there was no electrical or mechanical activity in the heart when I began to defibrillate.

Only I knew of my mistake. And fortunately, my mistake caused no harm to the patient, as defibrillating a dead heart has no effect. In fact, if you're unsure whether there's a rhythm, you're better off to shock than not shock. But I'd still made an error.

Despite not having a negative outcome, this mistake caused me great anxiety, frustration and thoughts of failure. My body was telling me not to admit to my mistake and keep it a secret, but this would have gone against my values. I needed the courage to step up and take accountability for my actions. In fact, I probably should never have started CPR on the boy in the first place. His condition was incompatible with life.

The pressure of the small child, the hysterical parents, and everyone looking to me for a miracle forced me to go against the medical standards for commencing CPR instead of simply calling time of death immediately. I rang my immediate supervisor and informed him of my mistake, and sent him all the details.

I thought the worst: 'Am I going to lose my job? I won't be able to provide for myself or my family. What if I go to court?' But none of that happened; my negative self-talk was doing me no favours. My boss later thanked me for acknowledging my mistake. He had no concerns with my actions and was grateful that I came forward.

I learned a great deal from this case and have since found it much easier to have the courage and conviction to make the difficult call, regardless of the situation. I'm now a better paramedic for it, and I teach this lesson to others.

If I'd never had the courage to take accountability, I would most likely still be making similar mistakes, and wouldn't be the paramedic I am today.

Confident Communication

Leaders communicate with confidence. Confident communication is an important skill for anyone wanting to influence an emergency scene or get an important point across. It will help boost your self-esteem, and earn respect from people around you. It can also reduce stress by empowering you in pressure situations.

Communicate clearly, honestly, directly and precisely, without being too passive or too aggressive. Communicating confidently means not manipulating or lying to the people who are looking to you for assistance. It helps you discuss things and resolve conflicts in a way that expresses your opinion without disrespecting the opinions of others. In other words, it allows you to respect not only your own ideas, but also the ideas of those around you.

Here's one example. Two paramedics arrive at a car accident. They see the driver of the vehicle, who was not at fault, broken down in the middle of a busy road. He jumps out of his vehicle and says, 'Some idiot ran me off the road and tried to kill me. Where is he?'

The mentor looks at the scene and assesses the situation, realising that the man talking to them, being aggressive, is in danger of being hit by oncoming traffic. As the crash happened on the bend of a blind corner, his vehicle is also at risk of injuring those driving past in other vehicles, who may not see him.

The student might say passively: 'Any chance you could move off the road?'

Or perhaps the student would say aggressively: 'Get your arse off the road before someone gets killed.'

These statements are likely to either anger the already irritated driver still further, or fail to motivate him to act.

The mentor, by contrast, would say confidently: 'I recognise that you're frustrated with how this accident was caused, but we must now prevent this from happening to anyone else. We must move off the road now, away from the traffic.'

They've acknowledged the driver's frustration and anger, while highlighting the seriousness of the situation and the need for action.

If we communicate too passively in this scenario, the man will ignore your concerns and continue to do whatever he wants, putting more people in harm's way. If you act too aggressively, you will heighten the driver's already agitated state. He may become enraged, again preventing him from following your instructions.

Confident communication plays two main roles:

- It stops people from taking advantage of you.
- It stops you from taking advantage of other people.

Using a confident communication style allows you to express your true feelings and desires. Instead of hiding behind anger or shyness, you become your genuine self. This communication style will take you a long way towards achieving your desired outcome.

This method is very useful when you are approaching someone in a crisis. Essentially, you are saying, '*I see what you're saying, I hear you, I understand, I get it.*'

Another aspect of confident communication is body language, a non-verbal communication method that includes postures, gestures and movements. Our body language projects out into the world, expressing how we're feeling and identifying how confident we are. If you want to project poise, you need to develop techniques for confident body language. If you have poise, you will probably already be doing this naturally. Body language is said to influence between 65 and 93 per cent of all communication, so it's crucial to spend some time on it.

Communications expert Carol Fox is well versed in effective communication via body language. She explains how to use a confident stance to promote a perfect balance between empathy and strength. This stance involves standing up straight with shoulders back in a neutral position, and feet slightly apart with a slight bend in the knees. Place your hands in front of you, and grab one of your wrists, as if you were holding your watch. That's the confidence stance. It's a position of strength, as you won't be easily knocked off your feet, but you're still open and non-threatening.

Another great tool to have is the leveller. This is used to subconsciously calm down a person who is in a heightened state. Most people would use this body language when trying to tell someone to calm down, which is obviously not a good thing to say to someone who's stressed – especially, and I speak from experience, your wife. The leveller involves simply moving your arms up and down in a slow and steady manner, with palms facing the floor. People will recognise this symbol as reassurance and feel calmer.

It's easy to tell from looking at a patient's body language

whether they're nervous, anxious, bored, engaged, defensive or aggressive, so it's important that paramedics pay attention to their body language, because the patient will be able to recognise the paramedic's mood as well.

Tone of voice is also an important consideration when communicating with people who are most likely in a heightened state of stress. The best method to use, as explained by Carol Fox, is the voice of leadership – low, slow and deep. She explains that this is one of the reasons we are more likely to listen to elderly people, because they speak in a low, slow and deep tone.

When we're stressed, we're more likely to speak in a fast and high-pitched voice. This will be obvious to the people you're meant to help, and your anxiety will project onto them, only increasing the stress of the entire situation. The best thing to do is pause, then consciously try to speak in a low, slow and deep tone.

Great leaders can articulate their words and express their feelings with confidence. It takes courage to say what you think and share your truth with the world, but that is what's required if you want to command under stress.

Empathy versus Sympathy

Paramedics have empathy, not just sympathy.

Empathy is the ability to understand and appreciate the personal experience of the individual you're interacting with, to walk in their shoes and comprehend what they're going through. Rather than viewing it from a distance, you are beside them.

Nursing scholar Theresa Wiseman identified four attributes of empathy:

1. seeing the world as others do
2. being non-judgemental
3. understanding someone else's feelings
4. letting the other person know you understand their feelings.

Sympathy gives you the ability to share the person's feelings or interests, but doesn't allow you to form a connection that will help you to give support. Brené Brown explains sympathy as trying to put the silver lining around things to try to make them better.

This might be an example of sympathy:

Patient: I'm having a heart attack.
Student: That's unfortunate but I know how to treat it.

Compare that example of sympathy to the following example of empathy:

Patient: I'm having a heart attack.
Mentor: I understand that this must be an overwhelming experience, but I'll be with you the entire time and I'm here to help.

Tell the truth with empathy, and you will form a connection that calms the person.

It's also important for the paramedic to remember that the patient and bystanders are going through the same fight, flight or freeze response. Those people, however, will more likely be unable to relieve that response, especially during the time the paramedic is on the scene.

Even if you want to be sympathetic and try to solve people's emotional problems, it won't work, simply because they're in the fight, flight or freeze response. They're unable to activate the prefrontal cortex and focus their attention. They won't take your advice, even if given, because they don't have the ability to perform higher-level cognitive functions such as problem-solving, self-control and planning. They're in survival mode.

It's up to you to have the courageous self-leadership to protect them. Being empathetic isn't weakness, it's the opposite. It takes courage to show compassion and take on other people's problems as if they were your own. Empathy also requires telling the truth and realising that there might not be a happy ending. Sometimes the empathetic thing to do is the harder choice, and in those circumstances courage is required.

Personal Experience – Treating a Criminal

A few years ago, my partner and I were dispatched to the local jail for a 62-year-old man with chest pain. When we arrived, we were escorted through multiple security gates and protocols before arriving inside the prison cell.

What we found there was a prisoner sitting in civilian clothes with a bag next to him. I thought this was a bit strange, but I ignored any irrelevant thoughts and focused on completing a thorough assessment of the patient.

I confirmed that the prisoner was having an episode of unstable angina, which could potentially lead to a heart attack. After treating him at the scene, we went to transport the patient to the hospital.

Typically when we treat a prisoner, the patient is handcuffed, usually to our ambulance stretcher. Their feet are also cuffed, and there's one prison guard inside the ambulance as an escort and another following behind in another vehicle. This time, however, they said those measures were not required.

This was very irregular, so I asked why. I was informed that the patient was being released that day after being in prison for more than 18 years. This was the cause of his heart attack: the increased stress and anxiety of having to rejoin society. I was reassured that the prisoner was non-violent, compliant and should not be a threat to me.

I was then pulled aside into another room and told in private that the patient was being released from a conviction as a paedophile. He'd sexually assaulted several young children while in a position of power. Needless to say, this goes against all my own personal values and moral code. It's something that sends chills through my body and makes the hair stand on end. 'That's one of the most heinous crimes a human can commit,' I thought.

But still, I couldn't let this affect the way I treated the patient. I had to stand by my own moral values and find the empathy to treat him in a way that was free from judgement and bias.

After all, he was my patient, not my prisoner.

Be Aware of Bias

We're not always the rational creatures we think we are – considering all the options, judging all the evidence and weighing up all the options. In fact, we're driven by a number of biases that can make us resistant to either facts or reason. These biases make us judgemental.

If you want to have a paramedic mindset, then you need to work to become aware of your biases and make decisions based on evidence and facts – not personal preference or ideology.

Cognitive dissonance is the mental discomfort experienced when we have to reconcile conflicting attitudes or beliefs, and can lead us to make unconscious biased decisions. For example, if a paramedic has to treat someone who is racist, their feelings about treating the racist person will conflict with their role as a healthcare provider seeking to provide inclusive care. Their unconscious mind immediately tries to find some way of reconciling that inconsistency.

There are stories of Jewish doctors treating Nazis during World War II, which demonstrates incredible altruism and dedication to the value of human life. When our feelings and the facts are at odds, though, we're at risk of finding a way to reconcile them that could be the worst course of action.

If you are treating a patient who comes from a different cultural background or religion than you, one with which you don't identify, you may unconsciously change the facts of the situation to match your beliefs. In effect, you're distorting the evidence, which could lead to a catastrophic decision. The internal inconsistency of cognitive dissonance, which feels worse to the mind than the idea of further disasters, suggests that people's beliefs can be shaped not just by reason and evidence, but by an unconscious desire for consistency. The mind will try and find a way to bring about consistency through changing our beliefs or making up justifications and rationalisations to explain the conflict. It's important to try to pay attention to the thoughts and emotions going on in our mind if we are to avoid this bias.

Another type of bias is confirmation bias, which is the consistent need to seek out evidence that supports our ideas and values, while at the same time looking for reasons to discredit evidence that runs counter to our existing beliefs. In 1620, the English philosopher Francis Bacon wrote, 'The human understanding when it has once adopted an opinion . . . draws all things else to support and agree with it.'

Be mindful that you're not using evidence primarily to support your own viewpoint; it's not about you, in the best way possible – it's about the person you're trying to help or the goal you're trying to achieve.

It can be hard to identify how much your biases are influencing your decision-making, but it's worth taking a moment to pause and ask yourself why you're doing what you're doing. Is it because of the evidence, or because you don't personally agree?

Having the courage to recognise your bias and identify the conflict within your mind takes moral courage and personal leadership of the kind we have been discussing.

POISE CYCLE

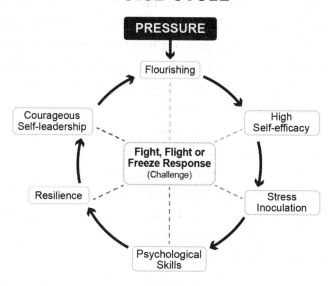

Figure 19. Courageous self-leadership, derived from taking responsibility for one's actions and communicating with confidence, promotes flourishing under pressure and the paramedic poise mindset.

INTERVIEW WITH THE AUTHOR
Do you have nightmares or flashbacks?

I have had difficult nights trying to get to sleep or mental flashes of scenes, but not nightmares. Fortunately, when this has happened it's only occurred for a few days after a major incident; it's never been a chronic or crippling incident of the kind that has affected many of my colleagues.

One case that kept me up at night was a result of a passing comment made by a forensic police photographer. I attended a multiple-casualty incident and quickly identified that a patient had died at the scene – they were trapped under the car with no pulse and not breathing. I would have needed superhuman strength to lift the car off them to perform any medical interventions. Despite knowing this, though, I lost sleep over the policeman telling me the next day that he was surprised she died because when they lifted the car off she had no obvious deformities and looked normal.

This comment created great doubt in my mind, and I was tossing and turning in my bed replaying the scene over and over again, questioning my decision, trying to reassure myself that I did the right thing. It took a conversation with one of my mentors to help me move on.

CALL TO ACTION

'Leadership is about having an ethical framework to determine what is the least bad of bad options. Take that bad option, knowing that everyone's going to tell you, you took a bad option.' – **Andrew MacLeod, former aid worker**

Key Takeaways

- Self-leadership is the process of learning who you are, being confident about that and staying true to it. It's taking responsibility for your decisions and having a clear sense of your intentions in life.
- Conquer your fears, recognise your response to stress, and have the courage to act and be resilient.
- Take responsibility for your actions and circumstances.

Key Tasks

- Challenge yourself to not tell a single lie for the next 48 hours after reading this sentence. You might be surprised how often you hold back the truth to satisfy others or avoid your fears.
- Watch the movie *Sully*.

Conclusion

Personal Experience – A 12-hour Night Shift

I hadn't worked in the city for about five years when I decided to take an overtime shift: a 12-hour night shift. I looked forward to working with another paramedic after doing it solo for so long. I was eager to refresh my practice in an urban environment, too – it was exciting to have backup minutes away instead of hours, and to be 30 minutes from two major hospitals.

I arrived at the station 40 minutes early because I wanted to make sure I completed a good vehicle check and familiarisation. I knocked on the door, but no one was inside – a station of 50 staff was empty. I didn't have the access codes for the building, so I rang a supervisor. He gave me the codes, but also informed me that my partner had called in sick and they couldn't find a replacement. I had to work alone again.

It wasn't a great start, but I moved forward. I found the vehicle keys. They had a vehicle roster sheet written in bold on the whiteboard, so I knew which ambulance to take. I was making progress. Next I had to gain access to drugs in the safe. I didn't know any of the codes, so that was another phone call to the supervisor. I signed out the drugs for my shift and walked to the ambulance.

It was a brand-new ambulance. I'd never driven a model of this vehicle so new, but I had done an online training module and seen a few pictures about it. How hard could it be? Maybe I could rely on my experience to adapt to a new vehicle, I thought. I made sure to spend extra time checking where the equipment was kept. Everything was slightly different from what I was used to. In an emergency, when you want to reduce your cognitive load, having to waste precious bandwidth on locating equipment can throw you completely. As I went through the vehicle, I found that it also had the latest medical suction device, something I'd only used once. The city always got the good stuff first.

My next job was to log on and say I was available to respond to calls. I was running 30 minutes late by this point; I'd needed extra time to get through my checks. The city used a mobile data terminal (MDT) for cases – a touchscreen device in the vehicle that relays all of the dispatch information for a case. I had used a more primitive MDT before, but I was still used to text messages and UHF radios. Luckily, it was pretty self-explanatory and I managed to enter my payroll details and log on to the ambulance. I was ready.

I ended up using the MDT immediately. I was dispatched to a two-vehicle car crash and I was the only available unit. I worked quickly to figure out how to navigate the map system on the MDT because I had no idea where I was going.

I jumped in the driver's seat. I reached for the gear stick, but it wasn't where I remembered from driving older vehicles. I located the new gear stick on the steering wheel column, knocked it into drive, turned on the flashing lights and I was away. Looking for another indicator, I accidentally knocked the car into neutral. I put the ambulance back into drive and continued on my way.

A call over the radio said that another vehicle had become available and would respond to the accident as my backup. I arrived on the scene of the accident after an interesting drive through the city. After treating the patients, I loaded one into the back of the ambulance ready for transport to the hospital. The only problem here was that I didn't know what the closest and most appropriate hospital was to transport the patient to. Feeling embarrassed, I jumped out of the ambulance to ask the other crew for directions. I entered the hospital address into the navigator and off I went.

I arrived at the hospital to let the patient into the emergency bay, but I didn't know the code to the hospital door. More embarrassment ensued, but I was able to find a way in quickly and easily.

The first two hours of my first night shift in a long time had put plenty of obstacles in my way. Despite this, I speedily overcame the many barriers I faced that night and rapidly adapted to the environment. Although this was different, I had been exposed to higher stress and problems before.

My next case was a very sick seven-year-old boy with a terrible disease called Marfan syndrome, a disorder that affects the fibres that support and anchor the organs in place. It can affect the heart and blood vessels. This unfortunate young boy was suffering from heart failure.

I couldn't tell you the last time I'd treated a patient with Marfan syndrome, as it had been a long time. I was trying to remember what I learned about Marfan syndrome in university – trying to revisit the stored files from deep in the back of my brain from years ago.

I arrived on the scene to find a very skinny, gaunt-looking kid. His bones were protruding and he looked as grey as a ghost. Alarm bells immediately went off. I'd developed a feeling for what critically ill people look like, so I was able to identify it as soon as I walked in the door.

I called for backup and received it straight away: magic! I treated the patient and supported the distressed family without concern. I jumped into the ambulance to transport them to the hospital. The patient's mother asked if she should call the children's hospital to let them know we were coming. I informed her that we would do that. Meanwhile, I updated the navigator to take us to the children's hospital. I'd forgotten that there was even a children's hospital in the city. I wasn't used to such luxury.

Over the course of the night, I attended to several non-eventful patients and visited some patients in nursing homes. It was now 4 am, nine hours into the shift. I was tired and on my third coffee of the night. I hoped the sun would start to break the darkness of the night sky, giving me a needed boost of energy and alertness to get through the rest of my shift.

I was driving back to the station when the MDT notified me of a new case: a cardiac arrest. I felt an adrenaline rush that woke me up. I was the only ambulance available at the time. Realising I'd volunteered for this shift, I began to question my sanity.

I arrived on the scene carrying every bag ready to perform advanced life support on a patient whose heart had stopped. But when I walked into the room I found a man who had clearly died hours before my arrival. I double-checked and made sure I was making the right decision before informing the family of the death of their loved one.

Given that the patient was middle-aged and there was no obvious cause of death, I had to inform the police of the incident. It had to be treated as suspicious until the police were able to rule out any foul play. The communications centre informed me that the police were notified, but they were extremely busy on other cases and would attend when they could.

An hour and a half later, I'd made two cups of tea for the family members, hugged several of them, and paced around the house. I couldn't leave the body unattended, as I had to keep a potential crime scene clean from contamination. Paramedics are notorious for making a mess of crime scenes when desperately trying to save someone's life, and rightly so – we have a lot to do.

At least the sun was finally shining. The police eventually turned up and I could leave. I needed a shower and a bed with blackout curtains.

I arrived back at the station 13 hours after I started. Despite the problems I faced, the obstacles of unfamiliarity and having to manage difficult scenes, I felt good. Every patient received the best medical care, and I was able to solve problems, stay composed and be self-assured. I had the paramedic mindset.

Decision-making Under Poise

The ultimate purpose of having poise under stress – the paramedic mindset – is to make competent decisions when faced with tremendous pressure. A good decision-maker weighs up the alternative options and settles on an appropriate one. They consider the risk and revisit the outcomes of their decision.

The most consistent finding in pressure research is that pressure is the nemesis of sound decision-making, and as we've seen, the heart of the paramedic's role is making good decisions. Decision-making is the process of making choices by gathering information and assessing alternative resolutions. Stress narrows our focus so that decision-making becomes risk-taking without poise.

Dealing with an enormous number of variables and unpredictable information in a stressful environment makes it extremely difficult to make high-quality decisions. Having poise allows us to eliminate those variables and unpredictability.

There is a plethora of research and information on decision-making that I encourage you to explore, but what is clear is that we cannot make a good decision in a state of panic, when we've lost our moorings. Possessing poise in a crisis will allow you the time and space to collect the critical information you need to make the correct decision. Decision-making first starts with the acquisition of all the information to hand, and you can't collect what you need if your mind is lost.

Start Small and Build

At this stage, you may be feeling a little overwhelmed or perplexed as to how to achieve everything we've covered in this book, but we need to remember that, in the end, we cannot be all things all of the time. That would require complete mastery of all the skills, all the time. Humans aren't perfect. It's adversity and setbacks that make us who we are. How we react to the adversity and our perceived weaknesses is what counts.

I would recommend taking incremental steps every day: make the 1 per cent gains. As the saying goes, Rome wasn't built in a day. To avoid feeling overwhelmed, pick one particular skill or area in which you believe you need improvement, or could achieve, and focus solely on that task. Don't try to multitask, because we know that doesn't work. When you focus on one item, one skill, you will start the ball rolling at the top of the hill. Those incremental improvements of that one thing will lead to greater improvements in the other areas: it's a snowball effect.

In making incremental improvements, I personally started with sleep. I got rid of my streaming video subscriptions and other distractions. I went to bed earlier and got up earlier, which changed my entire day. That led to me wanting to exercise in the morning because I'd created an environment for it. I drank more water and didn't need as much coffee because I was well rested.

This then led to more focus at work and in training. I felt more energised, and I let go of a lot of things holding me back, like the fear of failure. I started to trust the process and let the outcome work itself out. All of this was achieved by choosing one thing and focusing on that.

The Paramedic Mindset Journey

By now, you have a pretty good understanding of how to think like a paramedic who has poise, one who can face pressure with composure and self-assurance. I love sailing, so let me illustrate poise with the following analogy.

Poise is having an even keel. You don't need to be a sailing aficionado to know that an even keel refers to keeping our emotions under control. In sailing, an even keel is when the boat is level and balanced. This phrase of course refers to the keel of the boat, a structural beam at the bottom of a sailing vessel. It helps the boat remain stable while it's travelling on the water. An even keel ensures smooth sailing.

Having poise is like sailing on an even keel. As we travel through life and crises, we want to keep ourselves travelling along this line, in a zone of good decision-making and problem-solving. But life isn't that simple, and pressure can pose a challenge. We're human and we're governed by our biology, and so we take knocks along the way.

A boat's hull will constantly be hit by wave after wave, and with each impact, the hull will pull against you, likely to send you off course into the weakened side. This push and pull is analogous to the medical world: when you're fighting to save someone's life, there is tremendous pressure to perform. This pressure is like trying to move your sailing vessel against the tide, which is constantly pushing you back, trying to slow you down. And just when you thought you'd worked it all out, the tide changes.

The expression 'on an even keel' can be used to describe someone who can function normally after a period of difficulty. They're not tilting to one side, feeling like they're seeing the world sideways. In this scenario, like all goal-orientated endeavours, the keel will become more difficult to keep steady and level, but with your training and psychological skills, you'll be able to trim, or adjust, your sails to counter the pressure you face.

When you're sailing, the wind's strength and direction are constantly changing, requiring you to be ready for any outcome, just like life during a crisis. You'll be able to take control of the rudder and turn the wheel to reduce the impact of the wind and waves (the obstacles of life). You will, of course, also have to deal with reefs and rocks (unexpected surprises), but with your knowledge and composure, you'll be able to navigate your way around them.

The odd storm cloud may appear before you, but you'll be able to reduce your sails, i.e. make them smaller, to mitigate the risk of failure and severe damage to the vessel. You may have to take shelter and find a secure bay to drop anchor for the night and avoid the worst of the storm, but once it passes, you'll have learned from the experience and gathered more resilience to take on new challenges.

If you persist for long enough, despite the multiple course redirections, and at times being pushed backwards in the wrong direction, against the tide, you will eventually achieve what you set out to achieve: it just may not be in the manner that you expected.

For example, if I wanted to start at the X and sail around the island on the map below, the most direct and quickest course would be as marked.

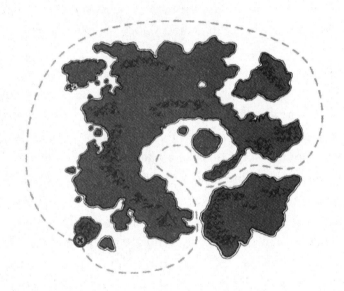

Figure 20. The map above shows a hypothetical course for someone who wishes to sail around an island.

The reality is that it isn't possible to sail a course as straight and as perfect as this. There are varying components that will influence your ability to stay on course, and this is what it's like when facing pressure. Your goal is to stay on course and complete the task as quickly and smoothly as possible, but when the outcome matters and time is limited, it's easy to be pushed off our even keel.

Your course will actually look more like this.

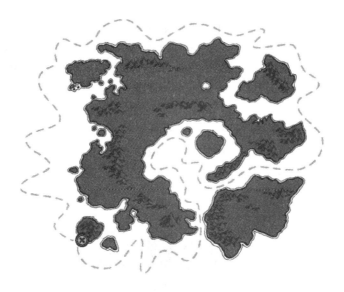

Figure 21. This map depicts a more realistic course to sail around an island than the ideal but logistically impossible route shown in Figure 20.

During your journey you will be hit by wind, tide and waves, but the good thing is that you didn't go too far off course. You held fast to the changes and obstacles thrown in front of you, adjusted as required and problem-solved your way through it. Despite being knocked around a few times, you managed to get to your destination; you had poise.

If you can treat disaster and triumph in the same way, then you will have poise. You're not being thrown off course from what you value, or how you act, because of internal or external pressures. When you have poise, you will be able to perform under stress and reach your full potential. You won't falter under strain. You will know what you're meant to do and how to do it, even when the odds are stacked against you.

Being in the middle of a crisis can be daunting and frightening, but with poise you will face it with composure and self-assurance.

The Ultimate Toolbox

A quick reference guide to all the available tools that will build your poise.

Tool	Use
Growth mindset	When we have a growth mindset, we believe that we can use hard work, consistency and dedication to develop our skills, rather than relying on our innate brain power or natural abilities.
Four levels of mastery	As we learn, we move through four psychological states until we reach a stage of mastery: ignorance, awareness, learning and, ultimately, mastery.
Perception of challenge	With the challenge perception, we understand that we have a great opportunity to improve and actively pursue positive change.
Flourishing	Flourishing adults have high levels of emotional wellbeing. They are happy and satisfied with life. They tend to see their lives as having purpose.

Tool	Use
Self-efficacy	If we have self-efficacy, we believe we can manage any situation by relying on our organisational and executive skills.
Performance outcomes	To develop self-efficacy we need to look to our past experiences. They indicate whether or not we can achieve the desired outcome. The best way to influence performance outcomes is through positive past experiences.
Vicarious experiences	We can develop high or low self-efficacy by watching other people, and comparing their competence with our own.
Verbal persuasion	Receiving positive feedback when we're attempting to complete a task gives us the self-efficacy to believe we can do it.
Physiological arousal	The way our physiological body responds to stress heavily influences our feelings and beliefs about a particular situation. The fight, flight or freeze response dramatically influences how we react to a task.
Heart rate conditions	As the level of arousal increases, we can begin to associate the 'Condition' levels with specific heart rate levels. Dave Grossman's research links heart rate and performance conditions.
Heart rate individualised zone of optimal performance	The heart rate individualised zone of optimal performance combines Grossman's work, the Borg rating of perceived exertion (RPE) scale and the individualised zone of optimal functioning (IZOF).
Stress inoculation training (SIT)	SIT provides the opportunity to practise our skills while performing under stressful conditions that approximate the operational environment.
Environment training	Get out of the classroom and air conditioning. Do the training when it's raining, when it's dark and when it's cold.

Tool	Use
Peer pressure	There's nothing quite like doing scenarios in front of your classmates or colleagues. No one wants to be seen as a novice in front of their peers.
Exercise-induced stress	Using exercise before performance training to increase our heart rate and induce fatigue and weakness is an excellent SIT technique.
Audience	Performing training tasks in front of an audience is similar to peer pressure. A great way to place pressure upon a learner is to make them do things among a crowd.
Auditory stress	Playing loud metal music or crowd noises to distract the learner in any way, or to make communication difficult, is a great strategy to induce stress.
Use what you have	You don't need the perfect, the best or have the latest training equipment or facilities to achieve your goal. Take advantage of what you have.
Learn continually	People who flourish are generally very committed to learning and development, and they seek out new challenges. They look for means of continually extending themselves.
Always challenge yourself	Challenging ourselves is a way to learn and grow. When we're learning, we must set a task that exceeds our current level of competence.
The physiological sigh	This is a way to reduce stress and anxiety in the moment. It involves inhaling twice through the nose, then a long exhale through the mouth.
Box breathing	This quick relaxation technique involves breathing in deeply for four seconds while engaging the diaphragm and attempting to pull the breath down into the abdomen, holding the breath for four seconds, exhaling slowly for four seconds, then holding the lungs empty for four seconds.
Door breathing	To reduce stress, take a single, deep, exaggerated breath in, followed by a single exhale, preferably with pursed lips.

Tool	Use
Positive self-talk	We should all endeavour to allow positive thoughts to define who we are and what we do.
Visualisation	Visualisation is a purposeful, intense imagination technique that can improve our performance or help us achieve a goal. We imagine every aspect of a scenario so that when we have to perform under pressure we already know what to do.
Focus words	Develop and use a one-word mantra. Use this word just before starting any procedure or taking any action. It should be a word that will brings us to full attention and focus, snapping us out of endless thought.
Dark humour	Humour, especially the dark kind, can help us deal with traumatic situations and change our perception of the doom and gloom.
Scanning	Scanning helps us quickly detach from what we're currently focused on so that we can re-engage and act.
The cognitive pause	The idea behind taking a cognitive pause is to disengage our attention and reduce the amount of information we must keep in our working memory at once.
Drinking water	Staying hydrated is one of the most important things we can do. When our body is deprived of an adequate level of water, it produces the stress hormone cortisol.
Acceptance	We need to accept our situation as if we have chosen it.
Self-reflection	The ability to engage in self-reflection in an open and honest way can be the difference between learning and growing, and avoiding and declining.
Cognitive offloading	In cognitive offloading we use physical aids such as checklists to reduce the cognitive demand of tasks.

Tool	Use
Reframing	When the frame is shifted, the meaning changes, and our thinking and behaviour often change along with it.
Savouring	Savouring is the capacity to appreciate and enhance the positive experiences in our life.
Prioritising	Instead of trying to multitask, we need to focus on prioritising tasks.
Focusing	What we focus on we amplify.
Focus on action	Any approach that involves confronting the problem directly and taking action is the best strategy for eliminating the stressor.
Focus on control	We must control what we can and let go of the rest.
Focus on process	Outcomes will take care of themselves if you focus on the process.
Focus on solutions	We want to be part of the solution, not part of the problem. When we construct solutions rather than fixating on problems, we will be more likely to act and have a positive impact.
Focus on task	Fulfilling the task directly addresses the situation and provides a result in a stressful, performance-based setting.
The power of routine	Having routines makes things familiar and expected.
Knowing your goal	Keeping our goal in mind can help us succeed by keeping us goal-oriented.
Social support	Social support greatly improves our resilience to trauma and sets us up to flourish.
Journalling	Keeping a journal, writing down our thoughts and feelings, can change our thought patterns and perspective on our problems. It may even change our trajectory.
Exercise	Exercise not only has health benefits but changes brain chemistry to improve mental function.

Tool	Use
Meditation	Resilience is more pronounced in people who meditate.
Sleep	We can die from the lack of sleep faster than from a lack of food.
Predictable surprises	These occur when disaster strikes because of deviance from best practice. These disasters are predictable, and we need courage to prevent them. If not, they will be a surprise.
Normalisation of deviance	This occurs when people within an organisation become so insensitive to deviations from standard practice that those deviations no longer feel wrong.
Courageous self-leadership	A courageous self-leader determines what their future will be by the way they see life and prepare themselves to face its realities.
Being accountable	You are the right person to do something about your situation, regardless of what it is and who is to blame: no one else can do that for you.
Being honest	Speak the truth in spite of possible negative consequences.

Afterword:
The Paramedic Mindset Study

During the process of putting this book together I had the privilege of interviewing high-performing individuals on the *Paramedic Mindset* podcast. In each interview, these experts discussed performing under stress and possessing poise. It was an absolute privilege to tap into the vast experience of a range of very talented people.

The interviewees told great stories and helped bring context to this book. They are not only entertaining but also downright captivating. Guests included Mike Mullane, a former NASA astronaut who has completed three trips to space; Andrew MacLeod, a former humanitarian aid worker for the United Nations with deployments to war zones and natural disasters throughout the world; Dr Michael Lauria, a former US Air Force Pararescueman turned critical care flight paramedic; Matt Pepper, a special operations tactical medicine paramedic; Daniel Cooper, a Special Air Service Regiment soldier in the Australian Defence Force; and Dave Grossman, retired Lieutenant Colonel in the US Army.

So as to not waste the great opportunity to collect and extract all of their collective knowledge and wisdom, I decided to conduct a qualitative study of the interviews.

By critically analysing the interview transcripts, I sought to answer the whys and hows of human behaviour, opinion and experience. I've written the results and discussion of my study in a scientific style reminiscent of a university assignment. I deliberately wrote it this way to lend greater authenticity and validity to the findings. By writing this way I was able to identify common themes and findings regarding how to perform under stress.

Qualitative studies have been defined as those undertaken by 'researchers who are interested in understanding the meaning people have constructed, that is, how people make sense of their world and the experiences they have in the world'.

In my research, I sought to get to the heart of how paramedics and people who face disaster perform under stress and how they make sense of the stressed world around them. This helps reinforce the incredible value of the tools and strategies shared in this book.

Figure 22. This word cloud shows some of the words used by respondents to describe ways to perform under pressure and flourish.

Qualitative Analysis

After conducting 15 interviews with experts who all perform at a high level, have vast experience with performing under pressure, and have shown poise in high-stress, high-consequence environments, I performed a qualitative analysis of our conversations. I transcribed all of the interviews, and coded them using a computer software program called NVivo.

My goal was to look for common themes among the responses from the 15 interviewees, to discover what strategies and tools the experts use, and the value of possessing poise. The questions throughout the interviews did vary depending on the interviewee, but the theme remained the same: extracting information from their personal experiences of performing under pressure.

I have used quotes from these interviews throughout the book to help reiterate the information spoken in each chapter, but now it's time to share what these 15 high performers had most in common and valued most.

Themes Mentioned in the Interviews

	Codes	Number of interviews in which referenced (out of 15)	Number of times referenced in the interviews
1.	Breathing techniques	11	34
2.	Exercise	11	28
3.	Continual learning	10	30
4.	Skill and training	9	34
5.	Reflection	9	28
6.	Task-centredness	9	23
7.	Resilience	9	20
8.	Positivity	8	24

9.	Nutrition	8	12
10.	Process orientation	7	23
11.	Talk therapy	7	18
12.	Acceptance	7	15
13.	Openness	7	11
14.	Experience	6	20
15.	Preparedness	6	21
16.	Detachment	6	14
17.	Cognitive pause	6	13
18.	Empathy	6	9
19.	Practice	5	14
20.	Kindness	5	13

Discussion

Current teaching methods and practices operate by instilling knowledge and skills in a controlled environment. However, the majority of work and emergency situations occur in an uncontrolled environment involving natural human biological responses. The goal for conducting this quantitative analysis was to analyse key elements used by high-performing, successful people to control their physiological arousal and perform under pressure.

Paramedics, in particular, are taught how to perform medical interventions and to develop a sound knowledge base for the emergency medical profession. What is missing, however, is the ability to apply the knowledge under pressure. The aim in this study was to understand the critical components for performing when the stakes are high and the correct decision-making is essential.

In this study, the 15 interviews were transcribed, then a text analysis performed to search for common themes and subjects. Through a combination of qualitative questioning and interviewing a multitude of high-performing people, some interesting findings came to light.

Surprisingly the key attributes allowing the interviewees to possess poise under pressure were more often based on the individual's wellbeing than their experience or preparedness. The top four common themes among the experts were: breathing techniques, exercise, continual learning, and skill and training. Out of 15 interviewees, 11 mentioned using breathing as a way to control their arousal and bring down their heart rate, and it could be argued that all 15 people do this on some level. Breathing has been shown to be one of the most effective psychological skills we can possess.

Exercise was the second most common theme among all the experts. All interviewees were clearly fit and healthy; they prioritised exercise throughout their daily routine and emphasised its importance. Exercise also played multiple different roles for interviewees; they used it to maintain a minimum standard of fitness but also to help unwind and let go of stress as a means to detach and recharge. The majority of interviewees who mentioned exercise as a key characteristic exercised outdoors. They found peace and energy in exercising in the environment, amongst nature.

The third most common theme among all the interviews was continual learning, which along with challenging oneself played a critical role in the success and lives of all of the interviewees. They saw adversity as a way to improve and learn. They all admitted to going through difficult times and failing on multiple occasions. What they did to overcome those failings was learn, adapt and improve. Their career progression may have looked like the stock market, going up and down constantly, but over ten or more years, that line kept creeping up.

Furthermore, nine out of the 15 interviewees highlighted fervently the need to master fine motor skills, mentioning it 34 times overall. This reinforces the fact that even if you learned all the teachings in this book, without sound theoretical knowledge and possession of the fundamental skills necessary for your particular field, psychological skills wouldn't help. The experts I talked to all possessed a solid foundation of knowledge in their chosen field, and used psychological skills to turn that knowledge into high achievement.

This informal analysis of my podcast guests' interviews is not peer-reviewed or large scale and is therefore limited in its use. But that doesn't mean you can't listen to them and hear for yourself what they have to say.

Overall, the interviewees all possessed a strong resilience to adversity, and encouraged challenging situations. They were passionate about their profession or mission. They set goals that were difficult to achieve but not unachievable. They were prepared for any situation by having a high level of problem-solving and adaptation skills.

Most importantly, they had a paramedic mindset. They were motivated by a strong belief in their ability to reach their goals. They didn't make excuses or blame others. They controlled what they could control. They had positive self-talk. Throughout their lives, they had shown great courage and taken action.

Contact Me

If you wish to further your knowledge and research into the mindset of a paramedic, please reach out to me via the following links. I would love to hear from you and offer any assistance I can to help you save a life.

Saving lives is my passion.
Website: www.paramedicmindset.com.au
Email: leigh@paramedicmindset.com.au

Scan the QR code to take you to the interviews on the *Paramedic Mindset* podcast, which is designed to reinforce the lessons learned from the poise model of flourishing under stress. I hope you enjoy listening to the interviews as much as I enjoyed conducting them.

The purpose of the podcast was to complement the book, and help inspire you, the reader, with stories of courage, failure and triumph.

Acknowledgements

It's crystal clear to me that none of this would have been possible without the unwavering support of my incredible wife, Chloe. You have not just been my partner; you've been the guiding light of this endeavour. Your sacrifices, both seen and unseen, have breathed life into these pages. During the late nights at my desk, your love and encouragement have been my rock, sustaining me through moments that felt insurmountable.

To all those who invested their time in exploring the various drafts and versions of this story, my gratitude runs deep. It's challenging to mention everyone individually, but each of you knows the invaluable role you played.

The guidance and wisdom from my publishing team moulded *The Paramedic Mindset* from a rough, scratched stone into a polished, sparkling diamond. Alex Lloyd, I can't thank you enough for taking the leap of faith on my project. You have influenced the words within this text greatly, but it is your courage to back me and the story that I'll forever be grateful for. I've never received better feedback than from Belinda Huang – I wish I was as tactful and proficient as a paramedic providing constructive advice. You can simplify the difficult and detect the obvious. And Nicola Young, I will forever be jealous of your command of the English language.

I want to express a special acknowledgment to Andy Bell, Lieutenant Colonel Dave Grossman and Dr Michael Lauria. Your contributions to the scientific research within these pages have elevated this work. Your insights and guidance have not only improved the accuracy of the research discussed but also deepened the impact. Thank you for allowing me to share my passion with you and for your invaluable support.

Andrew Macleod, you are an inspiration and a mentor who has taught me so much. Simply listening to your experiences, stories and wisdom has profoundly influenced my worldview. Thank you for the immeasurable contribution you've made to humanity.

Finally, Dr Wade Jacklin, you have been pivotal in the development of not only this book but also my personal growth. Thank you for your patience and direction.

Appendices

Appendix A: The Mental Health Continuum Short Form

Here are my results for the Mental Health Continuum Short Form.

During the past month, how often did you feel . . .	Never	Once or twice	About once a week	About 2 or 3 times a week	Almost every day	Every day	
Emotional wellbeing							
happy				X			3
interested in life					X		4
satisfied with life				X			3
Social wellbeing							
that you had something important to contribute to society					X		4

During the past month, how often did you feel . . .	Never	Once or twice	About once a week	About 2 or 3 times a week	Almost every day	Every day	
that you belonged to a community (like a social group or your neighbourhood)		X					1
that our society is a good place or is becoming a better place, for all people			X				2
that people are basically good					X		4
that the way our society works makes sense to you					X		4
Psychological wellbeing							
that you liked most parts of your personality			X				2
good at managing the responsibilities of your daily life				X			3
that you had warm and trusting relationships with others			X				2
that you had experiences that challenged you to grow and become a better person					X		4
confident to think and express your own ideas and opinions					X		4
that your life has a sense of direction and meaning to it					X		4

My total score is 44 out of 70, and I answered *every day* or *almost every day* to one of the three signs of emotional wellbeing (questions 1–3) and six of the remaining 11 signs of positive functioning (questions 4–14). According to the definition, I am flourishing, but only just.

If you would like to be part of the Paramedic Mindset study, please send your results to the Mental Health Continuum Short Form (page 63) to: leigh@paramedicmindset.com.au

Your information and results will be kept completely anonymous. We would love to collect the results and data to form a better understanding of the mental health of those who are engaged in stressful pursuits.

Please include in the email your:

- gender
- age
- occupation
- nationality.

Appendix B: Generalised Self-efficacy Scale

Here are my results for the Generalised Self-efficacy Scale.

	Not at all true	Barely true	Moderately true	Exactly true	
I can always manage to solve complex problems if I try hard enough.				X	4
If someone opposes me, I can find means and ways to get what I want.			X		3
It is easy for me to stick to my aims and accomplish my goals.		X			2
I am confident that I can deal efficiently with unexpected events.				X	4
Thanks to my resourcefulness, I know how to handle unforeseen situations.				X	4
I can solve most problems if I invest the necessary effort.				X	4
I can remain calm when facing difficulties because I can rely on my coping abilities.				X	4
When I am confronted with a problem, I can usually find several solutions.			X		3
If I am in a bind, I can usually think of something to do.			X		3
No matter what comes my way, I'm usually able to handle it.				X	4

I scored 35 out of a possible 40 points, well above the threshold of 20, which means I possess high self-efficacy.

If you would like to be part of the Paramedic Mindset study, please send in your results to the Generalised Self-efficacy Scale (page 74) to: leigh@paramedicmindset.com.au

Your information and results will be kept completely anonymous. We would love to collect the results and data to form a better understanding of the mental health of those who are engaged in stressful pursuits.

Please include in the email your:

- gender
- age
- occupation
- nationality.

Appendix C: Borg Rating of Perceived Exertion

Here are my results for the Borg RPE. First, I listed my emotions, both relating to success (positive affect) and negative affect, then listed them on each respective Borg scale for positive and negative affect. Next, I rated them and calculated the results to determine my optimal heart rate during performance.

Step 1: Success Emotions Table: Positive and Negative Affect

Positive Affect Emotions that Can Improve Performance

Motivated	Willing	Purposeful	Alert	Resolute
Active	Confident	Showing off	Vigorous	Energetic
Charged	Brisk	Certain	Glad	Enthusiastic
Cheerful	Rested	Eager	Easy-going	Brave
Relaxed	Exalted	Peaceful	Fearless	Excited
Satisfied	Stimulated	Calm	Pleasant	Good
Daring	Nice	Happy	Comfortable	Composed
Sleepy	Free	Overjoyed	Animated	Carefree

Negative Affect Emotions that Can Improve Performance

Attacking	Vehement	Intense	Aggressive	In pain
Pressure	Disappointed	Tense	Provoked	Furious
Angry	Irritated	Mad	Nervous	Restless
Concerned	Tired	Tight	Worried	Alarmed
Exhausted	Sluggish	Indignant	Overloaded	Dispirited
Irresolute	Weary	Doubtful	Unhappy	Sorrowful
Sad	Afraid	Distressed	Down	Lazy
Uncertain	Depressed	Unwilling	Strained	Terrified

Step 2: Borg Rating of Perceived Exertion Scale
Positive emotions that improve performance

		Positive Emotion				
		1	2	3	4	5
Score	Level of Exertion	Purposeful	Alert	Composed	Daring	Resolute
6	No exertion at all					
7						
7.5	Extremely low					
8						
9	Very low			X		
10						
11	Mild	X	X			X
12						
13	Somewhat high				X	
14						
15	High					
16						
17	Very high					
18						
19	Extremely high					
20	Maximal exertion					

If I add up the scores, I get a total score of 55.

Negative emotions that improve performance

Score	Level of Exertion	Negative Emotion				
		1	2	3	4	5
		Pressure	Concerned	Irritated	Provoked	Alarmed
6	No exertion at all					
7						
7.5	Extremely low					
8						
9	Very low					
10						
11	Mild					
12						
13	Somewhat high	X	X			X
14				X	X	
15	High					
16						
17	Very high					
18						
19	Extremely high					
20	Maximal exertion					

If I add up the scores, I get a total score of 69.

Calculating my total score and heart rate conversion

Total score = 55 + 69 = 124

Average score = 124/10 = 12.4

Heart rate conversion = 12.4 x 10 = 124 beats per minute

Appendix D: Heart Rate Individualised Zone of Optimal Performance

Here are my results for the heart rate individualised zone of optimal performance.

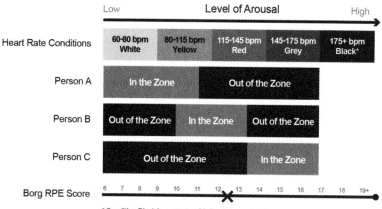

INDIVIDUALISED ZONE OF OPTIMAL PERFORMANCE

* Condition Black is a catastrophic breakdown of performance

With a Borg RPE score of 12.4 (see Appendix C), my heart rate individualised zone of optimal performance would be Paramedic B and the early stages of Condition Red. This means I prefer a moderate level of arousal and tend to perform well in most fine motor skills once I have mastered them. Please note, however, that this will still vary depending on the task being completed.

Recommended Reading

Paramedic Books

Connelly, Joe, *Bringing Out the Dead*, Vintage, 1999 (adapted into a 1999 movie of the same name)

Gilmour, Benjamin, *Paramedico: Around the World by Ambulance*, The Friday Project, 2013

Hazzard, Kevin, *A Thousand Naked Strangers: A Paramedic's Wild Ride to the Edge and Back*, Scribner, 2016

McCarthy, Jon, *Hard Roll: A Paramedic's Perspective of Life and Death in New Orleans*, Pelican, 2017

Whitfield, Sunny, *Here Hold My Drink and Watch This: Tales from the Lighter Side of Paramedicine, Adventure and Life*, Tablo, 2021

Mindset Development Books

Aurelius, Marcus, *Meditations*.

Brown, Brené, *Daring Greatly: The Courage to Be Vulnerable Transforms the Way We Live, Love, Parent, and Lead*, Hay House UK, 2020

Bungay, Stephen, *The Art of Action: How Leaders Close the Gaps between Plans, Actions and Results*, Nicholas Brealey, 2011

Dweck, Carol, *Mindset: The New Psychology of Success*, Random House, 2006

Kross, Ethan, *Chatter: The Voice in Our Head, Why it Matters, and How to Harness It*, Crown, 2021

Leaf, Caroline, *Cleaning Up Your Mental Mess: 5 Simple, Scientifically Proven Steps to Reduce Anxiety, Stress, and Toxic Thinking*, Baker Books, 2021

Pronk, Dan, Ben Pronk & Tim Curtis, *The Resilience Shield: SAS Resilience Techniques to Master Your Mindset and Overcome Adversity*, Macmillan, 2021

Ratey, John & Eric Hagerman, *Spark! How Exercise Will Improve the Performance of Your Brain*, Quercus, 2009

Vaughan, Diane, *The Challenger Launch Decision: Risky Technology, Culture, and Deviance at NASA*, University of Chicago Press, 2016

Walker, Matthew, *Why We Sleep*, Penguin, 2017

Wooden, John & Steve Jamison, *Wooden on Leadership: How to Create a Winning Organization*, McGraw-Hill, 2005

Interviewee Books

Ford, Justine, *The Good Cop: The True Story of Ron Iddles, Australia's Greatest Detective*, Pan Macmillan, 2018

Fox, Carol & Kathryn Gorman, *Confident Communication for Leaders*, Life Performance, 2018

Grossman, Dave with Loren Christensen, *On Combat: The Psychology and Physiology of Deadly Combat in War and Peace*, Killology Research Group, 2012

MacLeod, Andrew, *A Life Half Lived: Surviving the World's Emergency Zones*, New Holland, 2013

Mullane, Mike, *Riding Rockets: The Outrageous Tales of a Space Shuttle Astronaut*, Scribner, 2006

Sundahl, Daniel, *Portraits of an Emergency*, DanSun Photo Art, 2021

References

Chapter 1

17   The ideal attitude is of calm indifference . . .: Inwood B, 'Stoicism', in L Gerson (ed.), *The Cambridge History of Philosophy in Late Antiquity*, Cambridge: Cambridge University Press, 2000, pp. 126–39.

17   American author Ryan Holiday, the foremost researcher . . .: Holiday R, *The Obstacle Is the Way: The Timeless Art of Tuning into Triumph*, London: Profile Books, 2014.

17   Holiday's beginner guide says that 'Stoicism doesn't . . .': Holiday R, '7 Stoic Practices To Help You Become Your Ideal Self in 2020', <dailystoic. com/7-stoic-practices-to-help-you-become-your-ideal-self-in-2020>.

17   His work has generated . . .: Aurelius M, *Meditations*, 9.13, New York City, New York: Random House, 2002.

18   One of the most famous samurais . . .: Quoted in Abbasi M, 'To be a samurai', Mohammed Abbasi (blog), 22 July 2018, <mmabbasi. com/2018/07/22/to-be-a-samurai>.

19   The entire nation showed true . . .: Carlin D, 'How to handle a crisis: lessons from Churchill's darkest hour', *Forbes*, 25 November 2019, <www.forbes.com/sites/davidcarlin/2019/11/25/how-to-handle-a-crisis-lessons-from-churchills-darkest-hour>.

22   A study on paramedic health found that . . .: Lulla A, LL Tian, PM Hawnwan et al, 'The EMS Suicide Threat', *EMS World*,

February 2020, <https://www.hmpgloballearningnetwork.com/site/emsworld/1223779/ce-article-ems-suicide-threat>.

22   In 2010, an Australian psychosocial health study revealed . . .: Dawson DA, *Ambulance paramedic psychosocial health study*, (unpublished doctoral dissertation), Victoria University, Melbourne, Australia, 2018.

22   In 2019, an Australian Senate committee reported . . .: Education and Employment References Committee, *The people behind 000: mental health of our first responders*, Police Federation of Australia, February 2019.

Chapter 2

32   The word 'mindset' was first used . . .: Emmanuel I, 'Mindset', 7 October 2018, <wwwemex.wordpress.com/2018/10/07/mindset>.

32   In simple terms, our mindset is our view of . . .: Buchanan A, 'The nature of mindsets', *Medium*, 17 March 2017, <medium.com/benefit-mindset/the-nature-of-mindsets-18afba2ac890>.

34   Our personality is to all intents and purposes . . .: Dweck CS, *Mindset: The New Psychology of Success*, New York: Random House, 2006.

35   This prevents us from succeeding or learning from . . .: Parrish S, 'Carol Dweck: a summary of the two mindsets and the power of believing that you can improve', *Thrive Global*, 31 August 2017, <thriveglobal.com/stories/carol-dweck-a-summary-of-the-two-mindsets-and-the-power-of-believing-that-you-can-improve>.

35   A study completed by Dave Collins . . .: Collins D, A MacNamara & N McCarthy, 'Super Champions, Champions, and Almosts: Important Differences and Commonalities on the Rocky Road', *Frontiers in Psychology*, 2016, vol. 6, <doi.org/10.3389/fpsyg.2015.02009>.

39   A 2019 study by John vonRosenberg . . .: vonRosenberg J, 'Cognitive appraisal and stress performance: the threat/challenge matrix and its implications on performance', *Air Medical Journal*, 2019, vol. 38, no. 5, pp. 331–33, <www.sciencedirect.com/science/article/abs/pii/S1067991X19300021>.

39   Deciding to actively engage in problem-solving . . .: Ngui GK & YF Lay, 'The relationship between resilience and perceived practicum stress: the mediating role of self-efficacy', *Sains Humanika*, 2017, vol. 9, no. 1–4, <sainshumanika.utm.my/index.php/sainshumanika/article/view/1123>.

40   A paramedic's need is to fix the problem . . .: Minhaz M, 'Perception: definition, importance, factors, perceptual process, errors', iEduNote, <www.iedunote.com/perception>.

44   Dr Michael D. Yapko, who has written several pieces on depression . . .: Yapko MD, *Depression is Contagious: How the Most Common Mood Disorder Is Spreading Around the World and How to Stop It*, New York: Simon & Schuster, 2013.

45   Eventually, we start to think as they think . . .: Quoted in Chase J,

'You are the average of the five people you spend the most time with', Linkedin, 2 December 2020, <www.linkedin.com/pulse/you-average-five-people-spend-most-time-josh-chase>.

Chapter 3

54   'Health is . . . not merely the absence . . .': Constitution of the World Health Organization, in *Chronicle of the World Health Organization*, 1947, vol. 1, nos 1–2, p. 29.

54   Psychologist Dr Barbara Fredrickson's research on positivity . . .: Fredrickson BL, 'What good are positive emotions?', *Review of General Psychology*, 1998, vol. 2, no. 3, pp. 300–19, <www.ncbi.nlm.nih.gov/pmc/articles/PMC3156001>.

54   Among other answers, an important . . .: Rizo CA, AR Jadad & M Enkin, 'What's a good doctor and how do you make one?', *BMJ*, 2002, vol. 325, no. 7366, <dx.doi.org/10.1136/bmj.325.7366.0/g>.

54   In other words, the 'good' doctor is a . . .: Ninivaggi FJ, 'What makes a good doctor "good"?', *Psychology Today*, 6 October 2020, <www.psychologytoday.com/us/blog/envy/202010/what-makes-good-doctor-good>.

55   Mental health could thus be considered . . .: Doll DK, *Building Psychological Fitness: How High Performers Achieve with Ease*, Karen DeCasare Doll, 2022.

55   It could be considered a precursor or . . .: Magyar JL & CLM Keyes, 'Defining, measuring, and applying subjective well-being,' in MW Gallagher & SJ Lopez (eds), *Positive Psychological Assessment: A Handbook of Models and Measures*, 2nd edn, Washington DC: American Psychological Association, 2019, pp. 389–415.

55   If someone suffers from poor mental health . . .: Keyes CLM, 'The mental health continuum: from languishing to flourishing in life', *Journal of Health and Social Behavior*, 2002, vol. 43, no. 2, pp. 207–22, <dx.doi.org/10.2307/3090197>.

56   A 2005 study using these definitions estimated . . .: Keyes CLM & JG Grzywacz, 'Health as a complete state: the added value in work performance and healthcare costs', *Journal of Occupational and Environmental Medicine*, 2005, vol. 47, no. 5, pp. 523–32, <dx.doi.org/10.1097/01.jom.0000161737.21198.3a>.

56   They have self-belief, feel like they know what . . .: 'Ask an expert: What is "positive psychology"?', CNNfyi.com, 24 January 2001, <edition.cnn.com/2001/fyi/teachers.tools/01/24/c.keyes>.

56   Around 80 per cent of the population is not . . .: Keyes C, 'The mental health continuum: from languishing to flourishing in life', *Journal of Health and Social Behavior*, June 2002, vol. 43, no. 2, pp. 207–22.

57   Stoics believed that a life is eudaimonic when . . .: Garrett J, 'What is Stoicism? Explained in 3 beliefs', *The Collector*, 9 May 2023, <www.thecollector.com/what-is-stoicism-the-stoics-beliefs>.

57 Those who are languishing are not mentally ill . . .: Keyes CLM & JL Magyar-Moe, 'The measurement and utility of adult subjective well-being', in SJ Lopez & CR Snyder (eds), *Positive Psychological Assessment: A Handbook of Models and Measures*, Washington DC: American Psychological Association, 2003, pp. 411–25.

57 The risk of major depression is significantly higher . . .: Keyes CLM, 'The mental health continuum: from languishing to flourishing in life', *Journal of Health and Social Behavior*, 2002, vol. 43, no. 2, pp. 207–22, <dx.doi.org/10.2307/3090197>.

58 These discussions centre on the negative and . . .: Knipfer K & B Kump, 'Collective rumination: when "problem talk" impairs organizational resilience', *Applied Psychology*, 2022, vol. 71, no. 1, pp. 154–73, <dx. doi.org/10.1111/apps.12315>.

60 Positivity is beyond simple feelings of happiness: 'It consists . . .': Quoted in Robinson B, 'The 3-to-1 positivity ratio and 10 ways it advances your career', *Forbes*, 16 October 2020, <www.forbes.com/ sites/bryanrobinson/2020/10/16/10-ways-the-3-to-1-positivity-ratio-can-advance-your-career/?sh=cce76e170c42>.

61 Epicurus, a Greek philosopher, believed . . .: O'Connor, EM (trans.), *The Essential Epicurus: Letters, Principal Doctrines, Vatican Sayings, and Fragments*, 1993, Prometheus Books, Connecticut, USA.

61 Another interesting study by Barbara Fredrickson . . .: Catalino L & Fredrickson B, 'A Tuesday in the life of a flourisher: the role of Positive emotional reactivity in optimal mental health', *Emotion*, 2011, vol. 11, no. 4, pp. 938–50, <www.ncbi.nlm.nih.gov/pmc/articles/ PMC3160725>.

61 In comparison to non-flourishers and depressed people . . .: ibid.

62 Coming up is a quick questionnaire called the . . .: Keyes C, 'Atlanta: brief description of the mental health continuum short form (MHC-SF)', Sociology Department, Emory College, 2009, <www.sociology. emory.edu/ckeyes>, accessed 9 Mar 2022, no longer available.

Chapter 4

70 Recent research has identified a significant relationship . . .: Giblett A & G Hodgins, 'Flourishing or languishing? The relationship between mental health, health locus of control and generalised self-efficacy', *Psychological Reports*, 2021, vol. 126, no. 1, pp. 94–116, <journals. sagepub.com/doi/10.1177/00332941211040432>.

71 The term 'self-efficacy' was coined by Canadian American . . .: Bandura A, 'Self-efficacy: toward a unifying theory of behavioral change', *Psychological Review*, 1977, vol. 84, no. 2, pp. 191–215, <pubmed. ncbi.nlm.nih.gov/847061>.

71 In other words, it's our belief in our ability . . .: Lopez-Garrido G, 'Self-efficacy theory, SimplyPsychology, 10 July 2023, <www. simplypsychology.org/self-efficacy.html>.

71 It helps us determine which goals to set . . .: ibid.

73 According to Bandura, our self-efficacy can determine . . .: Bandura A, 'Self-efficacy: toward a unifying theory of behavioral change', *Psychological Review*, 1977, vol. 84, no. 2, pp. 191–215, <pubmed. ncbi.nlm.nih.gov/847061>.

73 Our belief in our own ability to succeed under stress . . .: ibid.

73 This was confirmed in a study conducted by Australian researchers . . .: Giblett A & G Hodgins, 'Flourishing or languishing? The relationship between mental health, health locus of control and generalised self-efficacy', *Psychological Reports*, 2021, vol. 126, no. 1, pp. 94–116, <journals.sagepub.com/doi/10.1177/00332941211040432>.

73 They concluded that 'a prospective belief in one's capacity . . .': ibid.

73 German researchers Ralf Schwarzer and Matthias Jerusalem . . .: Schwarzer R & M Jerusalem, 'Optimistic self-beliefs as a resource factor in coping with stress', in SE Hobfoll & MW Vries, *Extreme Stress and Communities: Impact and Intervention*, Dordrecht: Springer Netherlands, 1995, pp. 159–77.

77 Bandura wrote, 'Positive and negative experiences . . .': Redmond BF, 'Self-efficacy theory: do I think that I can succeed in my work?', *Work attitudes and motivation*, Pennsylvania State University, World Campus, 2010.

78 You develop the skills and ability to influence . . .: ibid.

78 Bandura wrote, 'People can develop high or low self-efficacy vicariously . . .': Bandura A, 'Self-efficacy: toward a unifying theory of behavioral change', *Psychological Review*, 1977, vol. 84, no. 2, pp. 191–215, <pubmed.ncbi.nlm.nih.gov/847061>.

79 Bandura wrote, 'Self-efficacy is also influenced by encouragement . . .': Redmond BF, 'Self-efficacy theory: do I think that I can succeed in my work?', *Work attitudes and motivation*, Pennsylvania State University, World Campus, 2010.

79 'I think I can climb up the mountain. I think I can. I think . . .': Piper, W, *The Little Engine That Could*, New York, NY: G P Putnam's Sons, 2001.

80 We experience sensations from our body...: Lopez-Garrido G, 'Self-efficacy theory', SimplyPsychology, 10 July 2023, <www.simply psychology.org/self-efficacy.html>.

Chapter 5

87 Our autonomic (involuntary) nervous system has two components . . .: 'Understanding the stress response', Harvard Health, 6 July 2020, <www.health.harvard.edu/staying-healthy/understanding-the-stress-response>.

88 The parasympathetic nervous system acts in . . .: Caroline NL, *Emergency Care in the Streets*, 5th edn, Philadelphia, PA: Lippincott Williams & Wilkins, 1995.

88   The amygdala interprets this information and immediately . . .: 'Understanding the stress response', Harvard Health, 6 July 2020, <www.health.harvard.edu/staying-healthy/understanding-the-stress-response>.

88   The hypothalamus will send signals through the . . .: Caroline NL, *Emergency Care in the Streets*, 5th edn, Philadelphia, PA: Lippincott Williams & Wilkins, 1995.

88   The adrenal medulla secretes hormones called . . .: Utiger RD, 'Adrenal gland', *Encyclopedia Britannica*, Accessed 2019, <www.britannica.com/science/adrenal-gland>.

89   In fact, the brain's wiring is so efficient . . .: 'Understanding the stress response', Harvard Health, 6 July 2020, <www.health.harvard.edu/staying-healthy/understanding-the-stress-response>.

89   This travels in the bloodstream to stimulate . . .: Carlton M, J Voisey, TJ Parker, C Punyadeera & L Cuttle, 'A review of potential biomarkers for assessing physical and psychological trauma in paediatric burns', *Burns Trauma*, 2021, vol. 9, article no. 49, <academic.oup.com/burnstrauma/article/doi/10.1093/burnst/tkaa049/6131418>.

91   We hyperventilate to increase our oxygen levels in the blood . . .: Caroline NL, *Emergency Care in the Streets*, 5th edn, Philadelphia, PA: Lippincott Williams & Wilkins, 1995.

91   Research completed by US psychologist Richard Dienstbier . . .: Dienstbier RA, 'Arousal and physiological toughness: implications for mental and physical health', *Psychological Review*, 1989, vol. 96, no. 1, pp. 84–100, <psycnet.apa.org/record/1989-14732-001>.

91   This was associated with favourable outcomes . . .: Kelley DC, E Siegel & JB Wormwood, 'Understanding police performance under stress: insights from the biopsychosocial model of challenge and threat', *Frontiers in Psychology*, 2019, vol. 10, article no. 1800, <www.frontiersin.org/articles/10.3389/fpsyg.2019.01800/full>.

92   In simpler terms, the heart can pump better . . .: ibid.

92   In a threat state, however, the purpose of this system . . .: ibid.

92   If this system becomes continuously activated . . .: Caroline NL, *Emergency Care in the Streets*, 5th edn, Philadelphia, PA: Lippincott Williams & Wilkins, 1995.

96   Working memory refers to the capacity to selectively . . .: Jha AP, SL Rogers & AB Morrison, 'Mindfulness training in high stress professions: strengthening attention and resilience', in RA Baer (ed.), *Mindfulness-based Treatment Approaches: Clinician's Guide to Evidence Base and Applications*, New York: Academic Press, 2014, pp. 347–66.

96   Our heart will start to pound, and our thinking . . .: Weisinger H & JP Pawliw-Fry, *How to Perform under Pressure: The Science of Doing Your Best when it Matters Most*, London: John Murray Learning, 2016.

98   Automaticity allows the brain to reduce . . .: ibid.

98   Your prefrontal cortex is into plausibility . . .: 'To reduce medical errors, take a cognitive pause', *Emergency Physicians Monthly*, 2013, <epmonthly.com/article/to-reduce-medical-errors-take-a-cognitive-pause>.

Chapter 6

105   First described in 1908, this law suggests that . . .: Yerkes RM & JD Dodson, 'The relation of strength of stimulus to rapidity of habit-formation', *Journal of Comparative Neurology and Psychology*, 1908, vol. 18, no. 5, pp. 459–82, <onlinelibrary.wiley.com/doi/10.1002/cne.920180503>.

105   It was clear from the experiment that the rats' stress . . .: ibid.

107   The catastrophe model hypothesises that physiological . . .: Hardy J & L Fazey, *The Inverted-U Hypothesis: A Catastrophe for Sport Psychology*, British Association of Sports Sciences Monograph No. 1, Leeds, UK: National Coaching Foundation, 1988.

108   The individualised zone of optimal functioning (IZOF) . . .: Gilbert M-A, DR Gould, Y Hanin et al., 'Sport psychologist's digest', *Journal of Sport and Exercise Psychology*, 1980, vol. 2, no. 3, pp. 175–80, <dx. doi.org/10.1123/jsp.2.3.175>.

108   The zone may also be different for individuals . . .: 'Zone of optimal functioning', *The Oxford Dictionary of Sports Science & Medicine*, Oxford Reference, <www.oxfordreference.com/view/10.1093/oi/authority.20110803133528142>.

109   This research also indicates that optimum performance . . .: Ruiz MC, JS Raglin & YL Hanin, 'The individual zones of optimal functioning (IZOF) model (1978–2014): historical overview of its development and use', *International Journal of Sport and Exercise Psychology*, 2017, vol. 15, no. 1, pp. 41–63, <www.tandfonline.com/doi/full/10.1080/161 2197X.2015.1041545>.

109   If it makes you perform worse, . . .: Svensson J, 'How to find your zone of optimal functioning', Evidence Based Training, 2020, <www.ebtofficial. com/perform-better/how-to-find-your-zone-of-optimal-functioning>.

110   Figure 7.: Adapted from Gilbert M-A, DR Gould, Y Hanin et al., 'Sport psychologist's digest', *Journal of Sport and Exercise Psychology*, 1980, vol. 2, no. 3, pp. 175–80, <dx.doi.org/10.1123/jsp.2.3.175>.

111   His groundbreaking 1997 work . . .: Grossman D & BK Siddle, 'Psychological effects of combat', in Lester Kurtz (ed.), *Encyclopedia of Violence, Peace, and Conflict*, 2nd edn, New York: Academic Press, 2008, p. 1796–1805.

111   I highly recommend that you read another . . .: Grossman D, *On Combat: The Psychology and Physiology of Deadly Conflict in War and in Peace*, 3rd edn, Millstadt, Illinois: Warrior Science Publications, 2008.

111   The beauty of this theory, though, is . . .: Jedick R, 'Combat stress response & tactical breathing', Go Flight Medicine, 2014, <goflightmedicine.com/on-combat>.

112   Grossman's five different conditions . . .: Grossman D, *On Combat: The Psychology and Physiology of Deadly Conflict in War and in Peace*, 3rd edn, Millstadt, Illinois: Warrior Science Publications, 2008.

117   When you imagine your previous best performance . . .: Hanin YL & P Syrj, 'Performance affect in junior ice-hockey players: a test of the IZOF model', *Medicine & Science in Sports & Exercise*, 1994, vol. 26, suppl. S56, article no. 314, <journals.lww.com/acsm-msse/citation/1994/05001/314_performance_affect_in_junior_ice_hockey.315.aspx>.

118   The Borg rating of perceived exertion . . .: Borg G, 'Rating scales for perceived physical effort and exertion', in *International Encyclopedia of Ergonomics and Human Factors*, 2nd edn, Boca Raton, Florida: CRC Press, 2006.

121   A score of 6 on the Borg RPE scale corresponds . . .: ibid.

Chapter 7

129   According to defence analysts J.D. Fletcher . . .: Fletcher JD & AP Wind, 'The evolving definition of cognitive readiness for military operations', in *Teaching and Measuring Cognitive Readiness*, Boston, Massachusetts: Springer US, 2014, pp. 25–52.

130   OCR is defined as 'the mental preparation (including . . .: Grier RA, JD Fletcher & JE Morrison, 'Defining and measuring military cognitive readiness', *Proceedings of the Human Factors and Ergonomics Society Annual Meeting*, 2012, vol. 56, no. 1, pp. 435–37, <journals.sagepub.com/doi/abs/10.1177/1071181312561098>.

130   In other words, through SIT we can attempt . . .: Robson S & T Manacapilli, *Enhancing Performance under Stress: Stress Inoculation Training for Battlefield Airmen*, Santa Monica, California: RAND, 2014.

131   SIT is typically organised into three distinct phases . . .: Meichenbaum D & R Cameron, 'Stress inoculation training', in D Meichenbaum & ME Jaremko (eds), *Stress Reduction and Prevention*, Boston, Massachusetts: Springer US, 1989, pp. 115–54.

132   Being exposed to the fight, flight or freeze response . . .: Grossman D, *On Combat: The Psychology and Physiology of Deadly Conflict in War and in Peace*, 3rd edn, Millstadt, Illinois: Warrior Science Publications, 2008.

132   US Air Force Pararescueman Michael Lauria says . . .: Lauria M & L Anderson, 'Episode 10: Michael Lauria, Beat the Stress Fool', The Paramedic Mindset, <www.paramedicmindset.com.au/expert-interviews>.

140   One of Canadian psychologist Dr Jordan Peterson's . . .: Peterson J, *Beyond Order: 12 More Rules for Life*, New York City, New York: Penguin, 2021.

Chapter 8

152   Forget about all the times you were told . . .: Ramirez J-M, 'The integrative role of the sigh in psychology, physiology, pathology, and neurobiology', *Progress in Brain Research*, 2014, vol. 209, pp. 91–129. <www.sciencedirect.com/science/article/abs/pii/B9780444632746000060>.

153   US neuroscientist Dr Jack Feldman explains that . . .: Del Negro CA, GD Funk & JL Feldman, 'Breathing matters', *Nature Reviews Neuroscience*, 2018, vol. 19, no. 6, pp. 351–67, <www.nature.com/articles/s41583-018-0003-6>.

153   Another US neuroscientist, Dr Andrew Huberman, explains . . .: Huberman A, 'How the brain makes sense of stress, fear, and courage', Finding Mastery (podcast), episode 237, <findingmastery.com/podcasts/andrew-huberman>.

153   Researchers have studied the behaviour of soccer . . .: Misirlisoy E & P Haggard, 'Asymmetric predictability and cognitive competition in football penalty shootouts', *Current Biology*, 2014, vol. 24, no. 16, pp, 1918–22, <www.cell.com/current-biology/fulltext/S0960-9822(14)00839-2>.

154   More recently, Huberman and his colleagues looked . . .: Balban MY, E Neri, MM Kogon et al., 'Brief structured respiration practices enhance mood and reduce physiological arousal', *Cell Reports Medicine*, 2023, vol. 4, no. 1, article no. 100895, <pubmed.ncbi.nlm.nih.gov/36630953>.

155   Diaphragmatic breathing involves contraction of the diaphragm . . .: Ma X, Z-Q Yue, Z-Q Gong, H Zhang et al., 'The effect of diaphragmatic breathing on attention, negative affect and stress in healthy adults', *Frontiers in Psychology*, 2017, vol. 8, article no. 874, <www.frontiersin.org/articles/10.3389/fpsyg.2017.00874/full>.

156   It's called door breathing because it gives you a small . . .: Lauria MJ, IA Gallo, S Rush et al., 'Psychological skills to improve emergency care providers' performance under stress', Annals of Emergency Medicine, 2017, vol. 70, no. 6, pp. 884–90, <www.annemergmed.com/article/S0196-0644(17)30314-1/fulltext>.

156   By employing positive self-talk, we can . . .: ibid.

157   We can choose to ignore the thoughts or let . . .: Kross E., *Chatter: The Voice in Our Head and How to Harness it*, London: Vermilion, 2022.

158   Essentially, it's thinking about how you will . . .: Kross E & O Ayduk, 'Self-distancing: theory, research, and current directions', in B Gawronski (ed.), *Advances in Experimental Social Psychology*, vol. 55, New York: Academic Press, 2017, pp. 81–136, <selfcontrol.psych.lsa.umich.edu/wp-content/uploads/2017/04/SD.pdf>.

158   Another small skill that can help increase . . .: Kross E., *Chatter: The Voice in Our Head and How to Harness it*, London: Vermilion, 2022.

159   In fact, our body's physiological response . . .: Lauria MJ, IA Gallo, S Rush et al., 'Psychological skills to improve emergency care providers' performance under stress', *Annals of Emergency Medicine*, 2017, vol. 70, no. 6, pp. 884–90, <www.annemergmed.com/article/S0196-0644(17)30314-1/fulltext>.

159   He says that 'Qualifying is very raw, so you spend . . .': 'Sebastian Vettel: why winning is all in the mind', *Autocar*, 23 July 2017, <www.autocar.co.uk/car-news/motorsport/sebastian-vettel-why-winning-all-mind>.

161   This word will bring you to full attention and focus . . .: Lauria MJ, IA Gallo, S Rush et al., 'Psychological skills to improve emergency care providers' performance under stress', *Annals of Emergency Medicine*, 2017, vol. 70, no. 6, pp. 884–90, <www.annemergmed.com/article/S0196-0644(17)30314-1/fulltext>.

166   Research has found that paramedics use humour . . .: Lancaster C & P Phillips, 'How does the use of humour in the UK ambulance service affect a clinician's well-being?' *British Paramedic Journal*, 2021, vol. 6, no. 2, pp. 26–33, <www.ncbi.nlm.nih.gov/pmc/articles/PMC8415210>.

166   Having said that, studies have shown that approximately . . .: Dexter L, K Brook & E Frates, 'The laughter prescription: a tool for lifestyle medicine', *American Journal of Lifestyle Medicine*, vol. 10, pp. 262–67, <doi.org/10.1177%2F1559827614550279>.

167   Other studies have suggested that emergency . . .: Moran C & M Massam, 'An evaluation of humour in emergency work', *Australasian Journal of Disaster and Trauma Studies*, vol. 1997-3, <www.massey.ac.nz/~trauma/issues/1997-3/moran1.htm>.

169   A New Zealand study found that when student . . .: MacIver K, 'Paramedic decision-making: expert evaluation of a new decision-making model', Masters thesis, Whitireia Community Polytechnic, New Zealand, 2017, <weltec.spydus.co.nz/cgi-bin/spydus.exe/FULL/WPAC/BIBENQ/44189491/67355886,1>.

170   'When you don't give your body the fluids . . .': Shaw G & B Nazario, 'Water and stress reduction: sipping stress away', WebMD, 7 July 2009, <www.webmd.com/diet/features/water-stress-reduction>.

Chapter 9

177   In mentioning self-actualisiation . . .: Maslow AH, 'A theory of human motivation', Psychological Review, 1943, vol. 50, no. 4, pp. 370–396. <doi.org/10.1037/h0054346>.

177   The knowledge that we'll survive no matter . . .: West H, 'What causes fear of failure and how to conquer it with self-acceptance', Harper West (blog), 22 December 2017, <www.harperwest.co/what-causes-fear-of-failure-how-conquer-with-self-acceptance>.

177   Our perception of the threat will determine . . .: Zhuang Q, L Wang, Y Tang & A Chen, 'Translation of fear reflex into impaired cognitive function mediated by worry', *Science Bulletin*, 2016, vol. 61, no. 24, pp. 1841–43, <link.springer.com/article/10.1007/s11434-016-1177-9>.

184   Psychologist Dr Tchiki Davis has defined self-doubt . . .: Braslow MD, J Guerrettaz, RM Arkin & KC Oleson, 'Self-doubt', *Social and Personality Psychology Compass*, 2012, vol. 6, no. 6, pp. 470–82, <psycnet.apa.org/doi/10.1111/j.1751-9004.2012.00441.x>.

184   More specifically, self-doubt makes us question . . .: ibid.

184   A common consequence of self-doubt is self-handicap . . .: 'Therapy for self doubt, therapist for self doubt', GoodTherapy, 23 September 2009, <www.goodtherapy.org/learn-about-therapy/issues/self-doubt>.

185   It refers to the phenomenon of doubting our . . .: Clance PR & SA Imes, 'The imposter phenomenon in high achieving women: Dynamics and therapeutic intervention', *Psychotherapy: Theory, Research & Practice*, 1978, vol. 15, no. 3, pp. 241–47, <psycnet.apa.org/record/1979-26502-001>.

186   Things around us become uncertain; we believe . . .: Braslow MD, J Guerrettaz, RM Arkin & KC Oleson, 'Self-doubt', *Social and Personality Psychology Compass*, 2012, vol. 6, no. 6, pp. 470–82, <psycnet.apa.org/doi/10.1111/j.1751-9004.2012.00441.x>.

186   You must acknowledge these experiences so that . . .: ibid.

186   One of our most primitive emotions, shame . . .: Miles S, 'Addressing shame: what role does shame play in the formation of a modern medical professional identity?', *BJPsych Bulletin*, 2020, vol. 44, no. 1, pp. 1–5, <dx.doi.org/10.1192/bjb.2019.49>.

186   Two hallmarks of shame are to . . .: Lewis HB, 'Shame and guilt in neurosis', *Psychoanalytic Review*, 1971, vol. 58, no. 3, pp. 419–38, <psycnet.apa.org/record/1972-21079-001>.

186   Brené Brown, a leading researcher in the field of shame . . .: Brown B, *Men, Women and Worthiness: The Experience of Shame and the Power of Being Enough*, Louisville, Colorado: Sounds True, 2012.

187   Shame activates our primal fight, flight or freeze . . .: Brown B, *I Thought it Was Just Me (But it Isn't): Making the Journey from 'What Will People Think?' to 'I Am Enough'*, New York: Gotham Books, 2007.

187   Remind yourself that you're not mentally ill . . .: Leaf C, '4 tips to drastically reduce anxiety in your life', Dr. Leaf (blog), 10 July 2019, <drleaf.com/blogs/news/4-tips-to-drastically-reduce-anxiety-in-your-life>.

189   Reflective practice pioneer Donald Schön defined . . .: Checkoway B & DA Schön, 'The reflective practitioner: how professionals think in action', *Journal of Policy Analysis and Management*, 1985, vol. 4, no. 3, article no. 476, <www.jstor.org/stable/3324262>.

190   Schön defines reflective practice as . . .: ibid.

190   By following Schön's model of reflection . . .: 'The Schön reflective

model', NursingAnswers.net, <nursinganswers.net/reflective-guides/schon-reflective-model.php>.

191   Going on big benders is worse than having a couple of beers . . .: Daviet, R, G Aydogan, K Jagannathan et al, 'Associations between alcohol consumption and gray and white matter volumes in the UK Biobank'. *Nature Communications*, 2022, vol. 13, no. 1175 <doi.org/10.1038/s41467-022-28735-5.

Chapter 10

197   Neuroscientist Andrew Huberman calls this . . .: Huberman A, 'The Science of Making or Breaking Habits, Huberman Lab, 2 January 2022, <www.hubermanlab.com/episode/the-science-of-making-and-breaking-habits>.

199   This is called the courage circuit.: Nili U, H Goldberg, A Weizman & Y Dudai, 'Fear thou not: activity of frontal and temporal circuits in moments of real-life courage', *Neuron*, 2010, vol. 66, no. 6, pp. 949–62, <www.cell.com/neuron/fulltext/S0896-6273(10)00467-8>.

201   South African neuroscientist Caroline Leaf . . .: Leaf C, '4 tips to drastically reduce anxiety in your life', Dr. Leaf (blog), 10 July 2019, <drleaf.com/blogs/news/4-tips-to-drastically-reduce-anxiety-in-your-life>.

201   Offloading can lead to improved performance on tasks . . .: Morrison AB & LL Richmond, 'Offloading items from memory: individual differences in cognitive offloading in a short-term memory task', *Cognitive Research: Principles and Implications*, 2020, vol. 5, no. 1, article no. 1, <cognitiveresearchjournal.springeropen.com/articles/10.1186/s41235-019-0201-4>.

203   When we shift that frame, the way we see the situation . . .: Morin A, 'How cognitive reframing works', Verywell Mind, 9 May 2023, <www.verywellmind.com/reframing-defined-2610419>.

203   Thomas Edison once said, 'I have not failed . . .': 'Importance of Thomas Edison's Quotes', Thomas A. Edison: Edison Innovation Foundation, <www.thomasedison.org/edison-quotes>.

203   Another good reframing tool . . .: Fox C., 'When you find yourself feeling negative', LinkedIn post, 2021 <https://www.linkedin.com/posts/carolfoxco_carolfoxco-reframetool-confidentcommunication-activity-6701963561607987200-7vQ6>

205   US entrepreneur Gary Keller, the author of . . .: Keller G & J Papasan, *The One Thing: The Surprisingly Simple Truth behind Extraordinary Results*, Portland, Oregon: Bard Press, 2013.

209   The law of attraction was made famous through . . .: Rhonda Byrne, *The Secret* , London: Simon & Schuster, 2006.

209   Dr Michael Yapko introduced an important concept . . .: Yapko, MD, 'Focus archives', Michael D Yapko, Ph.D., <yapko.com/tag/focus>, accessed 9 March 2022, no longer available.

210 All this does is amplify panic, which is defined as . . .: 'Panic', Dictionary.com, <www.dictionary.com/browse/panic>.

211 A study of paramedics and their behavioural responses . . .: Avraham N, H Goldblatt & E Yafe, 'Paramedics' experiences and coping strategies when encountering critical incidents', *Qualitative Health Research*, 2014, vol. 24, no. 2, pp. 194–208, <journals.sagepub.com/ doi/10.1177/1049732313519867>.

211 Marcus Aurelius, the great Stoic, wrote . . .': Aurelius M, 'Who is Marcus Aurelius? Getting to know the Roman emperor', Daily Stoic, <dailystoic.com/marcus-aurelius>.

211 The most influential theory of stress and coping . . .: Kavanagh DJ, 'Stress, appraisal and coping' (book review), *Behavioral and Cognitive Psychotherapy*, 1984, vol. 14, no. 4, p. 345, <dx.doi.org/10.1017/ s0141347300015019>.

211 They described two coping strategies for stress . . .: ibid.

212 As a consequence of using maladaptive coping . . .: ibid.

213 She has said that 'The loss of prefrontal function . . .': Quoted in Meier JD, 'How to feel more in control of your life with skill', Sources of Insight, <sourcesofinsight.com/feel-in-control>.

215 The only way to get optimal results is to focus . . .: Cohn P, 'How to focus on the process in golf', Peak Performance Sports, <www.peaksports.com/sports-psychology-blog/how-to-focus-on-the-process-instead-of-outcome-in-golf>.

216 His opponents, catching the basketball . . .: Krider D, 'John Wooden: An American beauty (1910–2010)', MaxPreps, 5 June 2010, <www. maxpreps.com/news/GIVf_XCkEd-lugAcxJTdpg/john-wooden-an-american-beauty-(1910–2010).htm>.

217 The task-oriented strategy involves taking direct . . .: Savage S, 'Task-oriented versus emotion-oriented coping strategies: the case of college students', RedOrbit, 5 April 2005, <www.redorbit.com/ news/health/141147/taskoriented_versus_emotionoriented_coping_ strategies_the_case_of_college_students>.

Chapter 11

225 It has been defined as 'a dynamic process . . .': Luthar SS, D Cicchetti & B Becker, 'The construct of resilience: a critical evaluation and guidelines for future work', *Child Development*, 2000, vol. 71, no. 3, pp. 543–62, <srcd.onlinelibrary.wiley.com/doi/abs/10.1111/ 1467-8624.00164>.

226 After surveying several experienced clinicians . . .: Hamlet O, A Irwin, R Flin & N Sedlar, *HeliNOTS: Non-technical Skills for Search and Rescue Pilots, Aberdeen: Applied Psychology and Human Factors Group*, University of Aberdeen, 2020, <research.abdn.ac.uk/ wp-content/uploads/sites/14/2020/08/HeliNOTS-S-Handbook.pdf>.

226 Review the markers below . . .: ibid.

227   The six layers of their shield were innate . . .: Pronk D, B Pronk &
       T Curtis, *The Resilience Shield: SAS Resilience Techniques to Master
       Your Mindset and Overcome Adversity*, Sydney, Macmillan, 2021.

227   'Firstly, for resilience to exist, there needs to be . . .': ibid.

228   Social support has been defined as 'support accessible . . .': Ozbay
       F, DC Johnson, E Dimoulas et al., 'Social support and resilience
       to stress: from neurobiology to clinical practice', *Psychiatry*
       (Edgmont), 2007, vol. 4, no. 5, pp. 35–40, <www.researchgate.net/
       publication/46095980_Social_support_and_resilience_to_stress_
       From_neurobiology_to_clinical_practice>.

228   And finally, flourishing people are socially tolerant, accepting . . .: 'Ask
       an expert: What is "positive psychology"?', CNNfyi.com, 24 January
       2001, <edition.cnn.com/2001/fyi/teachers.tools/01/24/c.keyes>.

230   As we discussed when talking about flourishing . . .: Catalino L &
       Fredrickson B, 'A Tuesday in the life of a flourisher: the role of Positive
       emotional reactivity in optimal mental health', *Emotion*, 2011, vol. 11,
       no. 4, pp. 938–50, <www.ncbi.nlm.nih.gov/pmc/articles/PMC3160725>.

230   While in prison, Senghor used reading and writing . . .: 'Returning
       Citizen Roundtable feat. Shaka Senghor, Jason Bryant, Eldra Jackson
       III and Robert Mosqueda', Compassion Prison Project, 8 August 2022,
       <compassionprisonproject.org/returning-citizens-roundtable>.

230   In his memoir, *Writing My Wrongs*, he recalls . . .: Senghor S, *Writing
       My Wrongs: Life, Death, and Redemption in an American Prison*,
       New York: Convergent Books, 2013.

232   Almost 60 per cent of the Western world's adult population . . .: Ratey
       JJ, *Spark: The Revolutionary New Science of Exercise and the Brain*,
       New York: Little, Brown & Company, 2013.

232   A growing body of research suggests that exercise . . .: ibid.

232   Researchers in Japan have found that as little as . . .: Park BJ,
       Y Tsunetsugu, T Kasetani et al., 'The physiological effects of *Shinrin-
       yoku* (taking in the forest atmosphere or forest bathing): evidence
       from field experiments in 24 forests across Japan', *Environmental
       Health and Preventive Medicine*, 2010, vol. 15, no. 1, pp. 18–26,
       <environhealthprevmed.biomedcentral.com/articles/10.1007/
       s12199-009-0086-9>.

233   A breakthrough study completed by US neuroscientist . . .: Cotman
       CW & NC Berchtold, 'Exercise: a behavioral intervention to enhance
       brain health and plasticity', *Trends in Neurosciences*, 2002, vol. 25,
       no. 6, pp. 295–301, <www.cell.com/trends/neurosciences/fulltext/
       S0166-2236(02)02143-4>.

233   This is important because the survival and . . .: Ratey JJ & E Hagerman,
       Spark: The Revolutionary New Science of Exercise and the Brain,
       New York: Little, Brown & Company, 2013.

233   Research has established that people learn vocabulary . . .: Winter
       B, C Breitenstein, FC Mooren et al., 'High impact running improves

learning', *Neurobiology of Learning and Memory*, 2007, vol. 87, no. 4, pp. 597–609, <www.sciencedirect.com/science/article/abs/pii/S1074742706001596>.

234   Ratey and Hagerman also highlight the importance . . .: Ratey JJ & E Hagerman, *Spark: The Revolutionary New Science of Exercise and the Brain*, New York: Little, Brown & Company, 2013.

234–5   'When adversity happens,' Davidson says . . .: Williams R, 'How mindfulness builds resilience', Sivana East, 2020, <blog.sivanaspirit.com/mf-gn-how-mindfulness-builds-resilience>.

235   This part of the brain controls behaviours and emotions . . .: Lou HC, TW Kjaer, L Friberg et al., 'A ^{15}O-H$_2$O PET study of meditation and the resting state of normal consciousness', *Human Brain Mapping*, 1999, vol. 7, no. 2, pp. 98–105, <www.ncbi.nlm.nih.gov/pmc/articles/PMC6873339/pdf/HBM-7-98.pdf>.

237   Dr Dan Pronk, co-author of *The Resilience Shield*, writes . . .: Campbell J, 'Always a little further: Dr Dan Pronk on building resilience in the every day', *Men's Health*, 5 October 2021, <menshealth.com.au/always-a-little-further-dr-dan-pronk-on-building-resilience-in-the-every-day>.

240   Psychologists have learned that negative experiences . . .: Tedeschi RG, 'Growth after trauma', *Harvard Business Review*, July–August 2020, <hbr.org/2020/07/growth-after-trauma>.

240   The concept of post-traumatic growth was developed . . .: Tedeschi RG & LG Calhoun, 'The Posttraumatic Growth Inventory: measuring the positive legacy of trauma', *Journal of Traumatic Stress*, 1996, vol. 9, no. 3, pp. 455–71, <onlinelibrary.wiley.com/doi/10.1002/jts.2490090305>.

240   If we're already resilient when we experience trauma . . .: Sword RKM & P Zimbardo, 'How we can grow during the pandemic', *Psychology Today*, 20 May 2020, <www.psychologytoday.com/intl/blog/the-time-cure/202005/how-we-can-grow-during-the-pandemic>.

240   To determine the extent of growth after trauma, Tedeschi . . .: Tedeschi RG & LG Calhoun, 'The Posttraumatic Growth Inventory: measuring the positive legacy of trauma', *Journal of Traumatic Stress*, 1996, vol. 9, no. 3, pp. 455–71, <onlinelibrary.wiley.com/doi/10.1002/jts.2490090305>.

Chapter 12

247   Vaughan noted that the root cause of the *Challenger* . . .: Vaughan D, *The Challenger Launch Decision: Risky Technology, Culture, and Deviance at NASA*, 2nd edn, Chicago, Illinois: University of Chicago Press, 2016.

248   This divergence occurs when people within an organisation . . .: Price MR & TC Williams, 'When doing wrong feels so right: normalization of deviance', *Journal of Patient Safety*, 2018, vol. 14, no. 1, pp. 1–2, <dx.doi.org/10.1097/PTS.0000000000000157>.

251   Predictable surprises require a sacrifice in . . .: Watkins MD &
       MH Bazerman, 'Predictable surprises: the disasters you should
       have seen coming', *Harvard Business Review*, 2003, vol. 81, no. 3,
       pp. 72–80, 140, <hbr.org/2003/04/predictable-surprises-the-disasters-
       you-should-have-seen-coming>.

252   Deviation occurs because of barriers that prevent us . . .: Price MR
       & TC Williams, 'When doing wrong feels so right: normalization of
       deviance', *Journal of Patient Safety*, 2018, vol. 14, no. 1, pp. 1–2, <dx.
       doi.org/10.1097/PTS.0000000000000157>.

253   Vulnerability has been described as 'uncertainty . . .': Brown B, *Daring
       Greatly: How the Courage to be Vulnerable Transforms the Way We
       Live, Love, Parent and Lead*, London: Hay House UK, 2020.

254   The following vulnerabilities have been identified . . .: Watkins
       MD & MH Bazerman, 'Predictable surprises: the disasters you
       should have seen coming', *Harvard Business Review*, 2003, vol. 81,
       no. 3, pp. 72–80, 140, <hbr.org/2003/04/predictable-surprises-the-
       disasters-you-should-have-seen-coming>.

256   Positive deviance is the idea that in every . . .: Pascale R, J Sternin &
       M Sternin, *The Power of Positive Deviance: How Unlikely Innovators
       Solve the World's Toughest Problems*, Cambridge, Massachusetts:
       Harvard Business School Press, 2010.

257   Pouring resources into trying to change the villagers' . . .: Sutton
       J, 'Positive deviance: 5 examples of the power of non-conformity',
       PositivePsychology.com, 21 August 2020, <positivepsychology.com/
       positive-deviance>.

257   By learning how those people were bucking the . . .: Pascale R,
       J Sternin & M Sternin, *The Power of Positive Deviance: How Unlikely
       Innovators Solve the World's Toughest Problems*, Cambridge,
       Massachusetts: Harvard Business School Press, 2010.

Chapter 13

263   Austrian American management consultant and educator Peter . . .:
       Swaim RW, *The Strategic Drucker: Growth Strategies and Marketing
       Insights from the Works of Peter Drucker*, Wiley, 2010

263   Self-leaders transform adversity into resilience.: Dening H, *Her Middle
       Name Is Courage: How Self-leadership Transforms Pressure into
       Performance, Chaos into Clarity, and Rage into Resilience*, Sydney:
       Heidi Dening, 2019.

263   A courageous self-leader is, to paraphrase William Ernest Henley's . . .:
       Henley WE, 'Invictus', Book of Verses, 1888, via Poetry Foundation
       <www.poetryfoundation.org/poems/51642/invictus>.

265   'Courageous leaders are not cowed or intimidated . . .': Gavin M,
       '5 characteristics of a courageous leader', Harvard Business School
       Online, 3 March 2020, <online.hbs.edu/blog/post/courageous-
       leadership>.

266   He has said that taking responsibility is 'about doing what . . .': Izzo J, *Stepping Up: How Taking Responsibility Changes Everything: How Taking Responsibility Changes Everything*, San Francisco: Berrett-Koehler, 2011.

270   He may become enraged, again preventing him from following . . .: Fox C & K Gorman, *Confident Communication for Leaders*, Melbourne: Life Performance, 2018.

271   Body language is said to influence between . . .: Mehrabian A, *Nonverbal Communication*, New Brunswick: Aldine Transaction, 1972.

271   The leveller involves simply moving your arms up and down . . .: Fox C & K Gorman, *Confident Communication for Leaders*, Melbourne: Life Performance, 2018.

272   Nursing scholar Theresa Wiseman identified four attributes . . .: Wiseman T, 'Toward a holistic conceptualization of empathy for nursing practice', *Advances in Nursing Science*, 2007, vol. 30, no. 3, pp. E61–E72, <dx.doi.org/10.1097/01.ANS.0000286630.00011.eK3>.

273   Brené Brown explains sympathy as trying to . . .: Brown B, The Power of Vulnerability (talk), Royal Society of Arts, London, 2013 <www.thersa.org/video/shorts/2013/12/brene-brown-on-empathy>.

275   When our feelings and the facts are at odds . . .: De-Wit L, *What's Your Bias? The Surprising Science of Why We Vote the Way We Do*, London: Elliott & Thompson, 2017.

275   The internal inconsistency of cognitive dissonance, which . . .: ibid.

276   In 1620, the English philosopher Francis Bacon wrote . . .: Bacon F, 'A.D. 1620–1. JANUARY–MARCH. ÆTAT. 60', in: J Spedding, RL Ellis & DD Heath DD (eds), *The Works of Francis Bacon*, vol. IV, Cambridge: Cambridge University Press, 2013, pp. 160–208.

Afterword

296   Qualitative studies have been defined as those undertaken . . .: 'Qualitative research', Physiopedia, <www.physio-pedia.com/Qualitative_Research>.

Index

Hurricane Katrina, 251
hydration, 169–71, 292
hyperkalaemia, 69
hyperventilation, 150–1
hypothalamic–pituitary–adrenal (HPA) axis, 89–93
hypothalamus, 88–90

ignorance, 47–8, 289
immune system suppression, 89, 93
imposter syndrome, 185
incompetence, conscious, 48
individualised zone of optimal functioning (IZOF), 108–11, 114, 121–4, 290, 313
instincts, 255–6
inverted-U concept, see Yerkes-Dodson law
Irukandji syndrome, 146–8
Izzo, John, 266

Jacklin, Wade, 66
Jerusalem, Matthias, 73
journalling, 230–2, 293

Keller, Gary, 205
Kennedy, Robert F., 260
Keyes, Corey, 55, 56, 228–9
Koehn, Nancy, 265
Kross, Ethan, 156, 158

languishing, 51–3, 55, 57–9, 66, 70–1, 75, 191
laryngoscopy, 126–8
laughter, 164–7, 203, 292
Lauria, Michael J., 132, 149, 150, 220, 295
Lazarus, Richard, 211
leadership
    moral courage, 260–3
    self-leadership, 263–5, 273–4, 277, 278, 294
    voice of leadership (tone of voice), 272
Leaf, Caroline, 201
learning
    continual, 35–7, 139–41, 256, 291, 299
    four levels of, 47–8, 110, 289
    improved by exercise, 233–4
    from mistakes, 180–4, 192, 245–6
    from others, 257
    see also practice (practising); training
Lee, Bruce, 48
A Life Half Lived (Macleod), 260
Lifeline Australia contact number, 23
limbic friction, 196–9, 200–1, 206–8, 220
linguistic distance, 158–9
lists, see checklists
lying, see honesty

McCandless, Christopher, 229–30
MacLeod, Andrew, 260–3, 278, 295
maladaptive coping, 211–12, see also avoidance behaviours

mantras, 161–2, 292, see also positive self-talk
mastery
    autonomous performance, 101, 110, 113
    fundamental skills, 46–7, 97–8, 299–300
    multitasking and, 205
    stages of competence, 47–8, 289
mediocrity, factors leading to, 59
meditation, 18, 234–6, 293
memory, 131, 169
    cognitive bandwidth, 98–9, 101, 113, 135–6, 205
    cognitive offloading, 103–4, 164, 201–2, 292
    stress-related impairment of, 96–7
    working memory, 96–9, 113
mental health, 27, 66
    assessment of, 62–5, 305–7
    defined, 54, 55
    mental illness definition and types, 54, 66
    of paramedics, 22–3
    positivity and, 60–2
    self-efficacy and, 73, 75
    statistics, 56
    see also flourishing
mental health continuum model, 56–9
Mental Health Continuum Short Form, 62–5, 305–7
mentors, 78–9
metronomes, 202
mimicked behaviour, 45, 257
mindfulness, 39, 212, 235
mindsets
    contagious nature of, 44–5
    defined, 32–3
    experience and, 33–4
    growth versus fixed, 34–7, 50, 139–40, 289
    paramedic mindset, 15–16, 20, 23–4, 27, 33–4, 283–7, 300
    paramedic mindset (personal anecdotes), 20–3, 279–82
    see also poise
mistakes
    accountability for, 266, 268–9
    circumstances and consequences, 26
    learning from, 180–4, 192, 245–6
    reframing, 195–6, 203
    stress-related, 91
    see also fear of failure
mnemonics, see checklists; mantras
moral courage, 260–3, 276
motivation
    lack of, 51–3, 59, see also languishing
    paramedics, 15
    stress and, 105–6
motor skills, see fine motor skills; gross motor skills
Mullane, Mike, 246, 253, 259, 295

multitasking, 94–6, 127–8, 204–5
muscle memory, 48, *see also* mastery

NASA *Challenger* disaster, 246–8
negativity, 60
   negative emotions, 109, 110–11, 116–17,
      211, 234–5, 310, 312
   negative rumination, 58–9, 234–5
nervous system, 87–8, 152, 156, 235
non-verbal communication, 271–2
noradrenaline, 88, 89–90
normalisation of deviance, 246–53, 259, 294
   positive deviance, 256–7
   prevention of, 253–6

Oliveri, Paul, poem, ix
operational cognitive readiness, 24, 129–30,
   206
optimal functioning, 108–11, 114, 121–4,
   290, 313
oxygen, 91, 92, 151, 153, 155, 166, *see also*
   breathing techniques

Pakistan earthquake humanitarian response,
   261–2
panic, 20, 44–5, 208
panic cycle, 25–6, 60, 80, 93, 191, 208, 250,
   256
Paramedic Mindset podcast, 295–301
paramedics
   heart rate condition for optimal
      performance, 112–13, 123–4, 233
   mental health, 22–3
   mindset, 14–16, 20, 23–4, 27, 33–4,
      283–7, 300, *see also* poise
   mindset (personal anecdotes), 20–3,
      279–82
   motivation, 15
   physical fitness, 232–3
   role and purpose, 11, 13–14
   students' level of competence, 47–8
   unique qualities, 20
parasympathetic nervous system, 87–8, 152,
   156, 235
past experiences, 77–8, 186, 290
Pasternak, Boris, *Dr Zhivago*, 229
patient assessment, 217–18, 219–20
peer pressure, 135–6, 290
Pepper, Matt, 144, 295
perceptions, 17, 38–41, 110–11, *see also*
   emotions
performance outcomes, 77–8, 290
   autonomous performance, 110, 113
   behavioural markers, 226–7
   catastrophe model, 106–8
   discovering optimal arousal level for
      performance improvement, 116–22
   expectation of poor performance,
      see self-doubt

incremental improvements, 283–4
individualised zone of optimal functioning,
   108–11, 114, 121–4, 290, 313
   stress and, 105–6, 107, 115–16
   see also fear of failure; focusing; learning
persuasion, *see* verbal persuasion
Peterson, Jordan, 13, 140
physical activity, *see* exercise
physiological sighs, 95, 152–4, 155, 291
physiological toughness, 91–2
physiology
   breathing, 150–2, *see also* breathing
      techniques
   fight, flight or freeze, 80, 87–93, 96–7,
      290, *see also* fight, flight or freeze
      response
   heart rate, *see* heart rate
pioneers, 79
pituitary gland, 89–90
podcast, 295–301
points of view (reframing), 194–6, 203–4,
   292
poise, 15–20
   analogy, 284–7
   benefit to bystanders, 44–5
   decision-making under stress, 283
   defined, 27
   inspirational figures, 16–20
   need for, 15–16
   personal anecdotes, 20–3, 279–82
   tools for building poise, 289–94
   see also coping strategies; mindsets;
      resilience
poise cycle, 23–5, 60, 80, 93, 143, 171, 241,
   277
positive deviance, 256–7
positive experiences, 33, 57, 58, 60–2
positive feedback, 70, 79, 189, 290
positive role models, 78–9, 257
positive self-talk, 57, 79–80, 149, 156–9, 291
positivity
   defined, 60–1
   positive emotions, 61–2, 116–17, 209,
      310–11
   positive risk-taking, 73
   reframing for, 194–6, 203–4, 292
   savouring positive aspects, 204
   see also self-efficacy
post-traumatic growth, 240–1
post-traumatic stress disorder (PTSD), 23,
   92
practice (practising), 18, 39, 47–8, 78, 101,
   113, 144, *see also* reflective practice;
   training
predictable surprises, 250–1, 256, 259, 293,
   see also normalisation of deviance
prefrontal cortex, 98, 169, 213
preparedness, *see* operational cognitive
   readiness; training